Studies of Modern Japan

Titles in the Series

Jews in the Japanese Mind: The History and Uses of a Cultural Stereotype, by David G. Goodman and Masanori Miyazawa

Chōshū in the Meiji Restoration, by Albert M. Craig

Japan and the Security of Asia, by Louis D. Hayes

The Web of Power: Japanese and German Development Cooperation Policy, by Kozo Kato

Unhappy Soldier: Hino Ashihei and Japanese World War II Literature, by David M. Rosenfeld

In the Shadow of the Miracle: The Japanese Economy Since the End of High-Speed Growth, by Arthur J. Alexander

Spanning Japan's Modern Century: The Memoirs of Hugh Borton, by Hugh Borton

Agony of Choice: Matsuoka Yosuke and the Rise and Fall of the Japanese Empire, 1880–1946, by David J. Lu

A Yankee in Hokkaido: The Life of William Smith Clark, by John M. Maki

Roadblocks on the Information Highway: The IT Revolution in Japanese Education, edited by Jane M. Bachnik

Limits to Power: Asymmetric Dependence and Japanese Foreign Aid Policy, by Akitoshi Miyashita

Constructing Opportunity: American Women Educators in Early Meiji Japan, by Elizabeth Eder

The Return of the Amami Islands: The Reversion Movement and U.S.–Japan Relations, by Robert D. Eldridge

Life and Resources in America, by Mori Arinori; edited and introduced by John E. Van Sant

The Return of the Amami Islands

The Reversion Movement and
U.S.–Japan Relations

Robert D. Eldridge

LEXINGTON BOOKS
Lanham • Boulder • New York • Toronto • Oxford

LEXINGTON BOOKS

Published in the United States of America
by Lexington Books
An imprint of The Rowman & Littlefield Publishing Group, Inc.
4501 Forbes Boulevard, Suite 200, Lanham, Maryland 20706

PO Box 317
Oxford
OX2 9RU, UK

British Library Cataloguing in Publication Information Available

Library of Congress Cataloging-in-Publication Data

Eldridge, Robert D.
    The return of the Amami Islands : the reversion movement and U.S.–Japan relations /
Robert D. Eldridge.
        p. cm.—(Studies of modern Japan)
Includes bibliographical references and index.
    ISBN 0-7391-0710-0 (hardcover : alk. paper)
 Amami Islands (Japan)—History. 2. United States—Foreign relations—Japan.
3. Japan—Foreign relations—United States. 4. United States—Military relations—
Japan. 5. Japan—Military Relations—United States. I. Title. II. Series.
    DS894.99.K339A4227 2003
    940.53'1424'095226—dc22

                                                                                2003018797

Printed in the United States of America

♾™ The paper used in this publication meets the minimum requirements of
American National Standard for Information Sciences—Permanence of Paper for
Printed Library Materials, ANSI/NISO Z39.48-1992.

To the people of the Amami Islands and to the memory of Nobori Naotaka, Izumi Horo, Kanai Masao, Okuyama Hachiro, Tanimura Tadaichiro, Toyoshima Itaru, and Nakae Saneyoshi, and the many others who worked toward a better future for Amami and a healthier U.S.–Japan relationship.

Contents

Figures and Tables

Figures

Tables

~

Acknowledgments

As the study of the political and diplomatic history surrounding the return of the Amami Islands has formed a special place in my own research interests, so have the people who I have been honored to know during its writing formed a special place in my heart.

First and foremost, I would like to express my deep gratitude to the Suntory Foundation (Suntory Bunka Zaidan) for providing me with a postdoctoral fellowship from April 1999 to September 2000, during which time I conducted the bulk of my research. In addition to providing a friendly atmosphere in which to work, the highly dedicated staff—Torii Shinichiro, Watanabe Hachiro, Sugitani Kenji, Kurosawa Kiyoharu, Bunno Junya, Hashimoto Noriko, Kojima Taeko, and Sangyoku Kazue—and the Foundation's intellectual supporters, such as Yamazaki Masakazu and Tadokoro Masayuki, provided a stimulating scholarly environment in which to study.

Secondly, I would like to thank the Eisenhower World Affairs Institute for financially sponsoring my research at the Dwight D. Eisenhower Presidential Library in Abilene, Kansas, in early 2000, as part of its Abilene Travel Grants Program. David J. Haight of the Library deserves special mention for his knowledge of the materials there on the Eisenhower administration (1953–1961) and for his passion for helping researchers uncover the lesser known aspects of U.S. foreign policy and bilateral relations. Likewise, I am grateful to the Eisenhower Foundation and, in particular, John R. Zutavern for the warm welcome the Foundation gave me during my enjoyable and productive stay in Abilene.

I also wish to thank the staff of the Nankai Nichinichi Shimbun in Naze City, Amami, for their support over the past three years in this research and related activities, such as introducing several articles of mine to their readers, including a long series on U.S. policy making with regard to Amami and Okinawa, and editing a collection of essays to which I contributed entitled *Sorezore no Amami Ron 50* (*50 Essays on Amami*), published by Nanpo Shinsha in 2001. I especially wish to thank its president, Murayama Michio, and Shigemura Akira, formerly director of the newspaper's Division of Research, who generously shared much material on the Amami reversion movement, including a copy of an important book on the reversion history published many years ago by the founder of the newspaper and father of Mr. Murayama.

I am grateful to Professor M. William Steele and the staff of the Institute of Asian Cultural Studies at International Christian University in Mitaka City, where I was a research fellow from September 1999 to September 2000. Professor Steele and the Institute warmly provided a wonderful atmosphere to undertake and introduce my research.

I would also like to express my gratitude to the International Exchange Committee of the Japan Association of International Relations (Nihon Kokusai Seiji Gakkai) for sponsoring my attendance at the Twenty-third Annual Meeting of the International Society of Political Psychology in Seattle in July 2000, allowing me to present my findings on the reversion movement. The stimulating debate and comparative perspectives of social movements were quite helpful in further developing this research.

Finally, and sadly, I wish to acknowledge my deep gratitude to the late Sakai Takayuki, a *sempai* of mine from Kobe University, who helped in much of the early stages of my research on the islands thanks to his position as an associate professor of International Relations at Kagoshima Kenritsu Tanki Daigaku, a small public college in Kagoshima Prefecture, in which Amami is located. Despite having just discovered that he had a rare form of leukemia, Sakai-san welcomed me to the campus and his home and made several important introductions for me. His loss is a big one for both his family and the field of international relations, not to mention an irreplaceable personal one for me.

One of the introductions I received from Sakai-san was to Professor Nishimura Tomiaki, also of the Kagoshima Kenritsu Tanki Daigaku, who authored an important study of the socioeconomic history of postwar Amami. Through Nishimura *sensei*, a native of Amami, I in turn was able to meet numerous people during my first visit to the islands with him in July 1999.

There are many other individuals who I wish to thank in Amami and elsewhere, including Hayashi Sokio and Takanari Osamu of the Naze City

Amami Musueum, Yamashita Fumitake, Kusuda Toyoharu, Sakida Saneyoshi, Yamaoka Hidetusugu, Satake Kyoko, and Migita Shoshin, all of whom helped me tremendously during and after my 1999 stay in Amami, and in the case of Mssrs. Kusuda and Migita, permitted the use of photographs in their collections for publication in this book. Kagoshima Governor Suka Tatsuro and his staff likewise kindly helped with hard-to-find materials on a former governor of the prefecture, Shigenari Kaku, who appears often in this book. My former advisor at Kobe University, Iokibe Makoto, now at Harvard University, remains the intellectual spring from which I continue to draw inspiration and insights. I also offer thanks to Watanabe Akio, the international relations scholar and author of *The Okinawa Problem: A Chapter in Japan–U.S. Relations*, who maintains a strong interest in the Amami Islands (and confided in me at one point that he had always wanted to write about them), for kindly introducing me to Nobori Amiko, the great-granddaughter of Nobori Naotaka, a leader of the reversion movement. International historian David Wolff gave me much advice on the early stages of the research and later continued to often ask the most important question: "So, how's it coming?" The help of Sakamoto Kazuya, an expert on U.S.–Japan relations in the 1950s, was also much appreciated in discussing the rearmament issue and the general significance of the return of the islands. Professor Emeritus Iwao Ishino kindly responded to my many questions with regard to his early involvement in public opinion polls in Amami around the time of the Peace Treaty. American diplomats James V. Martin Jr. and Clifton B. Forster, who attended the reversion ceremonies in December 1953, gave generously of their time in interviews for this book, which I hope meets their demanding standards. Likewise, Haraguchi Kunihiro, deputy director of the Diplomatic Records Office, Japanese Ministry of Foreign Affairs, who has a strong personal interest in the islands and was instrumental in getting the Amami reversion-related materials of the Foreign Ministry declassified and made available to researchers, also deserves special mention for his consistently helpful assistance, advice, and dedication, as well as for gaining permission to use the Foreign Ministry photos. The family of the late Araki Eikichi, ambassador to the United States during the time of the reversion of the Amami Islands, was generous with their time and insights. Nakamoto Kazuhiko, Washington, D.C. representative of the Okinawa Prefectural Archives, was a great help in many ways, but most of all, because he was a friend in times of need. I am also thankful to Hashimoto Yuko, a staff member at the Osaka School of International Public Policy (OS-IPP), for her technical and spiritual support.

In addition, I wish to thank the staff of Lexington Books who showed a strong interest in this book and worked with me all of the way, especially

~

Introduction: A Brief History of the Amami Islands

"I hope that the Amami Islands do not become another Alsace-Lorraine."

—Major General Takada Toshisada,
Surrender Signing Ceremony, Hedono Island, Amami Gunto
September 22, 1945

On September 22, 1945, a landing craft holding a ten-person contingent of American forces from the U.S. Tenth Army arrived in Hedono on the island of Tokunoshima, almost halfway between Okinawa and Amami.[1] Its task was to affect the disarmament of the Amami Islands, including the signing of a surrender document.[2]

Symbolic of problems that would emerge over the coming months and years with the geographical and historical understanding of the islands, as the Japanese Commanding Officer, Maj. Gen. Takada Toshisada, was about to sign the Surrender Agreement, he noticed that the Amami Islands were incorrectly written as Northern Ryukyu (*Hokubu Ryukyu*).[3] Putting down his writing instrument, Takada explained that "the Amami Islands were *not* the Northern Ryukyu Islands." "It must be made perfectly clear now," he continued, "that the Amami Islands belong to Kyushu and Kagoshima Prefecture." When his U.S. counterparts indicated through an American-born Nisei translator that they did not agree due to their own maps describing Amami as the Northern Ryukyus, Takada announced that he would not sign the document as it was, restating that Amami was a part of Kagoshima Prefecture. After a heated argument and long stand-off, the United States finally agreed to contact Gen. Joseph W. Stilwell at Tenth Army Headquarters in Okinawa.[4]

Stilwell approved the revision of the text, and Northern Ryukyu was changed to *Amami Gunto—Kagoshima Ken*, as first requested by Takada.[5]

The remainder of the afternoon surrender ceremony proceeded smoothly, but Takada was still obviously concerned. "I hope that the Amami Islands do not become another Alsace-Lorraine," he stated after the signing, repeating a concern he had written of in a letter to Gen. Stilwell some three weeks before.[6] "We will inform our superiors of your worry," his counterparts responded.

For the Amami Islands, the end of the war had officially arrived. So had the start of an unexpected journey that saw the almost eight-year unnecessary separation of their islands from Japan, a period that people in Amami understandably refer to as *ryuri no hibi* (the days of trial).[7]

As examined in this book, the separation was unnecessary for a number of reasons. In their planning, the State Department sought a formula by which the islands could be returned to Japan while base rights would be kept by the United States; eventually this formed the basis of the Security Treaty and Administrative Agreement, which could, in retrospect, have been applied to the Amami Islands much earlier. Secondly, the Japanese government was willing to permit the U.S. military to have base rights in the islands, so there was no need for the military to require absolute control including administrative rights over the islands. Finally, even the Far Eastern Command recognized that the islands were not necessary, but the Joint Chiefs of Staff (JCS) overturned that recommendation.

In this book, I argue that not only was the separation of the islands unnecessary, it was also politically unwise in that such a move opened the United States to criticism that it was imperialistic in nature and not respecting the ideals it had expressed in the Atlantic Charter. In addition, the separation endangered the still fragile postwar relationship with Japan, which even the preeminent military strategist of his time, President Dwight D. Eisenhower, argued (as discussed in chapter 4), was extremely important to the United States, and military control over the Amami Islands was not worth harming this relationship.

Purpose and Structure of Book

Although little known, territory in addition to Okinawa was separated from Japan in the immediate postwar period. Lying between 27° and 29° north latitude, the Amami Islands (as well as the Ogasawara, or Bonin, Islands) were politically and administratively detached from Japan in January 1946 and, unlike the rest of the country, were placed along with Okinawa under U.S. military government and remained under that status after the Treaty of Peace with Japan went into effect in April 1952.[8] Per Article 3 of the Peace Treaty, announced at the San Francisco Peace Conference in 1951, the Amami Islands continued to be separated from Japan, to the great disappointment of the Japanese government as well as the 219,000 islanders and 200,000 Amami residents on the Japanese mainland in the Kyushu, Osaka, and Tokyo areas.[9] At one minute after midnight on December 25, 1953, however, the islands were returned to Japanese administration in what was called at the time a "Christmas present" to the satisfaction and relief of the participants in the active and well-organized Amami reversion movement, or *Amami Fukki Undo*.

Despite being an important event in postwar Japanese history and U.S.–Japan relations, as well as being greatly intertwined with America's post-treaty Okinawa policy as a whole, the return of the Amami Islands has remained unexamined. U.S. historians have not explored the issue in a full study, instead focusing on the more contentious and well-known "Okinawa Problem." This is true among Japanese (and Okinawan) scholars as well. Likewise and curiously, the views and efforts of the Japanese government toward Amami (and Okinawa) have traditionally received little or no attention in the literature (both American and Japanese), although my *The Origins of the Bilateral Okinawa Problem: Okinawa in Postwar U.S.–Japan Relations, 1945–1952*, published in 2001 (with the Japanese language version appearing in 2003), went a long way to change that. In addition, little research exists on the Amami reversion movement itself, despite its having had an impact on the policy making of both the Japanese and U.S. governments and being a successful example of a sociopolitical movement in postwar Japan.[10]

Fortunately, however, there is a rich, multiarchival base from which to draw. Original documents from the reversion movement, for example, are preserved in Naze City, Kagoshima Prefecture, and several volumes of memoirs and remembrances, written by participants in the movement, also exist, shedding light on the activities of the various reversion groups. Moreover, adding to the different and sometimes colorful viewpoints, these accounts were written by individuals in local Amami-based groups as well as support groups on the mainland, by those of conservative as well as progressive and Communist political persuasion, by those who identified themselves closely with mainland Japanese as well as those who felt themselves to be more "Okinawan," or southern, and finally, by leader and follower alike. However, because these accounts did not access official papers on the U.S. and Japanese sides, the movement's *impact* has remained unknown. With the recent declassification of U.S. government and Japanese Foreign Ministry documents, the task of writing this history has now been made easier.

Indeed, these latter materials reveal a rich history and will be of great interest for those concerned with Japanese political and diplomatic history, U.S.–Japan relations, postwar Okinawa history, social movements, and studies on the bilateral alliance. Despite the availability of these materials and the fact that almost fifty years have passed since the Amami Islands were returned to Japan in 1953, no comprehensive study of the political and diplomatic history of this reversion process has been done to date.

This book attempts to correct that. Simply stated, the purpose of this book is to introduce an unknown episode in postwar U.S.–Japan relations: the return of the Amami Islands.

In this story, there are three major actors—the U.S. government, the Japanese government, and the Amami Reversion Movement, although, as will become clear, there were many subactors—groups and individuals—involved, which shows the many different forces influencing the actions of each larger actor. Each chapter is essentially centered around one of the main actors, with the interactions of one or both of the other actors intertwined throughout. For example, chapter 2, which deals with the Amami Reversion Movement, also discusses the affects of U.S. occupation policy on the islands as well as the impact of the movement on both U.S. and Japanese policies. This is done to show to what degree the statements and actions of each actor played on the others.

The book is divided into five chapters, an introductorion, and a conclusion. A set of six appendices, including the (until now) unknown, "unpublished minutes" on U.S. requests for post-reversion use of the Amami Islands, is included for easy reference. Finally, a detailed bibliography of Japanese- and English-language resources is provided.

Chapter 1 examines U.S. pre-reversion policy toward Amami and Okinawa, focusing on the clash between the State Department and the U.S. military, led primarily by the Joint Chiefs of Staff, over the postwar territorial disposition of these islands. Namely, it highlights the fact that the State Department, based on the desire to realize the ideals of the 1941 Atlantic Charter and to secure good relations with Japan in the postwar period, called for the retention of these islands by Japan, while the military argued for their separation from Japan and placement under permanent or semipermanent U.S. control for security reasons. Those debates and the respective policy recommendations that emerged were strongly at odds with each other and essentially run parallel for a decade into the start of the Eisenhower Administration in 1953. Importantly, the U.S. government, through the efforts of John Foster Dulles, the architect of the Peace Treaty allowed Japan to retain sovereignty over the islands in the end, a decision that I evaluate highly (and discuss in more detail in my *The Origins of the Bilateral Okinawa Problem*).

Chapter 2, entitled "The Amami Reversion Movement," shifts the discussion from the Pentagon to Amami, by looking first at the military administration of the islands and then at the start of the reversion movement in Amami and on mainland Japan, and argues that the evidence suggests the determined, well-organized efforts of the movement did have an impact on the national policies of the United States and Japan. I argue that, among other factors, the presence of talented, influential, forward-looking, moderate leaders and the legitimacy of their demands (to be allowed to return to Japan) kept the movement focused and unified and brought about its success.

Chapter 3 looks at the Japanese government and its efforts to resolve the "Amami–Okinawa Problem." Specifically, it highlights the fact that, despite the traditional interpretation (popular in Okinawa and fanned by some scholars) of Japan as indifferent to the plight of Okinawa, the Japanese government indeed made every effort to seek the return of Okinawa, Amami, and the Ogasawara Islands. Even though Japan did not have diplomatic rights until 1952, they were successful in convincing the U.S. government to recognize Japanese sovereignty over the islands (although administrative rights were ultimately retained by the United States).

Chapter 4 returns the discussion to Washington by looking at the start of the Eisenhower Administration and the rapid and prudent decision to return the Amami Islands. The chapter highlights how the clash in U.S. policy between security requirements and political considerations examined in chapter 1 eventually played out, and it explores the personal role, views, and leadership of President Eisenhower in this debate, as well as some of the other critical players, such as Secretary of State Dulles, Ambassador to Japan John M. Allison, and Assistant Secretary of State for the Far East Walter S. Robertson, all of whom labored strenuously in order to realize the return of the islands.

Chapter 5 examines the discussions and negotiations on the reversion agreement and the contents of the agreement itself in detail, first on the U.S. side and then between the two countries. In particular, it explores the "delay" in the return of the islands and highlights the fact that it took the United States some three months to come up with a combined draft agreement to present to the Japanese.

In the conclusion, I praise the decision of the United States to leave sovereignty over the Nansei and Nanpo Islands with Japan at the time of the Peace Treaty in 1951 (under Article 3) as well as their decision to return the islands peacefully (within the framework of this Article 3) in 1953, because both decisions showed the world that the United States could and would live up to the high ideals of the Atlantic Charter (the principles of "self-determination" and "no territorial aggrandizement") and that they valued their relationship with Japan. At the same time, I reemphasize my criticism of the military's shortsightedness in its view of strategic requirements at the time because it damaged U.S. prestige abroad and almost permanently endangered the U.S.–Japan relationship.

Before we look at chapter 1 and U.S. policy toward the islands prior to their reversion, it is necessary to briefly study the history of the Amami Islands and a general overview of the islands.

A Brief History of the Amami Islands

General Overview

The Amami Islands, whose name means "beautiful (or peaceful, friendly) rule," are located approximately halfway between Kyushu, the southernmost of Japan's four main islands, and Okinawa, the southernmost prefecture of Japan. Geographically speaking, the Amami Islands fall in between the coordinates 29° north latitude in the north to 27° north latitude in the south. (See figure I.1.)

The islands, also known as Amami Gunto, include Amami Oshima, Kikaishima, Kakeromajima, Ukejima, Yokoateshima, Tokunoshima, Okino Erabu, Yoronto, in the far south (near the main island of Okinawa), as well as several smaller islands. Amami Oshima is the largest of the island group, with an area of about 276 square miles (712 square kilometers), making it the third largest of Japan's offshore islands after Okinawa and Sado Island, off of Niigata.[11]

Eight of the islands are populated, with a total of 132,315 people living on them (according to fiscal year 2000 figures). Oshima, the biggest island in area and the most developed, has the largest population at 73,896.

The semitropical islands, while steep and hilly, are chiefly agricultural, with sugar cane, sweet potatoes, and fruits being the main products. The islands are fairly undisturbed and host many nature reserves, and they are a popular destination for divers, although they are not as well known as the more southern islands of Okinawa Prefecture and Ogasawara.

The main city is Naze, located on Amami Oshima, and serves as the business, political, and administrative center of the islands, although the Amami Islands fall under the administrative jurisdiction of Kagoshima Prefecture, located about 250 miles (400 kilometers) to the north. Many officials in Amami continue to come from Kagoshima, a practice that has its roots in prewar years.

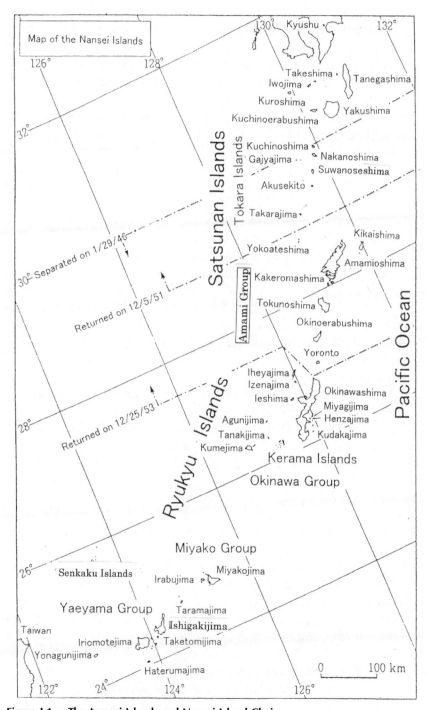

Figure I.1.   The Amami Islands and Nansei Island Chain
Source: Robert D. Eldridge, *The Origins of the Bilateral Okinawa Problem*.

Amami's relationship with Japan proper goes back considerably, which is not surprising, given its proximity to Kyushu. The Amami Islands are part of what is known as the Satsunan Islands.[12] The Satsunan Islands in turn make up the northern part of the Nansei Islands, with the Ryukyu Islands forming the southern part. In other words, the Satsunan Islands were (and continue to be) a part of present-day Kagoshima Prefecture, while the Ryukyu Islands after 1879 were (and continue to be) a part of present-day Okinawa Prefecture.

Early Times[13]

The name Amami means "beautiful (or peaceful, friendly) rule," but the reality was anything but peaceful and friendly. Its history prior to reversion can be described as one of *junan* ("hardship") as well as that of outside domination by its neighbors to the south, the former Ryukyu Kingdom, to the north, the former Satsuma domain (later Kagoshima Prefecture), and finally to the far east, the United States, which controlled the Nansei Islands at the end of World War II and occupied Japan from 1945 to 1952. Complex feelings still exist toward Kagoshima Prefecture today, such as inferiority and helplessness in some circles at the challenges the islands continue to face.

While it is difficult to confirm early historical accounts, contact between the islands and mainland Japan (the Imperial Court of Yamato) existed from at least 533 A.D. when government officials were dispatched to Amami, according to the *Nihon Shoki*, or *Chronicle of Japan*, compiled in 720 A.D. At this time, these officials established *miyake*, district taxation offices, and rice storehouses called *tonso*, finding the islands yielded good rice crops twice a year and had plentiful marine products.[14] Subsequently, beginning in about 614 A.D., Amami islanders, along with their southern neighbors from the Ryukyu Islands, went to pay homage to the Empress Suiko (593–628 A.D.), for which several received Court rank and thereafter visited the Imperial Court regularly.

With a well-established administration, including a governor (*Toshi*) and a post of administrative inspector (*Azechi*) to watch over the affairs of the islands established in 719 A.D., the islands prospered in a certain peaceful existence. However, beginning in the late ninth century (approximately 894 A.D.), infighting increased on the islands among local lords who are believed to have moved in from the Ryukyu Islands to the south when Japanese influence waned. This fighting, which continued for some 300 years, made the islands vulnerable to outside pressures, including Formosan and other pirates, and bandits ravaged the towns. Temporary alliances were formed to fight off these elements but, in the end, infight-ing continued.

During this time, the Taira (Heike) Clan, which had dominated Japan and to which the Heian Period is attributed, was driven out of power by the rival Minamoto Clan in the Civil War (known as the *Gempei* Wars) following the Battle of Dannoura. Defeated Taira clansman made their way to Kyushu and several went on to Amami and the Ryukyu Islands.[15] They suppressed the di-vided local lords on Oshima and took up residence on the islands.

Beginning in the 1260s, Ryukyuan leaders began to exercise greater influ-ence over the islands and a system of regular taxation was instituted, with offi-cials being sent to Amami in 1266 to assume control over the divided islands. The following year, the Amami islanders voluntarily submitted to the rule of King Eiso in Shuri, Okinawa, and began to pay tribute to *Oyako* (great father). When Eiso died in 1299, his son, Taisei, and grandson, Eiji, ruled in succession afterward, but when Eiso's great grandson, Tamagusuku, came to the throne in 1314, problems emerged in the family's rule. The nineteen-year-old Tama-gusuku, addicted to sensual pleasures, was known for his misrule. He gradually lost the support of the people. Eventually, powerful lords in the provinces re-fused to send tribute to the king, and Amami followed suit. The administration fell into confusion and open rebellion occurred in Urasoe, southern Okinawa, initiating a century of conflict.[16] The Ryukyu Kingdom subsequently broke in to three parts—Hokusan, Chuzan, and Nanzan.

Eventually, peace was restored under the Sho dynasty, but the century of conflict saw a rise in the influence of China in Ryukyuan affairs. Through its relations with China and wide trading routes, the Ryukyu Kingdom ex-panded its influence in the area, but mismanagement continued. Indeed, Shuri showed little interest in the north, and instead increasingly sought to expand its connections with the south. It did, however, send punitive expe-ditions on occasion against Amami and other islands, which increasingly were unhappy with domination by the Ryukyu kings. Adding to this humil-iation and anger among the islanders of Amami was an affair that King Sho-sei reportedly had with a young girl from the island. Finding itself overex-tended and facing dissatisfaction with its rule, the Ryukyu Kingdom began to decline in the late sixteenth century.[17]

The lord of the feudal domain Satsuma (present-day Kagoshima Prefecture), Shimazu Iehisa, organized an expedition in turn against the weakening Ryukyu Kingdom, nominally to force the resumption of tribute paid to the Shogun in Edo (and punish the Ryukyus for not sending a fighting force of 7,500 soldiers for the invasion of Korea), but in actuality to establish its own influence over the islands and acquire the rewards of its rich trade.

The Amami Islands served as a launching pad for the invasion of Okinawa after Setouchi, on Amami's southern tip, and Tokunoshima, to the south of the main island of Amami, had been occupied and Okino Erabu and Yoronto subdued. As a result, the Amami Islands came under the direct influence of the Satsuma domain.

In order to exert this control, Satsuma initially sent magistrates (*bugyo*) to Amami and Tokunoshima (subsequently appointing local magistrates, or *daikan*). Eventually, however, Satsuma came to find itself overextended and in debt and began to focus on introducing sugarcane into the islands and "monopoliz[ing] the wealth derived from Amami black sugar (*kokuto*)," which they could sell at a high price in the markets in Osaka. At the same time, Satsuma authorities banned the concealment of black sugar and its sales by individuals in Amami and required farmers to turn over their black sugar production, "reducing the Amami people to serfdom."[18] Satsuma authorities went all out to see that the quotas were met. In some areas, desperate parents sold themselves or their children off as indentured servants and prostitutes (a phenomenon that reportedly repeated itself during the U.S. occupation years). With the oppression too much to take, isolated riots brook out on Tokunoshima (at Inutabu and Boma). While the extent of the monopoly was such that it helped Satsuma temporarily ride out its financial crisis, during the Bakumatsu years (1850s), Satsuma found itself once again with an astronomical debt.

The Modern Era

With the coming of the Meiji Restoration in 1868 and a modern system of government, Amami became an official part of Kagoshima Prefecture, with the infrastructure of the islands modernized to some extent. In 1874, the Oshima Administrative Office was established, followed by the Oshima District Court in 1882 and *Shichoson* (City, Town, Village) Corporation in 1886. With the promulgation of the Meiji Constitution in 1889, limited elections were held in 1890 for the Diet. In addition, missionaries, mostly Catholic, were allowed to establish churches in the islands in 1891.[19]

Recognizing the islands' strategic importance, the Imperial Navy (and to a less extent the Army) began fortifying the islands in the prewar period.[20] Specifically, the Imperial Navy saw the Amami Islands performing two roles. The first was as the forward deployment of its battleships. The second role was a base for the protection of the sea lanes, as most of the imported items and raw materials coming into Japan passed along the Nansei, and thus, Amami, Islands. The Army also saw a presence in the islands as a way to monitor activity in the area for the defense of Japan.

Despite this strategic role, it was not until 1941 that the Imperial Navy had a large presence in the islands, having used them mainly for limited exercises in the past.[21] When the U.S. military began to successfully close in on Japan during its island-hopping campaign and subsequent bombing runs on the main islands, the military fortifications on the Nansei Islands were strengthened in an effort to head off the attacks and to prevent the loss of airspace control.[22] The bombing run on the Nansei Islands on October 10, 1944, reportedly by some 1,400 U.S. aircraft, suggested the desperateness of the situation Imperial Japan faced.

Economically, the islands, despite having become a part of the modern administration of Kagoshima, lagged far behind mainland Japan in most regards. With its weak economy (more than 80 percent having been poor farmers), many islanders sought work on the mainland, further strengthening the bond (or dependency) between the islands and Japan. As anthropologist Douglas G. Haring, who conducted extensive research on the islands in the early 1950s, wrote, "Japan Proper serve[d] as model and inspiration to Amami Oshima."[23] Indeed, the old proverb "Look North (to Japan)" exemplified both this trend and these feelings.

Interestingly, while many settled in Kagoshima Prefecture (and neighboring Miyazaki and Fukuoka), still more went on to the Kansai (Kyoto-Osaka-Kobe) and Kanto (Tokyo-Kanagawa-Saitama) areas, having faced discrimination in Kagoshima. Ironically, this situation benefited the reversion movement later due to the higher social standing that those from Amami had gained while in Tokyo because of their achievements in academia, politics, law, and government.

On the other hand, complicated feelings existed toward the Islands' southern neighbor, Okinawa, which had once dominated Amami. The Amami islanders began to adopt the discriminatory attitudes of mainland Japanese toward Okinawa. These feelings would continue into the postwar as well. Specifically, problems seen during the efforts to create one administrative system for the Amami and Ryukyu Islands during the occupation years exemplified these mixed feelings. With the occupation headquarters and numerous military bases being located in Okinawa, as well as new facilities being built, the much more heavily populated Okinawa became the administrative and economic center of the Nansei Islands, and the opinions of its leaders, who often held higher positions, carried more weight in many of the meetings. Moreover, to Amami residents, many Okinawans seemed indifferent about the question of reversion to Japan, as seen in statements by its leaders, while the Amami Islanders thought of nothing else. To the residents of Amami, the Okinawans were not Japanese, or at least not "as Japanese" as they felt themselves to be. During the reversion movement, they often made a distinction between their islands and Okinawa, calling for early reversion because their islands were less important strategically than Okinawa, and went out of their way time and time again to stress that they were a part of Kagoshima Prefecture and Japanese "to the bone." Indeed, as Haring observed at the time:

> Amami Oshima society and culture . . . are truly Japanese—with a difference. Often the people themselves are too close to the issues to see them in perspective, but there is no question about their basic loyalties and complete psychological identification with Japan. . . . The Meiji Government not only ended slavery, but introduced schools and gave the people a sense of dignity and importance. The twentieth century government of Japan subsidized Amami as a deficit area, provided agricultural education and agricultural experiment stations, introduced better breeds of pigs and horses, developed forestry services and controls, instituted weather forecasting and typhoon warnings, promoted shipping and fisheries, built roads and bridges, provided postal service and social insurance, welcomed Amami youths in mainland schools, effected the development of hydroelectricity, and held out glowing promises of a bright future in the impending conquests of Manchuria and East Asia—a new Empire with jobs for all and land for hungry peasants. This was the Amami Oshima picture of Japan. Unlike Okinawa, Amamians focused their dreams in Japan.[24]

Mainland Japanese, on the other hand, knew little about the islands, and, indeed, few could read the characters in the name "Amami" properly, instead pronouncing the name as "Enmi," or, even worse, "Ebimi" (as the character for Amami is similar to the character for *ebi*, or "shrimp"). Curiously, these incorrect readings happened during the height of the postwar reversion movement as well, saddening those from Amami who were organizing the rallies and signature drives, and who probably were made to feel "less Japanese" than they believed themselves to be.

Postwar and Occupation
Although they had been subject to aerial bombardments (with the one on Naze on April 10, 1945, shortly after the start of the horrendous Battle of Okinawa, reportedly destroying about 90 percent of the city) and submarine attacks, the Amami Islands did not experience an invasion or the horrendous ground fighting that Okinawa saw and which took approximately 140,000 civilian lives. The islanders did however live in constant fear of air raids, particularly following the successful taking of Okinawa and its surrounding is-

lands by U.S. forces that spring and in light of the islands' hosting of important Imperial Army and Naval bases, such as Koniya Air Field on the southern tip of Amami, as mentioned in the previous section.

With the signing of the Instrument of Surrender in Tokyo Bay on September 2, 1945, Japan came under Allied Occupation, led by U.S. forces and an American commander, Gen. Douglas A. MacArthur. The Amami Islands, being a part of Kagoshima Prefecture, continued to be administered by Japan. This would change less than six months later however, when the Amami Islands were administratively and politically separated from Japan and placed under the U.S. military occupation command for the Ryukyu Islands.

During this time, the islands were in a "vacuum," as one report mentioned, as they fell between two occupation areas, that of the U.S. Army Forces, Pacific (AFPAC) under 30° north latitude, and that of the Supreme Commander for Allied Powers (SCAP) north of that line. On January 29, 1946, SCAP issued a directive (SCAP–IN) to the Japanese government in which all islands south of 30° north latitude, including the Amami Islands and the Ryukyu Islands, were placed outside of Japan's jurisdiction. Announced to the people of Amami on February 2, this directive, known as the "2/2 Proclamation," effectively and administratively separated the islands from Japan, presenting the Amami Islands with the same fate that was befalling Okinawa farther to the South.

On March 13 of that same year, Lt. Comdr. Paul F. Reilley arrived in Naze with nineteen others to establish the U.S. Naval military government. The next day, the American flag was raised at the former local district office of the prefectural government. The occupation had begun.

With the Amami Islands, being separated as they were (despite their very intimate ties to the mainland), combined with the restrictions of the military government, strong feelings for reversion growing into the reversion movement were clearly inevitable. It was as if, Haring observed, "the people of the State of Maine might feel were they suddenly cut off from the United States and incorporated into French Canada."[25] A reversion movement, bordering sometimes on the radical, thus built up throughout the occupation period despite attempts to suppress it, as the fate of the islands and its 220,000 inhabitants continued to remain unknown. It would become more open and active in 1951, with the movements for a peace treaty receiving national and international attention following John Foster Dulles' visit to Japan in January and February of that year for discussions with the Japanese government.

The movement and public opinion throughout Japan, as well as the strong appeals of the Japanese government, were successful in convincing the U.S.

government and the Allies of the desirability of allowing the islands to be retained by Japan. Japan was permitted to keep "residual sovereignty" over the islands, but the United States maintained administrative rights. The movement continued with its demands and the Japanese government kept up its pressure on the U.S. government, and, eventually, the Eisenhower Administration decided to return the islands to Japan in late 1953. It is to that story that we now turn.

Notes

1. See figure I.1. Okinawa and Amami (or O-Shima) form the two largest islands among the Nansei Islands, which represent the entire island chain south of Kyushu in western Japan. The Ryukyu Islands are technically those islands south of 27° north latitude. The Amami Islands are those immediately north of that parallel.

2. Murayama Iekuni, *Amami Fukkishi* (*The History of the Amami Reversion*), (Naze: Nankai Nichinichi Shimbunsha, 1971), pp. 35–36.

3. *Ibid.* Also see Takada Toshisada, *Unmei no Shimajima Amami to Okinawa* (*Destiny's Islands: Amami and Okinawa*), (Kagoshima: Amamisha, 1956), pp. 95–99; and Saneshima Ryuzo, *Ano Hi, Ano Toki* (*That Day, That Time*), (Naze: Nankai Nichinichi Shimbunsha, 1996), pp. 157–166.

4. Murayama, *Amami Fukkishi*, p. 36. Stilwell had replaced Lt. Gen. Simon B. Buckner, killed in action by artillery fire on June 18, 1945, in the last days of the Battle of Okinawa, as commanding general of the Tenth Army. In July, he succeeded Adm. Chester W. Nimitz as military governor of Okinawa, returning to Washington in October.

5. As Takada relates in his memoirs, cited above, to his great disappointment, U.S. occupation authorities inexplicably continued to use the phrase "Northern Ryukyus" in other documents, signs, and speeches.

6. In a September 3, 1945 letter to Stilwell, Takada explained that he would like to call on him because he "long[ed] for your lending us your powerful influence over [the] Amami Gunto problem not to make these islands 'the second Alsace-Lorraine.'" See Reel No. A–0146, *Nansei Shoto Kizoku Mondai Amami Gunto, Daiikkan*, p. 19. For more on this, see Takada, *Unmei no Shimajima*, pp. 20, 24–25, and 88–99. According to one historian of postwar Okinawa, Takada's "unswerving honor and duty impressed" the United States particularly because he "bore a humanitarian understanding for his own force and the civilians of the Amami O'shima Gunto." See Gordon Warner, *The Okinawan Reversion Story: War, Peace, Occupation, Reversion, 1945–1972* (Naha: The Executive Link, 1995), p. 33. As an example of this, Warner relates that Tanaka later requested permission from the United States to hand over moving equipment, carpentry tools, blankets, and other materials to the civilian leadership in Amami for the benefit of the residents (p. 39). As is mentioned at the end of chapter 2 in this book, Takada also paid a visit on the delegation from Amami who were in Tokyo in 1952 to appeal for the return of the islands.

7. This expression was used for example by Izumi Horo, a writer–educator and leader of the reversion movement on Amami, in a poem on the occasion of the return of the Islands entitled, "Imazo Sokoku e." For more on this, see Robert D. Eldridge, "The Amami Reversion Movement: Its Origins, Activities, Impact, and Meaning," *Asian Cultural Studies*, No. 27 (2001), pp. 77–98.

8. The Ogasawara (Bonin) Islands, forming part of the Nanpo Islands, also separated at the time of the peace treaty, were returned on June 26, 1968. For a recent study on their return, see Robert D. Eldridge, "Ogasawara to Nichibei Kankei, 1945–1968" ("Ogasawara and U.S.–Japan Relations, 1945–1968"), in Daniel Long, ed., *Ogasawara Gaku Koto Hajime* (*An Introduction to Ogasawara Studies*), (Kagoshima: Nanpo Shinsha, 2002), pp. 245–272.

9. Article 3 reads: "Japan will concur in any proposal of the United States to the United Nations to place under its trusteeship system, with the United States as the sole administering authority, Nansei Shoto south of 29° north latitude (including the Ryukyu Islands and the Daito Islands), Nanpo Shoto south of Sofu Gan (including the Bonin Islands, Rosario Island and the Volcano Islands) and Parece Vela and Marcus Island. Pending the making of such a proposal and affirmative action thereon, the United States will have the right to exercise all and any powers of administration, legislation and jurisdiction over the territory and inhabitants of these islands, including their territorial waters." As discussed later in this book, Japan was recognized as having "residual sovereignty" over the islands at the Peace Conference. See Robert D. Eldridge, *The Origins of the Bilateral Okinawa Problem: Okinawa in Postwar U.S.–Japan Relations, 1945–1952* (New York: Garland, 2001).

10. My study, "The Amami Reversion Movement," appearing in *Asian Cultural Studies,* was undertaken precisely to fill this gap in the scholarship.

11. If the islands of Etorofu and Kunashiri, which are 3,183 km and 1,499 km, respectively, and make up part of the disputed Northern Territories, are included, then Amami Oshima ranks fifth in size.

12. In addition to the Amami Island Group, the Satsunan Islands, which have a total area of 922 square miles (1,483 square km), are made up of the Osumi Group (Tanegashima, Yaku, Kuchino Yerabu Islands), and the Tokara Group (Kuchinoshima, Nakanoshima, Suwanose Islands). It was between the Tokara Group and the Osumi Group, at 30° north latitude, that the Occupation drew the line of demarcation.

13. In writing this section, I am indebted to the following works: Nobori Shomu, *Dai Amami Shi* (*The History of Greater Amami*), Rev. Ed. (Tokyo: Hara Shobo, 1975); and Shidehara Akira, *Nanto Enkaku Shiron* (*Studies on the History of the Southern Islands*), (Tokyo: Toyamabo, 1900).

14. U.S. Amami Civil Administration Team, ed., *Amami Oshima* (Naze: U.S. Amami Civil Administration Team, 1952), p. 2.

15. George H. Kerr, *Okinawa: The History of an Island People* (Rutland: Charles E. Tuttle Company, 1958), p. 49. Douglas G. Haring, "Amami Gunto: Forgotten Islands," *Far Eastern Survey*, Vol. 21, No. 16 (November 19, 1952), p. 170.

16. Foreign Office, Japanese Government, ed., *Minor Islands Adjacent to Japan Proper: Part II Ryukyu and Other Nansei Islands* (Tokyo: Foreign Office, Japanese Government, March 1947), p. 9.

17. Kerr, *Okinawa*, p. 60.

18. Haring, "Amami Gunto." Satsuma was anti-Tokugawa and naturally sought to limit the influence of the Tokugawa forces in its province.

19. Amami Senkyo ed., "100 Shunen Kinenshi Henshubu," *Katorikku Amami 100 Nen* (*100 Years of Catholicism in Amami*), (Naze: Amami Senkyo 100 Shunen Jikko Iinkai, 1992), pp. 52–53. At the time, the Catholic population of Japan was 44,505, with 27,909 based in Kyushu. In 1934, the churches were closed due to a fear of spies and some 4,000 believers were forced to renounce Christianity. Today, some thirty-two Catholic churches can be found throughout the Amami Islands. For this history, see Miyashita Masaaki, *Seido no Hinomaru* (*The Cathedral's Hinomaru Flag*), (Kagoshima: Nanpo Shinsha, 1999).

20. Fujiwara Nanpu, *Shin Amamishi* (*New Amami History*), (Naze: Amami Shunjusha, 1980), p. 632.

21. *Ibid.*

22. *Ibid.*, pp. 632–634.

23. Douglas G. Haring, *Scientific Investigations in the Ryukyu Islands (SIRI): The Island of Amami Oshima in the Northern Ryukyus* (Washington, D.C.: National Research Council, 1952), p. 17. Haring adds, "unlike Okinawa, Amamians focused their dreams in Japan. Okinawans emigrated eagerly to Hawaii, to Brazil, to the Philippines—anywhere. Amami folk migrated only to Japan and to Manchuria, and still limit their hopes of self-improvement to moving to Japan Proper" (p. 18). Haring's article, cited previously, is based on this report. I would like to thank Yamashita Fumitake, who served as Haring's then-assistant in Amami, for his insights on the report. Author's interview with Yamashita Fumitake, July 18, 1999, Naze City, Amami. Yamashita later authored a small book entitled *Amami no Rekishi Samazama* (*Various Aspects of Amami's History*), (Sumiyoson: Amami Bunka Zaidan, 1994), and played a central role in the editing of *Kaitei Nazeshishi* (*Revised History of Naze City*) by the Kaitei Nazeshishi Hensan Iinkai, published in 1996.

24. Haring, *Scientific Investigations in the Ryukyu Islands*, pp. 18–19.

25. *Ibid.*, p. 18.

~

CHAPTER ONE

U.S. Pre-Reversion Policy toward Amami and Okinawa

It is the considered judgment of this Command, after a thorough examination of the whole problem, that the [proposed] course of action . . . is
impracticable under the present circumstances and fraught with such serious consequences as to jeopardize the prestige of the United States and
of Naval Administration in Far Eastern Waters.

—Rear Admiral John D. Price,
Memorandum to the Chief of Naval Operations,
January 20, 1946

The return of the Amami Islands can be said to have been a natural, if belated, outcome of the policy of the American government in favor of the
principle of "self-determination" and against territorial expansion as one of
the spoils of World War II as announced in the Atlantic Charter of August
1941. Due to a division within U.S. policy-making circles over diplomatic–political considerations and military–strategic requirements, however,
the decision to return to historically, legally, and culturally Japanese territory
was delayed for almost two years following the San Francisco Peace Treaty in
the case of Amami and twenty years in the case of the remainder of the Nansei Islands, namely Okinawa.

The following discussion examines U.S. policy toward these islands, and
the Amami Islands specifically, during the wartime and postwar periods leading up to the start of the Eisenhower Administration in 1953. Specifically,
this chapter focuses on the division within the U.S. government over Japan's

territorial disposition, namely the State Department's view that the islands should be retained by Japan and the U.S. military's strong desire to see the United States possess permanent or semipermanent control over them.

Early Planning: State and Military

From their earliest interagency discussions regarding the disposition of Japan's territory, the U.S. military, represented primarily by the Joint Chiefs of Staff (JCS), and State Department held almost completely opposing views. There would be numerous discussions and compromises in later years, particularly around the time of the Peace Treaty, but the basic positions, outlined above, remained essentially far apart.

Shortly before the outbreak of World War II, the State Department began its studies on the postwar world and its policies vis-à-vis Japan. These studies picked up in pace following America's entry into the war in December 1941. The summer before saw U.S. President Franklin D. Roosevelt and British Prime Minister Winston Churchill announce the "Atlantic Charter" which declared, among other important ideals, that the Allies would not seek territorial expansion through war and would respect the will of the people in any territorial changes. Adopting this as the basis for its policy for territorial disposition, the State Department sought to distinguish between territories Japan acquired by aggression and those historically a part of Japan. It also had to take into consideration the security requirements for the region. As a result, a tentative conclusion was reached in September 1942 that the Nansei (Luchu) Islands could "possibly be left in Japanese hands" but that further study was needed.[1]

In July of the following year, the so-called "Masland Paper," written by Dr. John W. Masland Jr. of the Territorial Subcommittee within the State Department, was completed suggesting that "conditional retention by Japan" was probably the best solution for the disposition of the "Liuchiu Islands," the Chinese name by which the State Department was then referring to the Ryukyus.[2] This paper would form the basic policy of the State Department over the years in seeking to return the Nansei Islands to Japan.[3]

In October 1944, the next time that serious discussions were undertaken regarding the disposition of the islands, the position that the Nansei Islands should be returned to Japan was confirmed, as seen in an October 7 draft of a paper presented to the secretary of the State Department's Inter-Divisional Area Committee on the Far East that stated, "It is recommended that no transfer of sovereignty take place for the Liuchiu Islands (the Amami, Okinawa, Sakishima, and Daito Islands)."[4] However, reflecting disagreement within the committee regarding the geographical composition of the Nansei Islands, the question of whether the Amami Islands should be considered a part of the Ryukyu Islands became the subject of debate.

On October 10, Joseph A. Ballantine, a Far Eastern specialist, asked Dr. Hugh Borton, secretary of the committee and a young Japan expert on loan from Columbia University, whether the "Amami Group [was] usually considered part of the Liuchiu Islands."[5] According to the minutes of the meeting, Borton responded that he believed that "the term usually was used to include the Amami group" but agreed to examine the question further. At the committee's next meeting held on October 12, Borton reported that, according to well-known Japanese geographers, the Ryukyu Islands were defined as extending from the Amami in the north to the Sakishima group in the south.[6] Two weeks later, reflecting the disagreement that continued to exist on this issue, the committee voted eight to five over the objections of the representatives of the Japan Affairs Division, Erle R. Dickover and Frank S. Williams, in favor of considering the Ryukyu Islands as a group and thus not subject to separate disposition.[7] As a result, the final recommendation of the committee, adopted at its 171st meeting on December 5, read

> As the Japanese have a strong claim to the Liuchiu Islands on the grounds of historical possession, nationality and propinquity, as well as on the basis of the ethnographic and linguistic similarities between the Japanese and the Liuchiuans, it is recommended that the United States should favor no transfer of sovereignty of the Liuchiu Islands (comprising the Amami, Okinawa, Sakishima and Daito Islands).[8]

Thus, the State Department, while importantly and correctly recognizing Japan's claim to sovereignty over all of the Nansei Islands and seeking to allow Japan to retain them, also incorrectly viewed the Amami Islands as a part of the Ryukyu Islands.

In 1945, following the end of the war, the U.S. military, which had become aware of America's vulnerability in the wake of the surprise attack on Pearl Harbor, began to clarify its postwar strategic requirements with the study known as JCS 570. These studies had actually been going on since 1942, but began to take shape near the end of the respective European and Pacific conflicts.[9]

On January 31, 1946, the JCS study (JCS 570/50) was given to Secretary of State James F. Byrnes, who had earlier requested it in order to know of the actual military requirements of the Joint Chiefs. The JCS study, to the shock of the State Department, delineated the Nansei Shoto Islands south of 31°

north latitude (see figure I.1) as a strategic trusteeship in order to allow for U.S. bases, in other words, the entire Nansei Island chain immediately south of Kyushu. The next day, State Department committee reviewed the JCS study in an attempt to bring the paper it had been working on in line with that of the JCS. There, Dr. Edwin O. Reischauer, a young Japan expert on loan to the State Department from Harvard University (and later to become Ambassador to Japan), who was in favor of the entire island chain's return, stated that he "thought that the committee should decide on a definite line (preferably 28°/40°), south of which they would agree to a trusteeship if such was to be established at all. The islands north of 28°/40° were traditionally a part of Satsuma territory, while those south of the line belonged to the ancient kingdom of the Liuchius.[10] Reischauer's suggestion was adopted, as seen in the February 11 revision of the paper drafted by Dr. Rupert Emerson, which recommended that

> If such a base is established, the remainder of the central and southern Ryukyus should be made a non-strategic trust territory with either the United States or the United Nations Organization itself as the administering authority, depending upon the extent of the strategic area required by the United States. The northern islands (north of 28°40°N. Lat., or north of such line as may be found to separate islands primarily inhabited by Okinawans from islands primarily inhabited by Japanese) should be returned to Japan.[11]

In his memoirs, Reischauer refers to this debate (particularly as it related to a revised version of the document on March 6, 1946). "I argued that the whole chain should if possible be returned to Japan," he writes, "but that if American bases were felt to be absolutely necessary, all the islands north of Amami Oshima should be returned to Japan and the central and southern Ryukyus should be made a non-strategic trust territory. My own memory is that I included Amami Oshima among the islands which should be returned, but possibly I was talked out of this before I wrote the March 6 draft."[12] By suggesting the new line of 28°/40° north latitude, Reischauer probably sought to reduce the areas acquired by the United States and thereby allow Japan to retain as much of its territory as possible. However, in doing so, he seems to have repeated the mistake made by his State Department colleagues earlier in their geographical definition of the Amami and Ryukyu Islands.

In the end, representatives from the State Department and the JCS were unable to resolve their differences over trusteeship arrangements for the Nansei Islands during discussions in 1946, and further talks were shelved for the time being. Instead, U.S. President Harry S. Truman announced that the former Japanese Mandated Islands would be placed under a United Nations

Strategic Trusteeship (with nothing mentioned as to the fate of the Nansei and Nanpo Island groups, both historically Japanese territory, as opposed to the Mandated Islands, which were administered after World War I by Japan on behalf of the League of Nations). In the meantime, as progress on preparations for an early peace treaty conference with Japan was being made, Borton—tasked to draft the treaty—finished a version of it (discussed below) that he had been working on since the fall of 1946. This draft, in line with the State Department's position to date, permitted the Ryukyu Islands to be retained by Japan.[13]

As this great debate continued in Washington, interestingly, locally in Okinawa, representatives of the Military Government had actually attempted to prevent the expansion of the occupation of Okinawa northward into the Amami Islands. Had these efforts been successful, the Amami tragedy of a badly run occupation and a poorly thought out partition of the islands and its people from mainland Japan could have been avoided. It is to that story that we turn next.

The Start of the Occupation of the Amami Islands

On February 2, 1946, the contents of a SCAP directive separating the islands from Japanese control was announced over the radio. Known as the "2/2 Proclamation," this directive essentially removed the islands from Japanese control.

Although the news came as a great shock to the people of Amami (a "thunderbolt out of the sky" in the words of one resident), the announcement was not completely unexpected.[14] Several days before, on January 29, GHQ officials had relayed to the Central Liaison Office (Foreign Ministry) of the Japanese government this directive, entitled "Governmental and Administrative Separation of Certain Outlying Areas from Japan," which stated that the "Imperial Japanese Government is directed to cease exercising, or attempting to exercise, governmental or administrative authority over any area outside of Japan, or over any government officials and employees or any other persons within such areas."[15] The directive went on to define Japan as "includ[ing] the four main islands of Japan (Hokkaido, Honshu, Kyushu, and Shikoku) and the approximately 1,000 smaller adjacent islands, including the Tsushima Islands and the Ryukyu (Nansei) Islands north of 30°north latitude (excluding Kuchinoshima Island)." Although not specifically named, the Amami Islands were excluded from the geographical definition of Japan in this directive. The "invisible, artificial line" of 30° north latitude, just south of Kyushu, became, in fact, a real boundary.[16]

At noon that same day (January 29), Rear Adm. John D. Price, Commander, Naval Operating Base, Okinawa, and Chief Military Gov. Officer, USMC Col. Charles I. Murray, Deputy Commander, and the three others in their party arrived from Okinawa by landing ship tank (LST) at Naze Port and met with Ikeda Yasukichi, the director of the Kagoshima Prefecture Amami District Office (Kagoshima Ken Amami Shichocho), relaying the general gist of the directive.[17] During their two-hour meeting, Price explained that a further announcement would be made in February or March and asked Ikeda to inform the people of the island to begin preparing for the arrival of military government personnel.

The following morning, Ikeda called a meeting at the District Office, with 300 community leaders and other residents crowding into the second-floor meeting room.[18] Ikeda, wishing to put the "Price Notice" in a favorable light, expressed hope in the ideals of American democracy and in the belief that the occupation would not mean a change in the territorial status of the islands.[19] In this latter point, Ikeda was correct in thinking that the directive did not necessarily suggest a permanent separation of the islands, as paragraph 5 of the January 29 memo clearly stated that "Nothing in this directive shall be construed as an indication of Allied policy relating to the ultimate determination of the minor islands referred to in Article 8 of the Potsdam Declaration."[20] However, Ikeda could not have been aware of the very strong desire of the JCS to keep control of the Ryukyu Islands, which would indirectly or directly affect Amami's future status.

In any case, through Price's visit and Ikeda's holding of the conference, Amami's leaders and general public were informed of the approaching occupation, but likely still believed it to be far off. The sudden, public announcement four days later on February 2, therefore, was indeed a great surprise. It was extremely unsettling as well, as the islanders did not know what to expect with regard to the occupation and the future status of their islands. Two days later on February 4, interaction between Amami and mainland Japan was stopped. The free import and export of items was banned, as was unrestricted travel. Everything subsequently would require permission.

A committee known as the Oshima Gun Renraku Iinkai (Oshima County Liaison Committee) was established by Ikeda on February 6 for liaison purposes with the occupation forces to relay instructions and transmit desires from the residents.[21] However, the occupation forces had yet to arrive, and with no further instructions following, Amami fell into a state of limbo.[22] "Amami was," in the words of one observer at the time, "neither of Japan nor of the U.S. occupation."[23]

Interestingly, the headquarters of the U.S. Naval military government based in Okinawa, to whom the task of managing the occupation of the Amami Islands fell, initially opposed the extension of the military government to the islands, stating that "the only effective and economical method of administering [the] Northern Ryukyus is to continue them for the present under Kagoshima Prefecture."[24] Indeed, in a more strongly worded memo on January 20, approximately one week before the GHQ directive, Price reported to both CINCPAC in Hawaii and the Chief of Naval Operations in Washington that "it is the considered judgment of this Command, after a thorough examination of the whole problem, that the [proposed] course of action . . . is impracticable under the present circumstances and fraught with such serious consequences as to jeopardize the prestige of the United States and of Naval Administration in Far Eastern Waters."[25]

Price's appeal to Washington went on to explain the circumstances that made the extension of the occupation to the Amami Islands impractical:

1. The administrative resources of the U.S. Naval military government, Okinawa, have been reduced to a point where without further additions of mature and experienced personnel efficient performance of its mission in Okinawa alone is impossible. This command, therefore, has no personnel whatsoever available for the tasks required by the above directives.

2. O-Shima Gun, by virtue of its being a part of Kagoshima Prefecture, completely integrated politically and economically with the prefectural government, requires no American personnel, equipment or supplies. Its separation from the Prefecture as directed would necessitate immediate assignment of highly qualified officer personnel in considerable over and above what is needed for the administration of Okinawa. Similarly, whereas the present administration of O-Shima Gun requires no American equipment or supplies, the establishment of Naval military government there would require both if only for the maintenance of administrative personnel assigned to the task. As indicated in subsequent paragraphs, however, no amount of American personnel or equipment can prevent a prolonged period of political and economic chaos, which is completely avoided by retaining the present arrangement.

3. Under the highly centralized Japanese system, Kagoshima City is the irreplaceable center of the economic and political life of the Prefecture including O-Shima Gunto. At Kagoshima are located the offices and records of all departments of local government, including police, postal services, civil service, education, courts, finance and taxation, monopolies, and so

on, and the offices and records of all prefectural associations such as agriculture and fisheries, as well as the central banks and home offices of business concerns and publishing companies. In short, so closely woven is the fabric of prefectural society that no seam is apparent along with the islands can be separated from the mainland without leaving countless threads dangling at loose ends.

4. In contrast to Kagoshima, as a result of the war Okinawa is an economic and political vacuum. Any attempt to orient O-Shima Gunto southward to Okinawa, even if Okinawa had not been destroyed, would be an unnatural as to try to compel New England and Florida to look to Arkansas as their administrative and economic center.

Price's observations were essentially correct, as was his warning, meant probably as a last-minute wake-up call to those unfamiliar with the situation in the islands:

> The coming of Military Government administration to O-Shimas [*sic*] Gunto in accordance with the directives will be attended by an economic and political breakdown, and American prestige will have suffered a blow from which it will be possible to recover only through the expenditure of money, time, talent and effort which might have been saved by continuing the present arrangement. All sections of the population will resent American rule on account of the economic collapse. But especially resentful will be the civil servants and others who will lose such vested interests as seniority rights, retirement annuities, anticipated bonuses and the like. Yet it is upon these that the U.S. Military Government must rely for the conduct of local affairs, if the Military government is to avoid inordinate costs in American personnel and facilities. Furthermore, in view of the possible future status of the Ryukyus as wards of the United States, their interim administration must avoid if possible taking such form as to destroy the confidence of the population in American political know-how and in American justice.

Despite his prophetic warnings, Price's recommendations were not acted on. Importantly, it was not only Price who felt that way. Army officials in the Government and G-1 Administration Sections of GHQ also were concerned about the administrative political consequences of assuming command for the islands.

A staff study on military government in the Ryukyus conducted by G-1 in March 1946 recommended that the "line of demarcation" between SCAP and U.S. Army Forces, Pacific (charged with military government) be the "southern boundary of Kagoshima Prefecture" because "the occupants of this portion

Table 1.1.   U.S. Military Government Commanders in the Amami Islands, 1946–1953

Navy-led Administration	
Lt. Comdr. Paul F. Reilley, USN	March 13, 1946 to April 11, 1946
Lt. Comdr. John R. Potter, USN	April 11, 1946 to June 12, 1946

Army-led Administration	
Lt. Col. Ross H. St. Clair, USA	June 12, 1946 to November 1946
Maj. Carl B. Rauterberg, USA	November 1946 to November 1946
Maj. Fred M. Labree, USA	November 1946 to September 22, 1947
Lt. Col. Henry B. Joseph, USA	September 22, 1947 to August 1948
Col. Hugh D. Adair, USA	August 1948 to October 1949
Col. Raymond C. Barlow, USA	October 1949 to July 1950
Maj. Rockwell A. Davis, USA	July 1950 to July 1950
Lt. Col. Robert M. Shiels, USA	July 1950 to August 1950
Col. Raymond C. Barlow, USA	August 1950 to November 1951
Col. Wilson Potter, Jr. USA	November 1951 to March 28, 1952
Col. Howard H. Davis, USA	March 28, 1952 to May 1953
Maj. Carrol J. Freeman, USA	May 1953 to December 1953

adapted from Fujiwara, *Shin Amamishi*, vol. 1

of the Ryukyus regard themselves as mainland Japanese."[26] Moreover, the study continues, that area is "economically, socially, and politically within" the prefecture and has been "functioning without American personnel, equipment or supplies and is administered by Japanese Kagoshima Prefecture officials." The study went on to recommend that GHQ should reauthorize the Japanese government to exercise "governmental and administrative control over that portion of the Ryukyus included within Kagoshima Prefecture." The area administered would be under the supervision of the Eighth Army, headquartered in Yokohama, "just as any other prefecture of Japan." This recommendation "also precludes the necessity of reorienting economically that portion of the Ryukyus included within the boundaries of Kagoshima Prefecture." Importantly, it notes, "this solution will achieve maximum economy of military government personnel without necessitating a redefinition of the territorial limits of the sovereignty of Japan."

The Government Section of GHQ immediately concurred in the G-1 study, recommending that "for administrative and command purposes," Japan be "redefined to include all of Kagoshima Prefecture south of 30°north latitude."[27] GS explained its reasons in the following way.

GS argued that a revision of the boundaries of Japan to include all of Kagoshima Prefecture, including those islands south of 30°north latitude, was "in no way inconsistent" with the Potsdam Declaration or policies adopted in the JCS document of November 1945, JCS 1380/15, as any changes made now would not determine the extent of Japanese sovereignty or predetermine the ultimate fate of the minor islands—"Such final determination must be made under the final peace terms."

Similarly, by having the islands administered by Japanese authorities under SCAP, there was "absolutely no commitment concerning the ultimate disposition of the islands, direct or implied." Thus, the argument continues, "the proposed revision does not jeopardize [U.S.] interests in any base on Okinawa. . . . As long as Japan is demilitarized and occupied by predominantly American forces, it is inconceivable that either Japan herself or any Allied participant in the occupation could threaten American interests from a position established in the Northern Ryukyus." As a result, "the problem is," the report continued, "not one of prematurely establishing an arbitrary boundary, but of administering the islands by the occupation forces in the most efficient and economical manner, while still fully protecting our interests."

Additionally, according to GS, the islands were in a "twilight zone" because no military government had been established over them between September 1945 and February 1946, and the subsequent severing of administrative control and official communications in early February had left them in a "vacuum." The Naval military government was faced with setting up a separate administration on short notice and with limited personnel, a problem that would be faced when the Army was to take over. "A redefinition of Japan as suggested," the report points out, "will definitely clarify this situation by placing all of Kagoshima Prefecture under the jurisdiction of SCAP and the 8th Army and by placing Okinawa Prefecture under Army Forces, Western Pacific (AFWESPAC)."

Further, there was "no valid reason" for causing the "dislocation" at this time nor for "assuming direct responsibility for the 183,500 people involved," particularly in light of the fact that their economy has never been self-sufficient. "To saddle any additional burden on the people of the United States," the report warned, "requires positive justification." Instead of placing the islands under direct military government, which would create a large burden, the islands should be left under Kagoshima's administrative control.

Finally, the report warned of the lack of personnel trained in military government, noting that between then (April) and July 16, the numbers would decrease "rapidly" (due to demobilization back to the United States) while the "volume of work required by SCAP is increasing. Unless the personnel requirements for the occupation of Japan, including the Ryukyus, are reexamined and increased in the near future," the report observed, "increasing difficulties will result on the operating level."

Despite these and other convincing reasons, G-3 Operations within GHQ strongly opposed any change in the line of demarcation.[28] Indeed, the report's conclusions argued, "United States interests should be paramount in establishment of jurisdictions involved, and sees no insuperable difficulties in maintenance of the southern boundary of SCAP control at 30° north latitude as presently established." One wonders if G-3 had even read any of the reports written by the military government personnel.

In the end, despite all of these warnings, it was decided that the status quo would be kept with regard to the boundaries set in the January 29 Directive, and that, as scheduled, the Army would take over for the Navy in the administration of the Ryukyu Islands effective July 1. This boundary would not change until the time of the Peace Treaty, when 29°north latitude became the line of demarcation, and the islands north of those (and below 30°) were returned to Japan on December 5, 1951.

In the meantime, however, the decision taken in the spring of 1946, as was mentioned above, was not meant to prejudice the final outcome. Indeed, as events below show, efforts were made by the State Department to have the islands returned to Japan.

However, the raising of the Stars and Stripes on March 14, the day after the arrival of U.S. forces participating in the military government, outside of the headquarters certainly did not put the islanders at ease as to their long-term fate.[29] Nor did the fact that when the headquarters was established (at the old District Office), the sign outside in English read "United States Naval Government of the Northern Ryukyu Islands."[30] This was in spite of the heated arguments that took place at the time of the Surrender Ceremony in September, to which the United States finally agreed to change the wording (as discussed in the introduction to this book) from Northern Ryukyus to Amami Gunto—Kagoshima Ken. Being called the "Northern Ryukyus" would continue to bother Amami residents for some time to come.[31] Symbolic of this separation of the islands from Kyushu, Ikeda and other prefectural government officials were relieved of their duties the following week and repatriated to Kagoshima in May.[32] The military occupation of Amami had begun.

The Aborted 1947 Peace Treaty and Reexamining U.S. Policy for the Ryukyus

As discussed previously, Borton and his colleagues came up with a draft peace treaty by the summer of 1947. This August 5 version, however, was severely criticized by MacArthur in Tokyo and the JCS in Washington for allowing strategically important Okinawa to be left with Japan.[33] Although the JSC indirectly recognized that the "relationship in language and culture" between the "Northern Ryukyus" and Japan is "close," it also noted that "the natives [of the islands south of the Northern Ryukyus] consider themselves racially and culturally distinct from the Japanese."[34] This latter perspective on the identity of the inhabitants of the Nansei Islands was a view typical of the military.[35]

Interestingly, the JCS acknowledged in the same study of the State Department draft that the "northern Ryukyus . . . are of negligible military importance and . . . are adjacent to Japan and have always been administered as a part of [Japan]," suggesting that the Amami Islands might in the end be returned. In the same report, however, the JCS made clear that the "southern Ryukyus cannot correctly, from the military viewpoint, be considered 'minor' in view of the extreme potential strategic importance, both defensively and offensively, of Okinawa." Amami, in other words, was far less important to the United States than Okinawa and the islands south of it, although the JCS would continue to call for the strategic control over the entire area.

In light of JCS opposition to the peace treaty draft, as well as the refusal of the Soviet Union to participate in a peace treaty preparatory conference, Undersecretary of State Robert A. Lovett directed George F. Kennan, director of the State Department's Policy Planning Staff (PPS), to review the Borton draft. After consultations with military officers and Far Eastern specialists, a draft PPS paper on U.S. policy for the peace treaty was prepared on September 8, with a long section devoted to dealing with the question of the disposition of the Ryukyu Islands. It read:

> For strategic reasons the southern portion of the Ryukyus, including Okinawa, should be placed under U.S. strategic trusteeship. Because such a proposal represents an expansionist move on the part of the U.S., care should be taken that it is presented to our allies in the most acceptable context. That context is not territorial delineations—awarding China, Formosa and the U.S.S.R its Yalta gains. The most acceptable context is negotiations regarding future measures to ensure that Japan does not again become a threat to peace. Therefore, the U.S. should in its draft state that the disposition of the Ryukyus is reserved for subsequent negotiation and in the territorial negotiations postpone discussion on the Southern Ryukyus until disarmament of Japan is taken up by the conference. It will be observed that Annex A [see figure 1.1 below] shows the strategically unimportant northern Ryukyus as retained by Japan. However, at least until such time as the U.S.S.R. reveals its attitude on the disposition of the southernmost Kuriles, the U.S. should apply its reservations regarding the southern Ryukyus to the whole Ryukyus archipelago. Thus if the U.S.S.R.

should concede the southernmost Kuriles to Japan, the U.S. would be in position to make, without strategic cost, an offsetting gesture with regard to the northern Ryukyus. If the U.S.S.R. does not make this territorial concession, the U.S. should still reserve negotiations on the northern Ryukyus until it proposes the strategic trusteeship for the southern portion of the chain. At this time it should, for a desirable psychological effect, however slight, also propose that Japan retain the northern Ryukyus.[36]

In a subsequent draft, dated September 17, the PPS recommended somewhat similarly that

The initial U.S. proposal regarding the southern Ryukyus [which were to be placed under U.S. strategic trusteeship] should, for bargaining purposes, include the whole archipelago. Thus if the U.S.S.R. should unexpectedly agree to Japanese retention of the southern-most Kuriles, the U.S. would have a counter in the painless relinquishment of claim over the northern Ryukyus. Ultimately in the negotiations, if there is no need for the claim for bargaining purposes, the U.S. should propose that the Northern Ryukyus be retained by Japan.[37]

The PPS final report, "PPS/10," dated October 14, recommended that "A decision on the disposition of the Ryukyu Islands south of 29° would be held in abeyance pending the receipt from the State-War-Navy Coordinating Committee (SWNCC) of information regarding relative desirability of (1) a U.S. strategic trusteeship over those islands and (2) a long-term lease of base areas, nominal sovereignty over the islands being retained by Japan."[38] Symbolic of the difficulty of the territorial problem, the PPS prepared an additional recommendation, "PPS/10/1," entitled "Special Recommendation on Ultimate Disposition of the Ryukyus," in which it stated that it needed more information before a final decision could be made.[39] The map included in PPS/10/1 suggests, however, that the Amami Islands were to be separated from Japan.

The review conducted by the PPS on the peace treaty concluded in March 1948, following a trip to Japan and Okinawa by its director.[40] Kennan, who was critically aware of the strategic requirements, recommended in PPS/28, submitted on March 25 and revised as PPS/28/2 on May 26, that the United States continue to seek strategic control of the Ryukyu Islands south of latitude 29° north latitude.[41] PPS/28/2 was eventually adopted as NSC 13 and, after almost one year of discussions, was approved as NSC 13/3 by President Truman on May 6, 1949. NSC 13/3 also had the Ryukyu Islands south of 29° north latitude to be placed under long-term U.S. strategic control.

Although this would become official U.S. policy with President Truman's endorsement, the members of the Office of Far Eastern Affairs in the State Department were concerned about the possibility that Japan might not be allowed to retain the Nansei Islands, territory historically Japan's. This policy became clear after the completion of the drafty peace treaty in the latter half of 1950, worked out between the State Department and Defense Department, which stated that:

> The United States will also propose to the United Nations to place under its trusteeship system, with the United States as the administering authority, the Ryukyu Islands south of 29° north latitude . . . and pending affirmative action on such proposal the United States will have full powers of administration, legislation, and jurisdiction over the territory of these islands.[42]

Likewise the September 11 corresponding memorandum on the seven principles of a peace treaty (officially announced on September 14) explains the same point in a shorter way: "(Japan would) agree to U.N. trusteeship, with the U.S. as administering authority, of the Ryukyu and Bonin Islands."[43]

Attempts by representatives of the State Department, namely Dean Rusk, U. Alexis Johnson, William J. Sebald, Gerald Warner, Douglas W. Overton, and Robert A. Fearey, to convince their military counterparts to seek a basing agreement for the Ryukyu Islands (which would allow the islands to be returned to Japan) were met with objections that "exclusive control of those islands must be retained by the United States in order for us to be able to carry out our commitments."[44] It would be up to Dulles, named special negotiator for the treaty in 1950, to seek some sort of arrangement to bring together the conflicting security requirements and political considerations.

Japan's requests that the islands be returned to its administrative control were dismissed by Dulles due to strong pressure of the JCS and MacArthur (discussed in detail in chapter 3) during his talks in Tokyo with members of GHQ and the Japanese government in late January 1951, but the March draft treaty stated that the United States

> may propose to the United Nations to place under its trusteeship system, with the United States as the administering authority, the Ryukyu Islands south of 29° north latitude, the Bonin Islands, including Rosario Island, the Volcano Islands, Parece Vela and Marcus Island. Japan will concur in any such proposal. Pending the making of such a proposal and affirmative action thereon, the United States will have the right to exercise all and any powers of administration, legislation, and jurisdiction over the territory and inhabitants of these islands, including their territorial waters.

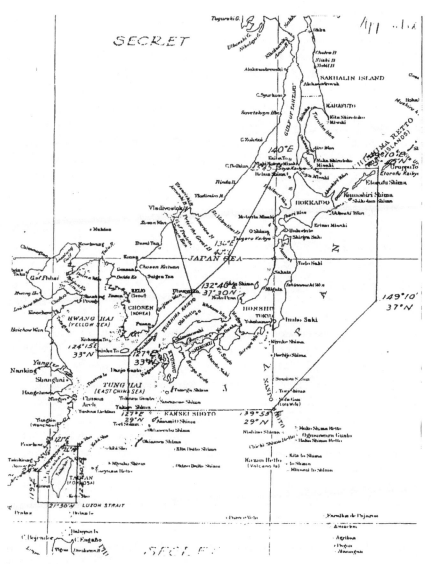

Figure 1.1 Map Appearing in PPS/10/1 Study, October 15, 1947

In an encouraging sign, "will propose" had been changed to "may propose."

In addition to this issue, the Japanese side was also concerned with the use of the word "Ryukyus." On March 27, following his arrival back to Japan from Washington, Sebald proceeded to give Prime Minister Yoshida Shigeru a copy of the treaty draft.[45] One week later, on the morning of April 4, Vice Minister Iguchi Sadao called on Sebald with his government's comments (approved by

Yoshida the day before).[46] The Japanese government, according to a memorandum handed to Sebald, requested that the phrase "The Ryukyu Islands south of 29° north latitude" (appearing in chapter 3, part 4, lines 3–4 of the draft) be replaced by "Nansei Islands south of 29° north latitude."[47] The explanation given by Iguchi for this was as follows: "The Amami island group, which belongs not to the Ryukyu Islands but to the Satsunan Islands, lies south of 29° north latitude, while the Nansei (Southwestern) Islands include both [the] Satsunan and Ryukyu groups, that is, all the islands between Kyushu and Formosa." Sebald agreed to forward this request to the State Department, which he did by telegram in the afternoon.[48] Sebald added his comment that the Japanese government's suggestion "appears historically correct according [to] Jap[anese] usage. 'Ryukyu Islands' not coextensive with 'Nansei Islands', former term applying only to those islands formerly included within Okinawa prefecture (Okinawa and Sakishima sub-groups, including Daito and Sento Islands)."[49] Upon receipt of Sebald's telegram, Fearey, who had been working on Okinawa-related issues since late 1946 and was one of the key proponents of seeking a base-leasing arrangement that would allow Okinawa to be retained by Japan in both fact as well as name, consulted on the question the same day with Samuel S. Boggs, the special adviser on geography in the Office of the Special Assistant for Intelligence and Research in the State Department since 1946. Boggs responded that indeed "'Nansei' was the more accurate term and should be used."[50] Fearey pointed out that "'Ryukyu' was a much more familiar name" and that the Japanese government probably had suggested "'Nansei' because it was a Japanese word" as opposed to the Chinese-sounding 'Ryukyu.'[51] "Nevertheless," Boggs replied, supporting the Japanese government's argument, "'Nansei' was technically more accurate."[52] Although this suggestion was not at first accepted by Dulles and the State Department, likely because such changes probably would open up a whole new round of discussions with and objections by the military, it was later adopted, as the final version of Article 3 would show.

The 1951 Peace Treaty and Calls for the Return of the Islands

It would not be inaccurate to say that up until the summer of 1951, the U.S. government did not have a clear or final separate policy toward the Amami Islands, nor was it likely aware of the degree of opposition there to a trusteeship. As we saw previously, the State Department still tended to consider the Amamis as part of the Ryukyu Islands rather than as part of the Nansei Island chain. As alluded to earlier in this chapter, perhaps the State Department chose to do so because it hoped to see all of the islands returned early together, rather than separately, in which case Okinawa might be permanently detached. In any event, it would result in underestimating feelings in the islands against their being a part of the Ryukyus on the eve of the peace conference.

On August 10, Overton, the deputy Japan desk officer in the Division of Northeast Asia Affairs since mid-1950, wrote a memorandum to U. Alexis Johnson, director of the Division of Northeast Asian Affairs, about the receipt of a petition containing the signatures of 99.8% of the residents in Amami Gunto over the age of fourteen. The petition, Overton's memorandum noted, stated that "in view of the strong historical, racial, cultural, and economic ties between Amami Gunto and Japan, failure to return the islands to Japan would be a violation of principles set forth at Potsdam and Cairo and in the Atlantic Charter."[53] Overton concluded in the following way:

> While it is obvious that many of the 139,348 persons who signed the petition have little active interest in political problems, there can be no doubt that the overwhelming majority of Amamians strongly desire that Amami Gunto be returned to Japan. Irredentist sentiment is, of course, strong throughout the Nansei Shoto; however, it is especially strong in the north, where geographical propinquity, intermarriage, and trade have operated to bind Amami Gunto closely to the Japanese mainland. On this basis, I believe that a special case can be made for the return of Amami Gunto to Japan, particularly in view of the fact that under the old Japanese Empire the Amami group of islands were [sic] included in Kagoshima Prefecture and had no administrative connection with the remainder of Nansei Shoto, which was lumped together and separately administered as Okinawa Prefecture.

Overton, it seems, had made a similar recommendation some four months before this, at the time of a visit by Amami Gunto Governor Nakae Sanetaka, who was in the United States along with several associates from Okinawa. On April 5, 1951, Overton and his immediate boss (and brother-in-law of Alexis Johnson), Warner, met with Nakae, who made an appeal for the return of the islands.[54] Overton, in his memorandum of the meeting's conversation, commented that:

> Unless the United States plans to develop military bases on Oshima, it might be considered desirable to ascertain whether this Island, and perhaps others in Amami-Oshima Gunto not of use to use, might not be returned to Japanese jurisdiction even though Okinawa and other islands to the south of Amami-Oshima are retained under U.S. trusteeship for purposes of development of bases.

Eventually Overton's recommendations would be realized, but not until 1953. Both Warner and Johnson, as well as Fearey, Sebald, and Rusk, also held sympathetic views. So sympathetic in fact, that in the fall of 1950, shortly after the seven principles of the peace treaty were announced, the Far Eastern Bureau made a rear guard effort to try to return the islands to Japan. In mid-November, for example, Fearey wrote a strongly worded memo to his superiors urging that the State Department "insist" that the military give "convincing reasons" why the United States should not seek the same military rights in the Nansei Islands as were expected to be acquired on the mainland (through a security treaty):

> The (State Department) suggestion that the U.S. keep bases in the Ryukyus under the same arrangement as in the main islands has always been met by the military reply that we must be able to count on holding the Okinawa base permanently. Even accepting this position, however, it has never as far as I know been satisfactorily explained why we must control the whole land area south of 29° north latitude permanently. Admitting the need for radar stations and the like some distance from the main base, why do we have to control the land and people in between? At most why should we require greater rights than the very broad military rights we will be acquiring in the main islands, where we have nevertheless not considered it necessary to take over the government of that country?[55]

Fearey added that although the State Department might be charged by the military with "reopening an issue already decided by the President," it was nevertheless important to reexamine the premise on which the government was proceeding.

The impetus for this memorandum was an October 26, 1950 despatch from Sebald in Tokyo to the State Department. Sebald had written that his office

> regards the deep-seated and widespread opposition of the Japanese people to the cession of such outlying island possessions as the Ryukyus, Bonins, and Kuriles as a political factor of primary importance which cannot be overlooked in our approach to the problem of the Japanese peace treaty. More specifically, the Mission believes that the long-term importance of this factor imposes upon the United States and the nations associated with it an obligation at least carefully to explore the feasibility of territorial provisions which, while allowing the retention of effective control over such areas as may be directed by security considerations, would avoid the appearance of an outright alienation of sovereignty from Japan, with a consequent rise of irredentism of considerable and possibly dangerous proportions.[56]

The views of Sebald, Fearey, and others were raised with Secretary of State Dean G. Acheson and with Dulles, who, in turn, raised them with the JCS at a meeting on January 3, 1951, but the JCS simply repeated its position that the islands should be kept under U.S. control and sovereignty "not restored."[57]

Dulles, faced with the strong urgings of the JCS and MacArthur to permanently separate the islands from Japan on the one hand, and, on the other, by the Japanese government and State Department to see to it that the islands were retained by Japan, not to mention the conflicting views of the Allies, eventually developed the "residual sovereignty" formula by which Japan would retain sovereignty over the islands but the United States would exercise administrative rights.[58] The decision by the United States, supported eventually by the other forty-eight Allied nations that signed the peace treaty, to leave the islands under Japanese sovereignty and not keep them as the price of war when there were strong calls for that both domestically in American and among the Allied powers, was a truly magnanimous one, rare in the history of mankind. However, because Japan was not able to exercise administrative rights on the islands, problems over the interpretation of the meaning of the article and the relationship between the islands and Japan emerged, leading to public rallies and protests by political parties.

Reports of these rallies and hunger strikes in the Amami Islands (discussed more fully in chapter 2) touched a sensitive nerve with Dulles and had the effect of angering Dulles on the eve of the peace conference. Receiving Yoshida on a courtesy call upon the latter's arrival in San Francisco on September 2, Dulles brought up the problem of public acceptance of the territorial provisions with Yoshida.[59] According to the memorandum of conversation by Nishimura Kumao, director of the Treaty Bureau of the Foreign Ministry, Dulles stated that "with the peace conference approaching, the one thing he regretted was the attitude of the Japanese people."[60] Dulles, whose delegation had been bombarded with last-minute petitions, "felt that it was shocking (*shingai*) that there is a hunger strike when it has already been said that the islands would be considered as a part of Japanese territory. America is to administer the Nansei Islands because of their strategic necessity—they are not to become our territory. It is exactly as I have often told you," he reminded Yoshida.[61] Dulles then gave some hints about the future as well. "It is clear," he continued, "that not only sovereignty will be left with Japan but other arrangements [can be worked out] as well. We want to think more about how it will be possible to realize the desires and requests you have made concerning allowing the inhabitants to keep their Japanese nationality. The demonstrative movements (*jii undo*) like the hunger strike puts the United States in a very difficult position. America is not going to take your wealth. The United States did not place any restrictions on Japan's maritime transportation or other economic relations [with the islands]."[62] Dulles ended

to the home islands without materially decreasing the overall security of the area." This latter issue—Japanese assumption of greater defense responsibility—would be a particular point of concern for Dulles, too, as seen in chapter 5.

Kenneth Young, director of the Division of Northeast Asian Affairs, and Charles C. Stelle, a China-born Asian expert on the State Department's Policy Planning Staff, were very critical of the above memorandum. They believed the study was "inadequate and unresponsive," providing "only the most cursory analysis" of base requirements.[68] Young observed that "the question . . . is how to proceed within the government" and "what the State Department wants to do about the Defense position." Young suggested that because the importance of the bases in the Ryukyus was "so substantial," the State Department should not initiate any action that would restrict U.S. "freedom of action" there; however, he felt that it was also necessary for the joint committee—set to start the following day—to draw up a joint study of possible solutions in order for the government to "be in a position to make a quick, reasoned decision whenever it becomes politically necessary to change the status quo." It was against this background that meetings between the State Department and Defense Department began to discuss the disposition of the islands.

The first meeting was held on September 12. In a follow-up letter dated September 17, State Department representative Young asked Charles Sullivan approximately ten questions, several of which pertained to the Amami Islands. Namely, Young asked his Defense counterparts if the strategic importance of the Ryukyus did not apply to the entire archipelago—could "it be possible to consider Japanese assumption of administration as well as sovereignty over certain selected islands, particularly the Amami group?"[69] In the end, these meetings were not successful in coming to a solution and Defense representatives continued to insist upon the issuance of a presidential statement explaining the need for U.S. control over the Ryukyu Islands, in essence supporting the status quo, while the State representatives pointed out the political implications of the retention by the United States and challenged the insistence on the status quo "as the sole basis upon which U.S. military facilities might be retained."[70]

These discussions continued off and on until December with the State Department participants gradually realizing that a compromise formula was increasingly unlikely. In fact, the State representatives were greatly disappointed, finding the "Defense position . . . an inflexible presentation of the JCS viewpoint" and that "future meetings on the State–Defense Committee level will not serve any useful purpose."[71] As a result, the State representatives decided to prepare a position paper for the Department for use in talks with the JCS and Defense Department. In a memorandum to John M. Allison, who had assumed the position of Assistant Secretary of State for the Far East, they warned that if a satisfactory outcome of such talks is not reached, "the question carries sufficient political importance to warrant its being presented to the President."[72]

The representatives'memorandum was comprised of four main arguments:

1. the Amami Oshima Group and the Ogasawara Islands should be returned to Japan at a time in the near future which would achieve the maximum political advantage for the United States upon making the necessary arrangements with Japan guaranteeing the rights needed on the islands;
2. at the time of the joint U.S.–Japan announcement of the return of the Amami group and Ogasawara Islands, there should be a carefully worked out statement by the president reaffirming Japanese residual sovereignty and the basic reasons for U.S. retention of some of the islands;
3. immediate steps should be taken to issue a revised directive for the Ryukyus and to increase the degree of self-government; and
4. it should be recognized that retention of U.S. control over Okinawa on a long-term basis is essential to U.S. security requirements in case Japan one day restricts use of facilities on the mainland or adopts neutrality.

These points would form the basis of the State Department's position on the eve of the birth of the Eisenhower Administration in January 1953. Before we look at Eisenhower's decisions with regard to the Amami Islands, it is necessary first to look at the activities of the Amami reversion movement, followed by the policies and goals of the Japanese government, to see how the islanders attempted to influence the U.S. and Japanese governments and to what degree they were successful.

Notes

1. "P Document 110, S Document 38, Tentative Conclusions of the Security Subcommittee Concerning the Disposition of Japanese Insular Possessions (September 22, 1942)," in Makoto Iokibe, ed., *The Occupation of Japan: U.S. Planning Documents, 1942–1945* (Bethesda, Md.: Congressional Information Service, Inc., 1987), microfiche 1-A-17.
2. "T-343, Liuchiu Islands (Ryukyu), (July 2, 1943)," *Ibid.*, microfiche 1-B-14.
3. Eldridge, *The Origins of the Bilateral Okinawa Problem*, p. 53.

4. "Minutes of the Inter-Divisional Area Committee on the Far East, Meeting No. 149 (October 12, 1944)," Iokibe, ed., *The Occupation of Japan*, microfiche 2-B-130.

5. "Minutes of the Inter-Divisional Area Committee on the Far East, Meeting No. 148 (October 10, 1944)," *Ibid.*, microfiche 2-B-129. For more on Borton and his work on the committee, see Hugh Borton, *Spanning Japan's Modern Century: The Memoirs of Hugh Borton* (Lanham, Md.: Lexington Books, 2002).

6. "Minutes of the Inter-Divisional Area Committee on the Far East, Meeting No. 149."

7. "Minutes of the Inter-Divisional Area Committee on the Far East, Meeting No. 153 (October 26, 1944)," *Ibid.*, microfiche 2-B-134.

8. "Minutes of the Inter-Divisional Area Committee on the Far East, Meeting No. 171 (December 5, 1944)," *Ibid.*, microfiche 2-B-152.

9. For more on the strategic planning, see Eldridge, *The Origins of the Bilateral Okinawa Problem*, chapters 2 and 4; and Gabe Masaaki, *Nichibei Kankei no Naka no Okinawa* (Okinawa in Postwar Japan–U.S. Relations), (Tokyo: Sanichi Shobo, 1996).

10. See "Minutes of the Inter-Divisional Area Committee on the Far East, Meeting No. 248 (February 1, 1946)," in Makoto Iokibe, ed., *The Occupation of Japan, Part 2: U.S. and Allied Policy, 1945–1952* (Bethesda, Md.: Congressional Information Service, 1989), microfiche 2-B-229. Two days before this meeting, on January 29 in Tokyo, General MacArthur had issued SCAPIN (SCAP Instruction) 677 which separated the Ryukyu Islands south of 30° north latitude from Japanese administrative control. Reischauer, after returning to academia, would later argue on the eve of the 1951 Peace Treaty Conference that the Amami Islands should be returned to Japan. See Nankai Nichinichi Shimbun Gojunenshi Hensan Iinkai, ed., *Nankai Nichinichi Shimbun Gojunenshi* (A 50–Year History of the Nankai Nichinichi Newspaper), (Naze: Nankai Nichinichi Shimbunsha, 1997), p. 138. Also see Edwin O. Reischauer, *The United States and Japan* (Cambridge, Mass.: Harvard University Press, 1950), pp. 238–239.

11. "PR-35 Final (Revision A), Disposition of the Ryukyu (Liuchiu) Islands (February 11, 1946)," *Post World War II Foreign Policy Planning, State Department Records of Harley A. Notter, 1939–1945* (Bethesda, Md.: Congressional Information Service, 1981), microfiche 1192-PR-35 Final (Revision A).

12. Edwin O. Reischauer, *My Life Between Japan and America* (New York: Weatherhill, 1986), p. 107.

13. "Draft Treaty of Peace with Japan (August 5, 1947)," in Makoto Iokibe, ed., *The Occupation of Japan, Part 3: Reform, Recovery and Peace, 1945–1952* (Bethesda, Md.: Congressional Information Service, 1991), microfiche 1-A-20. For explanations of the territorial clauses, see "Memorandum from Borton to Kennan on Sources for Clauses in Draft Treaty of Peace for Japan (August 19, 1947)," *Ibid.*, microfiche 1-A-19; "Memorandum from Borton to Davies on Background of Draft of Japanese Peace Treaty (January 30, 1948)," untitled folder, Box 4, Records Relating to Treaty of Peace, Office of the Historian, Bureau of Public Affairs, Record Group 59, General Records of the Department of State, National Archives, College Park, Maryland.

14. Nakamura Yasutaro, *Sokoku e No Michi: Kobei 8 Nen Amami no Fukki Un-doshi* (*The Road to the Fatherland: Opposing the U.S. for 8 Years, A History of the Amami Reversion Movement*), (Kyoto: Tosho Shuppan, 1984), pp. 44–48.

15. "AG 091, Memorandum for Imperial Japanese Government on Governmental and Administrative Separation of Certain Outlying Areas from Japan (January 29, 1946)," in Fukunaga Fumio, ed., *GHQ Minseikyoku Shiryo, Vol. 2 Senryo Kaikaku: Senkyoho-Seijishikin Kiseiho* (*Government Section, GHQ Materials, Vol. 2 Occupation Reforms: Election Law and Political Funds Law*), (Tokyo: Maruzen, 1997), pp. 141–142. It was not until the month before that all Japanese Imperial Navy and Army forces had been demobilized and relocated back to the mainland. The disarmament (*buso kaijo*) of Japanese forces had already taken place in late September and early October. See Takada, *Unmei no Shimajima*, pp. 112–113.

16. Saneshima, *Ano Hi, Ano Toki*, p. 166.

17. Murayama, *Amami Fukkishi*, p. 46.

18. *Ibid.*; Nakamura, *Sokoku e no Michi*, pp. 46–48.

19. Murayama, *Amami Fukkishi*, p. 47.

20. Paragraph 8 of the Potsdam Declaration ("Proclamation Defining Terms For Japanese Surrender") stated: "The terms of the Cairo Declaration shall be carried out and Japanese sovereignty shall be limited to the islands of Honshu, Hokkaido, Kyushu, Shikoku and such minor islands as we determine." Likewise, the related section of the Cairo Declaration stated "The Three Great Allies are fighting this war to restrain and punish the aggression of Japan. They covet no gain for themselves and have no thought of territorial expansion. It is their purpose that Japan shall be stripped of all the islands in the Pacific which she has seized or occupied since the beginning of the first World War in 1914, and that all the territories Japan has stolen from the Chinese, such as Manchuria, Formosa, and the Pescadores, shall be restored to the Republic of China. Japan will also be expelled from all other territories which she has taken by violence and greed. The aforesaid three great powers, mindful of the enslavement of the people of Korea, are determined that in due course Korea shall become free and independent."

21. Murayama, *Amami Fukkishi*, pp. 51–52. The committee was composed of twenty-two members, with Ikeda as chair, the president of the town and village heads association as vice chair.

22. In response to inquiries about food distribution and the actual start of the Occupation, Lt. Comdr. Neal Henry Lawrence was dispatched to Amami on March 2 to explain the status of the preparations of the military government command. See Murayama, *Amami Fukkishi*, p. 53; Nankai Nichinichi Shimbun, ed., *Gojunenshi*, p. 95; and William (Neal) Henry Lawrence, "Emergency Visit to Amami Oshima, 1946" (Unpublished essay, 2002).

23. Murayama, *Amami Fukkishi*, p. 53.

24. "The Problem of Administering the Northern and Southern Ryukyus (January 15, 1946)," in Committee Members for the Watkins Paper Publication, ed., *Papers of James T. Watkins IV: Historical Records of Postwar Okinawa: The Begining of U.S. Occu-*

pancy [sic], (Ginowan: Ryokurindo Shoten, 1993), Vol. 25, p. 41 (hereafter cited as *Watkins Papers*. The original collection is housed in the Hoover Institution Archives, Stanford University, Stanford, California). The Naval Military Government had sent officers several times to the Amami Islands to conduct research and investigations beginning in September 1945. An extensive study in turn was done in late October and early November led by Lt. Comdr. Robert P. Jackson, who stayed in Naze for six days. This was followed by subsequent visits later in November and December. See Murayama, *Amami Fukkishi*, pp. 36–38.

25. "A17-10, Memo from Commandant, Naval Operating Base, Okinawa to Chief of Naval Operations, Navy Department, Washington D.C. on Military Government of the Ryukyus (January 20, 1946)," *Watkins Papers*, Vol. 25, pp. 42–44.

26. "Staff Study on Military Government of Ryukyu Islands (March 27, 1946)," in Fukunaga, ed., *GHQ Minseikyoku Shiryo*, pp. 222–231.

27. See "Memo from Government Section to Chief of Staff on Military Government of Ryukyu Islands (April 3, 1946)," *Ibid.*, pp. 216–218.

28. "Memo from G-3 to Chief of Staff on Military Government of Ryukyu Islands (March 29, 1946)," *Ibid.*, pp. 219–221.

29. The twenty-person contingent was led by Lt. Comdr. Paul F. Reilley, who, upon his arrival at the Prefectural District Office, gathered local leaders and announced statements regarding the occupation.

30. Murayama, *Amami Fukkishi*, pp. 58–59.

31. In addition to the complicated historical and social dynamics involved with relations between Amami and Okinawa, Nakamura relates the views of Nakae Sanetake, who became Governor of Amami in 1947 and spoke with the head of the administrative affairs unit of the military government to request a change in the name of the way that the Amami Islands were written on the English sign: "We didn't like the name Ryukyu," Nakae explained to his American counterparts. "If [the Amami Islands are] looked at as a part of the Ryukyus, when thinking about the issue of reversion, there was a danger that it could take place only with Okinawa. We wanted to use a name in English other than 'Ryukyu' when translating. In Okinawa, more and more bases were being built and expanded but in Oshima there was nothing like that. Thus there was a chance that Amami could be returned before Okinawa. We then began to use 'Northern Nansei Islands' for the name of the government." See Nakamura, *Sokoku e no Michi*, pp. 49–50.

32. Murayama, *Amami Fukkishi*, p. 64. At this point, Toyoshima Itaru, who had been in charge of rehabilitation of the islands and had worked closely with his U.S. military counterparts, became director of the Amami Office. On October 3, the name of this office was changed to the *Rinji Hokubu Nanseishoto Seicho*, although the English name, Provisional Government for the Northern Ryukyu Islands, continued to use the Ryukyus. On that day, Toyoshima was appointed the first governor (*chiji*) of the islands. See *Ibid*, pp. 64, 93–95; and Saneshima, *Ano Hi, Ano Toki*, pp. 172–173.

33. See Eldridge, *The Origins of the Bilateral Okinawa Problem*, particularly chapter 6.

34. "JCS 1619/24, Review of United States Control Needed Over the Japanese Islands (August 26, 1947)," Section 30, CCS 360 (12-9-42), JCS 1946–1947, Record Group 218, Records of the Joint Chiefs of Staff, National Archives II, College Park, Maryland.

35. In contrast, locally, the Naval Military Government had been more attuned to the situation in Amami and the views of the residents there, as seen by a report written following a visit there in late 1945. "The people of O-Shima Gun regard themselves as mainland Japanese. They evince no tendence [sic] whatsoever to regard themselves as 'Ryukyuans' (as distinguished from mainland Japanese) or to resent the authority of mainland-born officials who have been sent to O-Shima Gun." See "Report of Northern Ryukyus Survey from Officer-in-Charge (Lt. Cmdr. Jackson), Northern Ryukyus Survey Party, to Deputy Commander for Military Government, Okinawa (Murray), (January 5, 1945)," Watkins Papers, Vol. 25, pp. 30–44.

36. "United States Policy Toward a Peace Settlement With Japan (September 8, 1947)," attachment to Minutes of 56th Meeting of the Policy Planning Staff, September 8, 1947, Box 32, Records of the Policy Planning Staff, RG 59. Interestingly, and almost prophetically, this issue would emerge at the time of the announcement (in August 1953) of the decision to return the islands. A Japanese scholar focuses on the Soviet factor in his 1994 article and cites this same PPS document. See Kajiura Atsushi, "Amami Shoto no Henkan o Meguru Beikoku no Tainichi/Taisokan" ("The Views of the U.S. toward Japan and the Soviet Union in the Reversion of the Amami Islands"), Kokusai Seiji (International Relations), No. 105 (January 1994), pp. 112–126.

37. "United States Policy Toward a Peace Settlement With Japan (September 17, 1947)," attachment to Minutes of 63rd Meeting of the Policy Planning Staff, September 22, 1947, Box 32, PPS Records, RG 59.

38. "PPS/10, Results of Planning Staff Study of Questions Involved in the Japanese Peace Settlement (October 14, 1947)," Foreign Relations of the United States [hereafter cited as FRUS], 1947, Vol. 6, The Far East (Washington, D.C.: Government Printing Office, 1972), pp. 536–543.

39. "PPS/10/1, Special Recommendation on Ultimate Disposition of the Ryukyus (October 15, 1947)," in Anne Kasten Nelson, ed., The State Department Policy Planning Staff Papers, 1947 (New York: Garland Publishing, 1983), pp. 116–117.

40. For a discussion of the trip and its significance, see Eldridge, The Origins of the Bilateral Okinawa Problem, pp. 201–216.

41. PPS/28/2 can be found in Anna Kasten Nelson, ed., The State Department Policy Planning Staff Papers, Volume II: 1948 (New York: Garland Publishing, 1983), pp. 175–243.

42. "Draft of a Peace Treaty with Japan (September 11, 1950)," Foreign Relations of the United States, Vol. 6, East Asia and the Pacific (Washington, D.C.: Government Printing Office, 1976), p. 1298. This was adopted as official policy as NSC 60/1.

43. "Unsigned Memorandum Prepared in the Department of State (September 11, 1950)," Ibid., p. 1296.

44. "JCS 2180/2, Report by the Joint Strategic Survey Committee to the Joint Chiefs of Staff on United States Policy Toward Japan (December 28, 1950)," *Ibid.*, p. 1391.

45. Diary entry for March 27, 1951, *The Diaries of William J. Sebald*, Special Collections Division, Nimitz Library, U.S. Naval Academy, Annapolis, Maryland (hereafter cited as *Sebald Diaries*). Nishimura mistakenly records (or there simply was a typing mistake) that Sebald visited Yoshida on February 27, but the actual date was March 27. See Nishimura Kumao, *Nihon Gaikoshi, 27: San Furanshisuko Heiwa Joyaku (Japanese Diplomatic History, Vol. 27: The San Francisco Peace Treaty)*, (Tokyo: Kajima Heiwa Kenkyusho, 1971), p. 102.

46. Diary entry for April 4, 1951, *Sebald Diaries*.

47. "1951 Nen 4 Gatsu 4 Nichi Iguchi Jikan Kara Shiiborudo Taishi ni Kofu shita Heiwa Joyaku Soan ni Taisuru Wagaho Ikensho (Eibun) (Memorandum of Our Opinions on Peace Treaty Passed to Ambassador Sebald from Vice Minister Iguchi on April 4, 1951 (English Version)," Flash Number 4, Reel Number B'0009, *Tainichi Heiwa Joyaku Kankei, Daresu Rinichi Yori Dainiji Kosho Made no Katei (Files Relating to the Peace Treaty With Japan, The Process from Dulles' Departure from Japan to the Second Stage of Negotiations)*, DRO-MOFA, pp. 54–60.

48. "The United States Political Adviser to SCAP (Sebald) to the Secretary of State (April 4, 1951)," *FRUS, 1951, Vol.* 6, pp. 960–961.

49. *Ibid.*, p. 961.

50. "Memorandum from Fearey to Allison on Nansei Shoto," Folder: Ryukyus-Old, Box 4, ONA Records, RG 59. This discussion is also cited in footnote 2, *FRUS, 1951, Vol.* 6, p. 961.

51. Footnote 2, *FRUS, 1951, Vol.* 6, p. 961.

52. *Ibid.*

53. "Memorandum from Johnson to Rusk on Petition for the Return of Amami Gunto to Japan (August 10, 1951)," in Roll 6, Microfilm C0044, ONA Records, RG 59. For Overton's views on this issue, see his oral history, "The Reminiscences of Douglas W. Overton," at the Oral History Research Office, Columbia University, New York.

54. "Memorandum of Conversation on Questions Regarding Ryukyus (April 5, 1951)," Central Decimal File, 1950–1954 (794c.0221/4-551), RG 59.

55. "Memorandum on Territorial Provisions of a Japanese Peace Treaty by Fearey (November 14, 1950)," Folder: 1/50–12/50, Intra DS Memos, Box 3, Records Relating to Japanese Peace Treaty and Security Treaty, 1946–1952, Office of the Historian, Bureau of Public Affairs, RG 59.

56. "Dispatch No. 628, Territorial Provisions of a Japanese Peace Treaty (October 26, 1950)," Central Decimal File, 1950–1954 (694.001/10-2650), RG 59.

57. For more on this, see Eldridge, *The Origins of the Bilateral Okinawa Problem*, pp. 287–292.

58. For more on this formula, see *Ibid.*, particularly chapters 7 and 8.

59. A memorandum of this conversation is also produced in the Foreign Ministry's Diplomatic Records Office. See "Yoshida Sori, Acheson Kokumu Chokan, Dares

Tokushi Kaidanroku (Memorandum of Conversation Between Prime Minister Yoshida, Secretary of State Acheson, and Special Representative Dulles), September 2, 1951," Flash Number 1, Reel Number B'0010, *Sanfuranshisuko Tainichi Kowa Kaigi* (*San Francisco Conference on the Treaty of Peace With Japan*), DRO-MOFA, pp. 4–15. Incidentally, the memorandum of this conversation appearing in FRUS is improperly dated and does not mention the discussion on the territorial problem and Japanese public opinion. See "Memorandum of Conversation by Sebald (September 3, 1951)," *FRUS, 1951, Vol. 6*, pp. 1315–1317.

60. Nishimura, *San Furanshisuko Heiwa Joyaku*, p. 190.

61. *Ibid.*, pp. 190–191. Nishimura, in his 1959 article on Dulles, uses the word "shocking" for the translation of *shingai* in his description of these events. See Nishimura Kumao, "Okinawa Kizoku no Kimaru Made—Motomeru ni Isoideatta Nihon no Seron (Until the Reversion of Okinawa is Decided—Public Opinion Demanded [the Return of the Islands] Too Quickly)," *Asahi Jaanaru*, Vol. 1, No. 15 (June 21, 1959), p. 20. Throughout 1951, Dulles, SCAP, the Allied Council of Japan, the Far Eastern Commission, and the Japanese government had received numerous petitions and "expressions of views" from individuals, associations, and political parties. Scholar Watanabe Akio suggests in his study of the Japanese side of the Okinawa problem that the Japanese Government, particularly the Foreign Ministry, in some cases early on encouraged such activities. See Watanabe Akio, *The Okinawa Problem: A Chapter in Japan-U.S. Relations* (Melbourne: Melbourne University Press, 1970), pp. 135–139.

62. Nishimura, *San Furanshisuko Heiwa Joyaku*, p. 191.

63. *Ibid.*

64. Yoshida's reply appears in the Foreign Ministry's original memorandum of conversation.

65. Note signed by McClurkin attached to "Memorandum from Robert D. Murphy to Assistant Secretary of State Allison (March 31, 1952)," Reel 7, Microfilm C-0043, Japanese Subject Files, Records of the Division of Northeast Asian Affairs, 1947–1956, RG 59. The note in full reads: "This question of the disposition of the Ryukyu and Bonin Islands has been decided as a matter of policy within the Department. The approach to the Department of Defense was delayed while the Administrative Agreement was being worked out and the Peace Treaty ratified. We should resume the battle promptly now."

66. The delay was caused (among other reasons) by the fact that the Defense Department would not name members to the working group until the Joint Staff of the JCS had completed its report on military requirements in the Ryukyus. See "Memorandum from Mr. Young to Mr. Frederick E. Nolting on State-Defense Planning on the Ryukyus (July 3, 1952)," Reel 7, Microfilm C-0043, Japanese Subject Files, Records of the Office of Northeast Asian Affairs, RG 59. Ironically, it was not only the Defense Department that was late in naming its representatives. In a memorandum dated September 11, Kenneth T. Young pointed out that Myron Cowen had not informed him and his colleagues as to their designation on the working group, and

they only learned about their role through their Defense counterpart Charles Sullivan. "Memorandum from Young to Allison on State-Defense Divergence on Disposition of the Ryukyus (September 11, 1952)," Reel 7, Microfilm C-0043, Japanese Subject Files, Records of the Office of Northeast Asian Affairs, RG 59. A second reason for the delay had to do with the president's request to have an overall policy paper for Japan developed within the NSC. This policy paper was eventually approved as NSC 125/1 and underwent further amendments.

67. "Memorandum by the Joint Chiefs of Staff to the Secretary of Defense Lovett on the Future Post-Peace Treaty Disposition of Ryukyu and Bonin-Volcano Islands (August 15, 1952)," attachment to "Memorandum from the Deputy Secretary of Defense Foster to the Secretary of State Acheson (August 29, 1952)," *FRUS, 1952–1954, Vol. 14, Part 2*, pp. 1318–1327. The study was conducted by the Joint Strategic Survey Committee as part of JCS 1380 series. The study was completed on August 6 as JCS 1380/148. See "JCS 1380/148, Report by the Joint Strategic Survey Committee to the Joint Chiefs of Staff on Future Post-Peace Treaty Disposition of Ryukyu and Bonin-Volcano Islands (August 6, 1952)," Section 31, CCS 383.21 Japan (3-13-45), JCS 1951–1953, RG 218, National Archives.

68. "Memorandum from Young to Allison on State-Defense Divergence on Disposition of the Ryukyus (September 11, 1952)."

69. "State Department Questions Regarding Defense Department Position on the Subject of Disposition of the Ryukyus (undated)," *FRUS, 1952–1954, Vol. 14, Part 2*, p. 1335.

70. "Memorandum of Conversation on the Disposition of the Ryukyus by Hawley (September 12, 1952)," Reel 7, Microfilm C-0043, Japanese Subject Files, Records of the Office of Northeast Asian Affairs, RG 59.

71. "Memorandum by the Director of the Office of Northeast Asian Affairs Young to the Assistant Secretary of State for Far Eastern Affairs Allison (January 12, 1953)," *FRUS, 1952–1954, Vol. 14, Part 2*, pp. 1376–1378; "Political Summary for Japan, January–February 1953, Prepared by the Office of Northeast Asian Affairs," Japan, January thru June 1953 (1) file, Box 5, Bureau of Far Eastern Affairs, Miscellaneous Subject Files, 1953, Lot File 55D388, RG 59.

72. "Memorandum by the Director of the Office of Northeast Asian Affairs Young to the Assistant Secretary of State for Far Eastern Affairs Allison (January 12, 1953)."

CHAPTER TWO

~

The Amami Reversion Movement and its Impact

> If the Ryukyus hide their desire to return to Japan for fear of upsetting America, the future generations of both countries will find themselves in a tragedy from which they cannot be rescued.
>
> –*Editorial in* Nankai Nichinichi Shimbun, *February 8, 1951*

The Amami Reversion Movement, or *Amami Fukki Undo*, is an example of one of the most successful sociopolitical movements in postwar Japan. As demonstrated in U.S. and Japanese diplomatic documents declassified in recent years, the reversion movement not only exercised a clear influence on the policies of the Japanese government, but it also had a significant impact on the decision making process of the U.S. government and, in particular, the Eisenhower Administration. The movement's story is told in this chapter.

As will be discussed below, the Amami Reversion Movement was actually two movements—one based in mainland Japan and centered in Tokyo led by the Amami Federation (*Amami Rengo*), which was the successor organization of the Amami Association of Tokyo, or *Tokyo Amami Kai*, and the other in Amami, the Council for the Reversion of Amami to Japan (*Amami Oshima Nihon Fukki Kyogikai*), or *Fukkyo*. These two groupings successfully worked together closely, despite the great distances and primitive communications that existed at the time.

The movement succeeded likely because of the following reasons:

1. the basic unity maintained throughout most of their efforts in seeking the return of the islands;
2. the widespread support among the people of the islands, who clearly identified themselves strongly as Japanese, for the movement's goals;
3. the high level of organization;
4. in the case of the Tokyo-based *Amami Rengo* (introduced more fully below), the high social standing and degree of contacts possessed by its members in the Diet, government, academia, legal, and media publishing world; and
5. the presence of forward-looking moderate leaders like Nobori Naotaka in Tokyo and Izumi Horo, locally in Amami.

Moreover, the movement had the support of the people and the governor of Kagoshima Prefecture, as the islands had been a part of that prefecture since its establishment in 1871, and the expressions of support and lobbying that Governor Shigenari Kaku undertook (discussed in this and subsequent chapters) would prove critical in raising awareness of the issue throughout the prefecture and Japan.[1]

While little research exists on the return of the islands, the few references to the reversion movement generally tend to focus on the year 1951 when the Treaty of Peace was signed with Japan and international recognition for the continuation of U.S. administration over the islands was gained. However, calls for reversion in the islands—cut off from interaction with mainland Japan—began well before that, as the following discussion shows, and thus the history of the reversion movement becomes inevitably intertwined with the history of the occupation and the development of the policies the Naval military government adopted and the army followed.

The following discussion of the reversion movement is divided into three sections corresponding to the three essentially chronological stages of the movement, namely the period from 1946 to 1950, when the islands were first cut off from the administrative area of Japan and the policies of the military government caused the situation to deteriorate; the two years from 1950 to 1952, during which time the Peace Treaty was discussed, signed, and went into effect; and the period following the Peace Treaty, from 1952 to 1953, when the reversion of the islands was decided on and they were successfully returned to Japan within the framework of Article 3 of the Peace Treaty.

Each section has a title and subtitle, with the latter meant to suggest the goals, or perhaps better put, the strategy, of the movement at the time.

The First Stage of the Reversion Movement, 1946–1950: Early Return to Japan

Following the shaky start of the military government (as described in chapter 1) in the Amami Islands in March 1946, a period of cautious optimism set in among the islanders. They were concerned of course about their islands being cut off from mainland Japan, but they also looked forward to the liberal, democratizing policies of the United States and the chance to work toward the creation of a peaceful and prosperous Amami under American guidance.

The arrival on April 11 (1946) of a youthful, liberal, forward-looking military government officer, Lt. Cmdr. John R. Potter, further strengthened these hopes.[2] Potter, who had studied political theory in college, often met with newspaper reporters to relay information of general interest to the islanders as well as to exchange opinions on the situation in Amami, and he often sought out the advice of those he met, according to one participant in these meetings.[3] He was in the words of that same person, "the epitome of the ideal democrat."[4]

The local government office, in an effort to clarify local sentiment in the islands and present these desires to the Naval military government, organized a survey of opinions in Amami that spring. This produced the following requests:

1. the establishment of a county (*gun*)-wide assembly and elections for its members;
2. concurrent elections for town and village heads and for local assembly members;
3. change in the name of the local government office;
4. consolidation and reduction in government offices and public personnel;
5. establishment of auditing system for local governments and the recruitment of those from the private sector; and
6. effective and immediate use of wartime tax revenues effectively and immediately.

On being shown the results, Potter, on June 4, announced the holding of public elections for the Naze City Assembly and other municipalities.[5] At the same time, Potter promulgated Proclamation No. 5 which guaranteed the rights of free assembly, speech, publishing, beliefs, peaceful association, and labor unions. A "renaissance" of sorts began, with new newspapers (*Nankai Nichinichi Shimbun* and *Amami Taimusu*) and magazines being started and discussions on culture, politics, and economics becoming more common.[6] One journal in particular, *Jiyu* (*Freedom*), first published in September 1946 and edited by Izumi

Horo, later the leader of the reversion movement, served as an important source of discussion on the political and economic policies toward the islands and played a critical role in shaping opinion in the reversion movement.[7]

Although Lt. Gen. Wilhelm D. Styler, who assumed the position of military governor when the Army took over for the Navy on July 1, 1946, had stated that all existing directives would continue, Potter's "present" of democratic freedoms was not long in lasting.[8] Potter's successors, Lt. Col. Ross H. St. Clair and Maj. Fred M. Labree, for example, found the need to increase censorship of the *Nankai Nichinichi Shimbun* and the *Amami Taimusu*, when these two newspapers took up more politically sensitive topics, including the worsening economic situation and the quality of the local administration. No political topic was more sensitive, however, than the question of reversion, an issue that would become a topic of great interest when movements were seen toward a peace treaty in 1947.

At a luncheon sponsored by the foreign press in March that year, MacArthur stated his desire to see an early peace treaty with Japan since it had fulfilled the obligations of demilitarization and democratization with the new Constitution (in May).[9] MacArthur, at that time also touched on the territorial issue, suggesting that the fate of Okinawa and the Amami Islands should be decided at a peace conference. With this statement, residents of Amami and local news organizations, not to mention those from Amami living on the mainland, began to carefully follow the debate over the territorial status of the Nansei Islands.[10]

With Foreign Minister Ashida Hitoshi's assumption of office on June 1, 1947, events began to move more quickly.[11] Expecting that a peace treaty conference would be held later that summer, Ashida expressed Japan's desires regarding a treaty in an interview with Tom Lambert of the Associated Press news agency at the foreign minister's official residence in Meguro, Tokyo. There Ashida stated that "while Okinawa is not very important to the Japanese economy," Japan desired to see the Ryukyu Islands (as well as the Kuriles) returned and noted that "the Japanese people question the applicability of the Potsdam Declaration toward Okinawa and a part of the Kuriles."[12] This argument was consistent with the Foreign Ministry's views and their planning toward a peace treaty, as will be discussed more fully in the next chapter.[13] However, Allied reaction was strongly critical of Ashida's statement because Japan as a defeated nation, the Allies argued, had no right to comment on the contents of a future peace treaty or to express its wishes. MacArthur, in what was likely meant as a rebuff to Ashida's comments, also stated in an interview with visiting American newspapermen that "there was no Japanese opposition to the United States holding Okinawa since the Okinawans are not Japanese."[14] Locally, Maj. Labree, senior Naval military government officer of the Northern Ryukyus, in early August warned the two local newspapers against spreading false rumors and "expressing private desires that are baseless."[15]

As movements toward a peace treaty continued at the international level, local speculation on the territorial issue did not stop with Labree's warning to the press. On August 19, a rally attended by 3,000 people from around the island was held at the lecture hall of Oshima Middle School (now Oshima High School) to debate the question of the public election of the governor and several other issues of democracy and improvements in the islands' economic and political administration, and to choose a twenty-person action committee to discuss these issues with the local commander, governor, and mayor.[16] On September 7, the action committee gave its report to another large gathering—this time about 1,500—at the same lecture hall. The committee members told the crowd that the military commander welcomed their comments, and they described their meetings with him. This report was followed by several committee members' speeches, including three that touched on the reversion issue. Although the first two speakers, careful of the admonitions of the military government, used the less inflammatory word *kizoku*, which means "belonging to," instead of *fukki*, which means "revert," the third speaker, twenty-one-year-old Tokuda Toyomi of one of the youth organizations (and a former student of Nakamura Yasutaro) spoke of the need to move forward toward reversion. The crowd reportedly went wild.[17] The sentiment of the people had seemingly moved from economic and administration problems to the reversion issue itself.

A few days later at a meeting of the Council of the Heads of the Cities, Towns, and Villages (*Shichosonchokai*) on September 10, attended by Governor Toyoshima Itaru, the discussion focused on the reversion issue.[18] A thirteen-point resolution was subsequently unanimously adopted, stating, among other items of importance, that "The interest of the people of Oshima in the territorial issue is very large and it is the earnest wish and desire of the people to return to Japan."[19]

The following day, after learning of the meeting and that the Council was preparing to present the resolution (and despite his reported desire to hear the public's comments), Labree decided to crack down, announcing (in Proclamation No. 13) that he was withdrawing the rights of free assembly, speech, publishing, beliefs, peaceful association, and labor unions that had been announced in June the previous year as Proclamation No. 5.[20] Although Labree was replaced shortly after this and his order was later withdrawn, open activities critical of the military government and in favor of reversion were not tolerated.[21] Symbolic of this was the reported comment on October 4 by Labree's successor, Lt. Col. Henry B. Joseph: "A military government is far from being a democracy. It is a sort of dictatorial politics."[22]

In line with this view, Lt. Col. Joseph released a written directive on October 7 confirming censorship over newspapers and journals, which had been in effect since January 1946. He also released a new directive (Proclamation No. 15) on October 16 that, while replacing Labree's September 11 order, clarified certain rights and liberties but also banned gatherings critical of the military occupation or local Provisional Government and any public statements or written materials that supported such views. In addition, existing organizations would need to reapply for permission to continue.[23] It was, in the words of one of the newspapers at the time, "The Non-Liberal Liberties Proclamation."[24] It goes without saying that these events were particularly disheartening for the islanders because, on the mainland, the new Japanese constitution securing these basic rights had already been promulgated and gone into effect half a year before.

With this, movements toward reversion died down until 1950, although dissatisfaction with the military government's political and economic policies remained strong as the occupation continued and Japan awaited a peace treaty.[25] The short period of democratic reform and optimism was over, and disillusionment set in, particularly when military government authorities began to crack down on activities it saw as political in nature and thus potentially threatening, such as the creation of politically motivated youth organizations and other types of associations, as well as groups addressing the issue of reversion.[26]

This desperation deepened with the worsening economic–social–political situation and the coming crisis over the food prices (in 1949) and would lead to the strengthened calls for reversion. Following the separation of the islands from Japan in 1946, the economic situation had worsened due to the severing of trade and other interaction. The islands were forced to purchase items from Okinawa and the U.S. military and were unable to export black sugar and other items to traditional markets in Japan. Moreover, between December 1945 and December 1946, more than 50,000 former islanders returned to Amami (an increase of approximately 25 percent) due to the islands potentially being cut off from Japan. Unsanitary conditions prevailed, resulting in a smallpox epidemic in the spring of 1946 as well as other major diseases, such as tuberculosis, and minor illnesses. Unemployment and inflation rose, with salaries not keeping pace with the changes, leading to the formation of several labor unions, including that for public workers, who demanded a doubling or tripling of salaries.[27] Black market activities also became common, with formerly law-abiding citizens forced to buy goods from these merchants. Unable to generate their own income, the islanders eventually were forced to rely on financial outlays from the military government, to the tune of 8,818,000 yen in fiscal year 1947 and 6,963,000 yen in 1948. Efforts by then-Governor Nakae toward fiscal retrenchment and new taxes, as well as price stabilization, were not enough to overcome the circumstances that were not of his islands' making. Sadly, the military government, due to the initial lack of qualified personnel, had not been comprised of commanders with backgrounds in business or economics—something that early officers had prophetically pointed out would create problems.

Because of this worsening situation, numerous able-bodied young men and women, many of the latter forced into prostitution, had to leave the islands to work in Okinawa, at a pace of about 1,000 Amamians a month. Eventually, some 40,000–50,000 residents of Amami made their way to Okinawa by mid-1953. Those that remained behind became dependent on the military government for their food and other commodities. This desperate situation made the somewhat sudden announcement by the Occupation authorities on April 29, 1949, of a threefold rise in prices for food distributed by them, to be effective retroactive as of April 1, all the more severe.[28] It became a "life or death matter" for the islands, one resident remembered.[29]

With Nakae temporarily away, Vice Governor Kasai Junichi warned Col. Hugh D. Adair, the new local commander, that "the new policy had no chance of succeeding economically, socially, or politically" and that "70,000 people would immediately become wards of the state."[30] There were also immediate and strong protests against the move by labor groups, youth organizations, housewives, the heads of the city, town, and village councils, and the Committee for Economic Rehabilitation (*Keizai Fukko Iinkai*), not to mention continued protests from Nakae and Kasai. The response from the military governor was quite bureaucratic in nature and lacked sympathy, however: "Once something is decided from above in Okinawa, we cannot change it here."[31]

With that being the response, the heads of the city, town, and village councils and the Committee for Economic Rehabilitation held joint, open discussions beginning on May 3, eventually leading to a decision to send a fifteen-person delegation to Okinawa to explain the local situation in Amami directly to the related economic officials in the Naval military government.[32] The delegation, comprised of Nakae and four others from the Provisional Government; six members from the city, town, and village councils and the Committee for Economic Rehabilitation; and four representatives of the residents from the assemblies, youth groups, and women's organizations departed Naze on May 8, having been seen off by a brass band from the Naze Middle School. After arriving by a military transport vessel, the delegates went to see the military governor and directors of the Economic and Finance Divisions, but they were told that they were away in Tokyo and not available. Instead, they left prepared materials "to plead Amami's case" with these divisions and other related sections. Importantly, the delegation did get to meet with the deputy commander for military government, Col. Guessey B. Green, but only twice (on May 13 and 17) and only with a few members at a time. "The reaction of the military to us," one of the participants recalled, "was extremely cold."[33]

Two months later, in early July, the delegation received a reply from Green to the effect that measures to stabilize prices were not appropriate at the time and that the military government would continue with its policy of price increases. As a means of bettering the situation, occupation authorities planned to adopt measures to improve the economy, such as by releasing currency and doubling the budget for war-related rehabilitation from 7.5 million yen to 15 million yen, requests that seem to have come from the Rehabilitation Committee.[34] These measures were widely reported in the press, which released a special edition (gogai) of the newspapers, but the islanders were still unsatisfied about the initial price rise. Anger also increased against the Rehabilitation Committee members for what the islanders saw as a sell-out during their talks with Green, and the members of the committee were forced to take responsibility by resigning.[35]

Meanwhile, Governor Nakae and Vice Governor Kasai felt they could no longer be held responsible for the unpopular policies of the military government, and, because they could not change these guidelines themselves as seen by the statement above, decided to submit their resignations on July 9, as did all other officials in the Provisional Government.[36] Their resignations were turned down, however, and Nakae was told that "it was the responsibility of the Governor to stay in his current position and help out."[37] As with Toyoshima before him (and Higa Shuhei in Okinawa during the 1950s), Nakae found himself in a very difficult situation, torn between the feelings of the people and the demands of the times and of the military government.[38]

The situation actually became even more tense. Shortly before this, on July 5 (the same day that Green's reply was announced with regard to the food prices), the All Oshima Council to Protect Livelihoods (Zen Oshima Seikatsu Yogo Kyogikai), with Minami Yasumitsu, (a devout Catholic who had participated actively in the summer 1947 rallies) as head, was formed bringing together numerous smaller committees that had been established throughout the island.[39] Its goal was to a lower the price of food and clothing, stabilize a minimum 2,400-calorie-per-day diet, and preserve emergency foodstuffs for times of need.[40] Being seen as comprising "some members not cooperating with the military government," a euphemism for suspected Communists and other outspoken troublemakers, the Council was banned a month later on August 5.[41] In its place, youth and labor groups set about reconstituting their own organizations, and, on August 6, a Housewives Association for the Protection of the Livelihoods of Housewives (*Fujin Seikatsu Yogokai*) was formed, led by Nakamura Mitsue, the wife of *Amami Taimusu* president and Communist activist/politician, Nakamura Yasutaro, and several others.[42]

In a gesture of compassion as well as perhaps a reflection of its helplessness, the Provisional Government in July relayed the directive on price increases to the respective communities but, at the same time, closed its eyes to the distribution of goods at the old prices.[43] This became known however to the military authorities early the next year, and on January 11, 1950, the new prices were implemented.[44] At the same time, the Provisional Government was ordered to pay for the loss in revenue (approximately 120 million "B Yen") from April to December 1949.[45] Nakae found himself forced to comply, stating that "Because this is a direct order from the military we must go along with it no matter what results emerge and what difficult situations occur. We can only hope that the military government comes quickly to recognize the bad situation and changes the prices accordingly."[46]

There was a sign that a new, however belated, recognition had occurred. After being shown the results of investigations conducted by the Social Division (*Shakaika*) of the Provisional Government, which suggested that numerous households on the islands were faced with malnutrition due to the high prices, Col. Raymond C. Barlow, the new commanding officer of the Northern Ryukyus military government, announced on January 24 that there would be a 30 percent reduction in the price of rice and a 50 percent reduction in that for soybeans, effective retroactively for January 10.[47] In one sense, this signaled the end of the food price crisis, particularly when Nakae went to Okinawa with his government's economic director, Okuda Kannosuke, to call for greater trade and an increase in the budget for rehabilitation.[48]

On the other hand, however, it probably came too late to restore the political situation in Amami, and, indeed, economically as well, the purchasing power never recovered and more and more islanders lost their places of employment and were forced to leave for Okinawa where there was plenty of work servicing the bases.[49] Essentially, during this time, every islander had been affected by the price increases, which embittered many to not only the poor administration and "strong-armed tactics" of the military government but also to the situation in which the military government even existed at all. This period also saw the rise of ordinary people becoming politically aware and organized. These individuals and the groups to which they belonged, many formed during this period, would become active in the reversion movement about to start.

The Second Stage of the Reversion Movement, 1950–1952: Opposition to Trusteeship and Return to Japan

With movements by the Allies toward a peace treaty beginning again in late 1949, discussion increased in Japan about the shape of the future treaty and the disposition of its territory—news that was watched carefully in the Amami Islands.[50] This debate carried over into 1950, just as the food price crisis was coming to a conclusion of sorts.

At the end of January, for example, Kawakami Yoshimi, a member of the opposition *Ryokufukai* (Green Breeze Society) from Kagoshima (originally Amami), asked Prime Minister Yoshida Shigeru during party questioning in the main session of the Upper House about the fate of the Amami Islands, pointing out that "for historical, administrative, economic, and ethnic reasons, the islands should be returned to Japan" and deploring the situation in which the islands were cut off administratively from Japan, forbidding normal commerce and exchange.[51] Yoshida responded that he "believed the Allies, which had the right to make a final decision, would take into consideration the various relations, such as historical and ethnic, that the islands had with Japan."[52] In a Lower House Budget Committee that same day, when asked by Kanbayashiyama Eikichi, a member of the Democratic Party from Kagoshima Prefecture, about the territorial problem, Yoshida, while noting that "he could not comment as it was before the peace treaty," stated that "the government was studying the issue and GHQ was watching public opinion."[53]

Upper House member Ito Ryuji, a former diplomat from the same village as Kawakami who had been Ashida's Administrative Vice Minister for Foreign Affairs (and later would become a House of Representatives member from the district including Amami Oshima), followed up by asking Yoshida in a session of the Upper House Foreign Affairs Committee the following month "just how in fact the question of the return of the Amami Islands problem was to be resolved."[54] Yoshida, who was also Foreign Minister, responded that "it was all right that the Japanese people expressed their hopes and opinions. It was natural for Japan to call for the return of the Amami Islands. Go ahead and continue to call for the return of the islands." Yoshida's comments were given big play in the national newspapers as well as in the local *Nankai Nichinichi Shimbun* and would have the effect of encouraging those calling for the reversion of the islands.

During this debate, Kagoshima Governor Shigenari, who would take a strong interest in the reversion movement as Amami had been historically a part of Kagoshima Prefecture, was in Tokyo.[55] While there, Shigenari met with Brig. Gen. Paul Shepard, chief of Civil Affairs in GHQ, to relay the feelings of the islanders.[56] According to reports, Shigenari left the meeting favorably impressed, believing that a solution would be found.[57] Returning to Kagoshima on February 6, he called upon the people of Amami "to put more effort into seeking the reversion of the islands, as it would be hard for the central government to do so (alone)."[58] A month after Gov. Shigenari's return, eleven members of the Kagoshima Prefectural Assembly, led by Yamanaka Sadanori (later involved with the Okinawa issue in his capacity as director of the Okinawa and Hokkaido Development Agency and longtime member of the Diet), submitted the motion "Amami Oshima Fukki ni Kansuru Ken (Item Regarding the Return of Amami Oshima)" which stated that the Amami Islands "were historically a part of Japan and had never been fought over with another country," and, furthermore, "the islands could not exist economically independent of Japan."[59] The resolution, adopted unanimously on March 28, also called for the adoption of immediate measures such as the restoration of transportation links with the islands and the transfer of registry authority back to Kagoshima Prefecture, as well as requesting members to make appeals to the government and the leaders of both Houses of the Diet to seek the return of the islands at the time of a peace conference.[60]

Importantly, around the same time, the Prefectural Assembly of Miyzaki, which also had a large population of former Amami Islanders, passed a similar resolution. Moreover, the Miyazaki Oshima Youth Group (*Oshima Seinendan*) issued a "reversion appeal" on February 17 and called on its counterparts throughout the country and in Amami to begin signature drives to raise awareness of the issue.[61] Likewise, the Tokyo Amami Student Association (*Tokyo Amami Gakuseikai*) took the lead in Tokyo by organizing rallies and signature drives in Shinbashi, Shibuya, and numerous other places.[62]

Locally, the Naze City Federation of Youth Groups (*Nazeshi Rengo Seinendan*), a Communist-led organization that had been reconstituted the previous summer, responded to this appeal by holding a youth rally (*seinen kekki shukai*) on March 24 on the grounds of Naze Elementary School.[63] Although the reason given for the gathering when applying for the permit (as was required) was to discuss the recent food crisis and rising unemployment, the real focus was the reversion issue. These problems were, of course, interrelated with the general feeling that "to improve the serious economic situation, reversion was the only road left open to them."[64]

The following day, the Federation began its movements for reversion, but, on March 27, in what became known as the "Amami Communist Party Incident" (*Amami Kyosanto Jiken*), some seventeen of its leaders were arrested for possessing communist literature, including the newsletter of the outlawed Amami Communist Party, as well as for conducting without authorization what military authorities considered a political rally. Because, for better or worse, these activists had played a central role in organizing many of the reversion-related activities, their removal effectively put a temporary stop to overt movements, although the flames of reversion had been lit.[65]

During the spring of 1950, movements were seen once again in the U.S. government and among the Allies for a treaty of peace with Japan, symbolized by the appointment on May 18 of John Foster Dulles, an advisor to Secretary of State Acheson, to be in charge of arranging a peace treaty and his subsequent trip to Japan in June. Despite the outbreak of the Korean War nearby, President Truman officially announced on September 14 that the U.S. government would go ahead with consultations with each of the governments of the Far Eastern Commission, and, by November, an official version of the "Seven Principles" of the future Japanese Peace Treaty was released, of which Point 3 stated that "Japan would . . . agree to U.N. trusteeship, with the United States as administering authority, of the Ryukyu and Bonin Islands."[66] Because the geographical definition of the Ryukyu Islands had been used loosely in the past by the United States (as discussed earlier), it was unclear to the Japanese government as a whole and the residents of Amami in particular what, in fact, was meant by the "Ryukyu Islands."

Due to this concern, the president of the Federation of Amami Islanders' Associations in Japan (*Zenkoku Amami Rengo Sohonbu*), Dr. Nobori Naotaka, and (soon-to-be Supreme Court Justice) Tanimura Tadaichiro, chairman of the Tokyo Chapter of the same Federation (*Zenkoku Amami Rengo Tokyoto Honbu Iinkai*), and Kamimura Kiyonobu and Seta Ryoichi, chairmen respectively of the Saitama and Kanagawa prefectural chapters of the above Federation, decided to petition MacArthur. On November 15 the group wrote to the Supreme Commander of the Allied Powers, noting that "to see an early reunion of the Island Group of Amami Oshima with Japan proper is indeed an ardent desire on the part not only of the 400,000 islanders [in Amami as well as on the mainland] but also of the entire people of Japan," calling for his "sympathetic understanding," and requesting that he "see to it that [the] islands are reunited with Japan proper as soon as practicable."[67] The four-page petition added that the permanent separation of the islands from Japan proper would be "tantamount to a death-blow for them (*seimei o tattaru no omoi*)."[68] As a show of support for their position, Nobori included in their petition a list of names gathered during a signature drive in Tokyo and said that gathering "many more thousands of hundreds of signatures" would be "easy" were more time allowed.

Nobori's claim was not mere boasting. *Amami Rengo*, which was formed on December 8, 1946, had thousands of members and, being a well established, influential, and nationwide organization, was able to play a crucial role in directing the reversion movement on the mainland.

The Federation was effectively the successor to the *Tokyo Amami Kai*, which had already been in existence for forty-five years at the time of the end of the Pacific War. In the immediate aftermath of the war and the subsequent separation of the islands from Japan, *Tokyo Amami Kai* spent a great deal of time, energy, and money to assist fellow islanders stranded on the mainland in matters of housing, health, finance, and legal questions, such as travel permits.[69] This type of support was repeated throughout the country by other groups that had newly formed, such as the *Nansei Shoto Renmei* (Nansei Islands League) and *Doshikai* (Brotherhood Association) in Kansai and the *Kanto Amami Renmei* (Kanto Amami League) in Tokyo. However, the help these organizations were able to give was scattered and haphazard due to the confusion of the times and the rivalries that inherently occur between and within organizations.[70] Recognizing the need for a more united effort, several members of the *Tokyo Amami Kai* made an appeal to its counterparts for the formation of a nationwide organization, resulting in being the creation of *Amami Rengo* on December 8, 1946, with chapters organized throughout the country.[71]

As figure 2.1 shows, *Amami Rengo* was essentially an umbrella organization that brought together these different organizations (with their different agendas, personalities, networks, and ideologies) to cooperate in overcoming the immediate hardships that residents from and in Amami were facing, as well as later to organize a reversion movement. Within *Amami Rengo*, the *Amami Rengo Tokyo Honbu*, or Tokyo Chapter, was established, and this *Tokyo Honbu* would play a central, if not the key, role.[72]

There are several reasons for this. Most obviously, being located in the capital city—the center of politics, administration, and diplomacy—the Tokyo Chapter was the best location from which to work. Moreover, the forerunner to this organization, *Tokyo Amami Kai*, was the oldest and most well organized of the existing Amami-related associations and thus its members had a significant network already established. Most important is the fact that the many members of *Tokyo Amami Kai* were highly educated, well connected, and very much respected in their individual fields. For example, several were lawyers, scholars, former (and future) members of the Diet, judges, and diplomats. With this impressive membership, and by using their

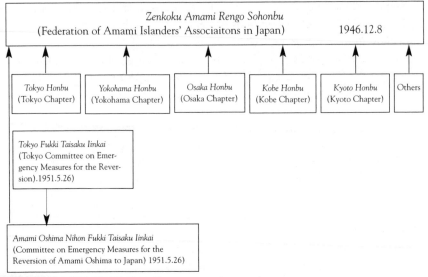

Figure 2.1. The Organizational Structure of *Amami Rengo*

connections and contacts in government and the political world, the Tokyo Chapter was able, as is discussed below, to gain valuable information and exert continuous pressure on the government to do more for the islands.[73]

The first example of *Amami Rengo* making its desires known came when it requested the liberalization of trade, transit, and money transfers between the islands and Japan in a petition given to GHQ on September 2, 1948, some ten months after Nobori had assumed leadership of the Federation.[74] The petition was titled "Amami Gunto to Nihon Honkokukan no Kotsu, Boeki, Sokin to no Jiyu Kyoka (Permission to Liberalize Transit, Trade, Money Transfers, etc. Between Amami Gunto and Japan Proper)" and was the Federation's first petition, but it would not be their last.

Significantly, in addition to this role, leaders from the Federation encouraged the creation of a reversion movement within the islands themselves, with the first real appeal being the suggestion by Kanai Masao, a lawyer, former member of the Diet (*Seiyukai* Party), and former governor of Wakayama Prefecture (who had recently been de-purged), to local leaders via telegraph in Amami to initiate a signature drive. As he later lamented, however, "it seems an open reversion movement was still impossible at the time there."[75]

This did not prevent the mainland-based groups, including *Amami Rengo*, *Tokyo Amami Gakuseikai*, and youth groups from holding rallies and con-

ducting signature drives on their own. For example, the Amami Student Association, formed in March 1950 and headed by Takaoka Yoshinari from
Bunri University (and later a well-known geologist), launched a signature
drive beginning that April that lasted forty days.[76] A similar signature drive
was not possible yet in the islands, however.

This was still true to some extent going into 1951, although expectations were high regarding the likelihood of a treaty. Prime Minister
Yoshida's January 5 statement to the first meeting of the Cabinet in the
new year expressed the hope that "the Ryukyu Islands eventually would be
restored to Japanese sovereignty because they have been Japanese territory
for a long time and were not taken through invasion," a report that received considerably large attention in the local newspapers.[77] Dulles's follow-up trip to Japan for consultations later that month and the first half
of February also received considerable attention as the territorial issue was
seen as one of the most "delicate" parts of the treaty.[78] Amid a great deal
of speculation, it became obvious, however, during the Dulles–Yoshida
talks, that Japan's desires to retain the Nansei and Nanpo Islands under
full sovereignty and administrative control were not going to be realized
and that the United States might be given the right to seek a trusteeship
arrangement for the islands.[79]

**Figure 2.2. Signature Drive by the Amami Student Association of Tokyo, April 1950,
outside East Exit, Shinjuku Station, Tokyo.**

Reaction in Amami was swift and strong and could no longer be kept under the surface. Following the appearance of Nobori and Tanimura as witnesses (*sankonin*) in an open hearing of the Upper House's Foreign Affairs Committee on February 6 in which they stated it was "natural that the islands should be returned," the *Nankai Nichinichi Shimbun* editorialized the following in its February 8 edition, entitled "On the Territorial Problem (Kizoku Mondai ni Tsuite)":

Debate on the territorial issue of the Ryukyus has increased dramatically in recent days. The argument that because the people of the Ryukyus are the same as in "Japan proper" and therefore the islands should be returned to Japan is convincing. Ryukyu islanders in Japan have been working in concert in gathering signatures expressing the desire to see the islands returned. Yet, in the critical local scene, such a movement has not yet appeared. That locally a curious business-as-usual attitude is being preserved may be said to be out of fear of bothering America, but as long as America's attitude toward the Ryukyus is decided is firm, this concern is absolutely unnecessary. In other words, if the Ryukyus believe in America as a guiding state, cooperates with America in its leadership role, faithfully tries to be America's friend, there is no reason that the islands should be separated from Japan because these ideas are also held by Japan itself. Therefore because the expression of the desire of the Ryukyus to return to Japan are in line with the views of Japan and are not meant to be in opposition to America, the people of the Ryukyus should be allowed to express their views freely. It seems in general that expressing the desire to return to Japan is something bad to America. What should be most feared by America and the Ryukyus is not this but covering truth in deceit. If the Ryukyus hide their desire to return to Japan for fear of upsetting America, the future generations of both countries will find themselves in a tragedy from which they cannot be rescued.[80]

The author and first president of the *Nankai Nichinichi Shimbun*, Murayama Iekuni, later recalled that he expected his "call for the desire to return to Japan be made clear" to be censored and was surprised that his "outburst" was allowed to go to print.[81]

Less than one week later, local leaders and activists answered his call when the Amami Oshima Social Democratic Party (*Amami Oshima Shakai Minshuto*) organized the Council on Measures for the Reversion Problem (*Kizoku Mondai Taisaku Kyogikai*), holding its first meeting on February 13 at the meeting room of the Naze City Office.[82] (For political parties in Amami prior to reversion, see figure 2.3.) There, some seventy people from thirty-two civic, youth, and media organizations participated in the five-hour discussions, which noted that the people of the islands "were at a fork in the middle of a racial divide." "Was a passive attitude simply quietly watching the way events turned out an appropriate response? The return of Oshima to Japan was racially correct. The reversion movement is not an anti-American one, but is instead one that is based on the principles of cooperating with the United States."[83]

In the end, representatives from fourteen of the groups agreed to form the Council for the Reversion of Amami Oshima to Japan (*Amami Oshima Nihon Fukki Kyogikai*), later known by its abbreviated form *Fukkyo*.[84] *Fukkyo*, as a result, came into being the next day, February 14, and, as described below, would play a crucial role in realizing the reversion of the islands to Japan by its numerous actions and petitions. (The organizations and groups making up the Council appear in table 2.1.)

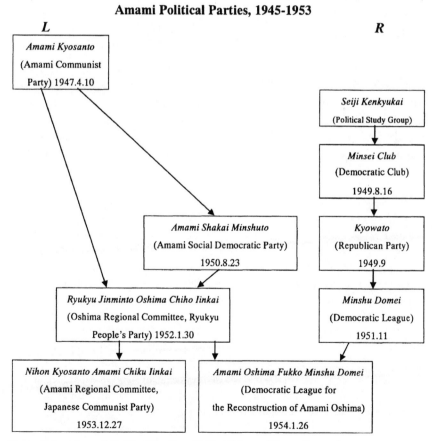

Amami Political Parties, 1945-1953

L   *R*

Amami Kyosanto
(Amami Communist Party) 1947.4.10

Seiji Kenkyukai
(Political Study Group)

Minsei Club
(Democratic Club)
1949.8.16

Amami Shakai Minshuto
(Amami Social Democratic Party)
1950.8.23

Kyowato
(Republican Party)
1949.9

Ryukyu Jinminto Oshima Chiho Iinkai
(Oshima Regional Committee, Ryukyu People's Party) 1952.1.30

Minshu Domei
(Democratic League)
1951.11

Nihon Kyosanto Amami Chiku Iinkai
(Amami Regional Committee, Japanese Communist Party)
1953.12.27

Amami Oshima Fukko Minshu Domei
(Democratic League for the Reconstruction of Amami Oshima)
1954.1.26

Figure 2.3. Amami Political Parties, 1945–1953, and Dates Formed

Table 2.1 *Fukkyo's* **Member Organizations**

Amami Oshima Nihon Fukki Kyogikai
(Council for the Reversion of Amami Oshima to Japan) 1951.2.14

Amami Shakai Minshuto	Amami Oshima Kyoshokuin Kumiai
Amami Seinen Rengo	Naze Shi Fujinkai
Naze Shi Seinen Rengodan	Oshima Gun Ishikai
Fujin Seikatsu Yogokai	Oshima Gun Shika Ishikai
ZenKan Kocho Shokuin Kumiai	Hokubu Oshima Shika Ishikai
Naze Shi Yuya Kumiai	Oshima Dengyosho
Daiko Ichibu Jichikai	Shakuchi Shakuya Jinkai
Daiko Nibu Jichikai	Chosen Jinkai
Daiko Sanbu Jichikai	Inshokuten Kumiai
Daisho Jinkai	Bunka Kyokai
Shiho Daisho Jinkai	Amami Bungeika Kyokai
Sakurakai	Nankai Nichinichi Shimbunsha
Amami Taimusu Sha	Jiyu Sha
Amami Hyoron Sha	Bunmei Sha
Shinseinen	Oshima Shinkyushi Kai

The representatives decided that *Fukkyo's* main office (*honbu*) would be located in Naze, with chapters (*shibu*) established in each of the towns and villages. It was to be suprapartisan in nature. Izumi Horo, a former educator, poet, and editor of the journal *Jiyu*, and who became chairman of the local Social Democratic Party the previous December, was chosen as its leader by unanimous vote.[85] Its goals were explained in the declaration, drafted by Nakamura, it adopted that day:

> We believe that the reversion of our homeland, Amami Oshima, to Japan should be realized because of our ethnic, historic, and cultural relations with Japan proper, which the more than 200,000 residents of the islands have earnestly desired since the end of the war.
>
> On the eve of the peace treaty, we have a good chance to make our views known now in some way to the entire world and the various international organizations that it is the strong desire of us, the inhabitants of these islands, to return to Japan.
>
> At this important time, we, the numerous groups represented, in forming on our own a peaceful "Council for the Reversion of Amami Oshima to Japan," have confidence in the fairness of the world's democratic Allied Powers when deciding the territorial problems as based on the Cairo and Potsdam declarations, and will work hard to make the desires and true ethnic feelings of the more than 200,000 of our compatriots realized.[86]

Fukkyo's first action became the collecting of signatures of all residents over the age of fourteen calling for the return of the islands to Japan as decided at the February 13 meeting. In order to raise awareness of the importance of this signature drive, *Shaminto* asked Shigeno Eizo, the chairman of Hyogo Chapter of *Amami Rengo* who happened to have returned to Amami from Kobe temporarily, to give a public speech on February 17 on the status of the reversion movement on the mainland.[87]

After another rally the next night, *Fukkyo* launched the signature drive the following day on February 19, ending it on April 10. During that time, some 139,348 signatures of individuals who supported the early return to Japan were collected.[88] These results were forwarded to Dulles who had arrived in Japan on April 16 for his third visit (mainly to calm Japanese fears about MacArthur's firing by President Truman, but also to consult with the Japanese government about the status of his talks with the Allies).[89] They were also forwarded to MacArthur's replacement (Lt. Gen. Matthew B. Ridgway), the eleven-country Far Eastern Commission (located in Washington, D.C.), the four-power Allied Council for Japan (located in Tokyo), Prime Minister Yoshida, the presidents of the Upper and Lower Houses of the Japanese Diet, and the Secretary General of the United Nations.

In addition to the signature drive, the so-called *denpo sakusen*, or "Telegram Operation," was conducted, in which appeals were sent by telegram with messages sent from *Fukkyo* and numerous supporting organizations, both in and outside of Amami, to MacArthur, the U. S. and Japanese government, the Diet, and others beginning on February 22.[90] This mass appeal did not go unnoticed by U.S. officials, as subsequent memorandum and comments suggest.

In the middle of these efforts and shortly after the March 12 draft of the Peace Treaty, which had the islands south of 29° degrees north latitude placed under trusteeship, was made public, the thirteen-member Amami Legislature (*Amami Gunto Kaigi*), established in November 1950, passed a unanimous resolution on March 26 calling for the early return of the islands to Japan, followed by the Naze City Assembly (April 4) and the assemblies of other towns and villages throughout Amami.[91]

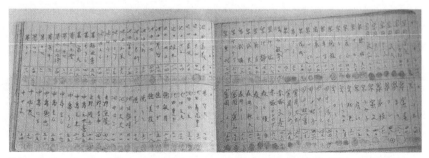

Figure 2.4. Some of the 140,000 Signatures Collected in Amami, February–April 1951

A week later, the final count of the signatures was made, showing that some 99.8 percent of the population over the age of fourteen desired the return of the islands to Japan. In addition to sending the results to the eight individuals and organizations named above, the leaders decided to make a special appeal to the Diet and mass media in an attempt to increase public awareness and expand the movement from a local one to a national one.

On May 8, the petition and signatures were placed on a Yokohama-bound boat, which arrived in the evening of May 12. Upon their receipt by Kanai Masao, who had become chairman of the Tokyo Chapter of the *Amami Rengo* on April 14, and other former residents of Amami, who went down to Yokohama the morning of the May 13, the petition and signatures were brought to the meeting of *Amami Rengo* on the 14th and then to the Diet on May 16.[92] Through introductions by Tokonami and Socialist Party (Left Wing) Diet member Sata Tadataka, also from Kagoshima, the signatures were shown directly to the leaders of both Houses and the other Diet members from Kagoshima and were officially submitted to the Lower House that day as proof of the islanders' desires for reversion.[93] Members of *Amami Rengo* also paid visits on Chief Cabinet Secretary Okazaki Katsuo (later Foreign Minister), GHQ (May 16), the Allied Council (May 18), and members of the Foreign Affairs Committees of both Houses.[94]

With the help of veteran Lower House member Uehara Etsujiro, a graduate of Washington State University and a former minister for Home Affairs in the first Yoshida Cabinet (1946–1947), who introduced a "Resolution Concerning Territory (*Ryodo ni Kansuru Ketsugi*)" on June 2 prepared by the Liberal, Democratic, and Socialist parties, the Lower House passed the resolution which requested the goodwill of the Allies when deciding the territorial arrangements and called upon the government to see that the desires of the residents were heard.[95] This was the first resolution to be passed specifically on reversion of Japanese territories. A similar resolution was passed by the Upper House the same day.

The successful passage, while widely reportedly in the newspapers, particularly the *Mainichi*, and on the *Yomiuri* International Movie News, was at best symbolic, and *Amami Rengo* realized that it would have to strengthen and increase its activities for reversion.[96] Meeting at the No. 2 House of Representatives Office Building on June 24, *Amami Rengo* decided to create a new coordinating body within the Federation to be called the *Zenkoku Amami Oshima Nihon Fukki Taisaku Iinkai* (National Committee on Emergency Measures for the Reversion of Amami Oshima to Japan). In particular, with the Peace Conference approaching, the group decided to petition the U.S. government once again and conduct another signature drive on the mainland.

On July 10, however, the final version of the draft Treaty of Peace with Japan was reported over the radio, causing great distress in the islands. Again, it seemed, Article 3 of the draft had the Amami and Ryukyu Islands separated from Japan and potentially to be placed under a trusteeship arrangement, an outcome that "completely disappointed" *Fukkyo's* chairman, Izumi.[97] That same day, he sent off a short but to the point telegram to Yoshida, the heads of both Houses and each party, as well as Lt. Gen. Ridgway, stating that the islanders were "ABSOLUTE[LY] OPPOSED TO TRUSTEESHIP [AND] WILL CONTINUE STRUGGLE UNTIL THE DAY OF RETURN TO FATHERLAND."[98]

With their appeals not apparently heard, *Fukkyo* leaders immediately met to consider their next move, the result being the organizing of a citizens' rally (*Shimin Sokekki Taikai*) in Naze on July 13.[99] Initially, the rally, attended by some several thousand people, was ordered to be called off by Col. Barlow, because it was considered illegal under Ordinance 32 of the military government. A one-hour stand-off emerged when Izumi and the other organizers refused to stop the rally and cautioned Occupation authorities that the people could turn "anti-American" if not allowed to proceed with their gathering.[100] Chants of "Go home, go home (*kaere, kaere*)!" coming from the crowd, which felt that they had a natural right to demonstrate their unhappiness with the terms of the Peace Treaty, no doubt made the warning more credible.[101] *Fukkyo* was eventually allowed to conditionally go ahead with the rally after Nakae intervened and acted as mediator. The conditions agreed on were: 1) elementary school students would go home; 2) signs and placards would be taken down; and 3) the demonstration to follow the rally would be cancelled.[102] Despite these promises, following the rally, the crowd picked up the placards and purposely took a longer route home, effectively creating a demonstration, with children lining the route.[103]

A second, larger rally, called the "Mass Meeting of all the People in Favor of Reversion to Japan" and comprising some 10,000 people, was held the following week in the late afternoon of July 19.[104] Importantly, the rally was also attended by Lower House member Nikaido Susumu from Kagoshima, who had stopped in Naze on his return from an inspection trip of the Nansei Islands and, having seen the situation himself, would take up the territorial problem in the Diet in late August following Yoshida's appearance to explain the treaty (see below).[105] The rally eventually adopted the following three resolutions: 1) to send a resolution calling for reversion to Prime Minister Yoshida; 2) to send a large delegation, including Nakae and Izumi, to Japan to appeal; and 3) to conduct a hunger strike.[106] Symbolic of the last decision, a hunger strike, the movement became more desperate and, at the same time, perhaps more convinced of the righteousness of its cause.

Figure 2.5. Izumi Horo, Leader of the Reversion Movement in Amami, Beginning a Hunger Strike at Takachiho Shrine in Naze City, August 1951

In August and September, one hunger strike after the other followed led by Izumi. The first one began on August 1 on the grounds of the Takachiho Shrine in Naze and was conducted until August 5.[107] This was followed by a second one on August 16, after Yoshida spoke to the Diet regarding the treaty, and a third one on September 5, the eve of the peace treaty signing. In the meantime, the movement had decided to send representatives to the mainland to present their case one final time before a Japanese delegation, led by Yoshida, left for San Francisco. However, as leaving Amami without permission was illegal and efforts to receive permission for the trip were unsuccessful, these eleven representatives had to be smuggled out (on August 6).[108] The plan was to split into groups of two to three and meet up by 6:00 P.M. on August 16 at the Tokyo Chapter of *Amami Rengo*.[109] On the way, however, three persons were apprehended by police and accused of entering the country illegally. They eventually were allowed to proceed when the police were barraged with appeals for their release from the public after their story was reported in the media.[110]

Around the same time, *Amami Rengo* held rallies in Tokyo and other parts of Japan—Osaka, Kobe, Kyoto, Kagoshima, Miyazaki, Fukuoka—to raise awareness through speeches, the passing of resolutions, and the launching of their own signature drive of one million (reached in early August). Importantly, these events were well attended and saw participation by high-ranking officials, including local governors, mayors, and Diet members, raising the prominence of the movement.[111] One rally, held at Shinbashi Station in Tokyo on August 10 with some 2,000 attendants, reflected the movement's determination in the resolution the rally passed that day: "We will continue to fight until the end in order to realize the return of Amami Gunto to Japan through our opposition to trusteeship."[112]

As we have seen, opposition to trusteeship—in effect the continued, if not permanent, separation of the islands from Japan—was strong. The month before, following the publication of the draft treaty on July 10, Nobori and Kanai requested on July 13, in a petition appealing to America's Christian and Wilsonian Democratic ideals drafted by Nishida Togen, vice chairman of the Emergency Measures Committee, that the treaty draft be amended to change the geographical designation in Article 3 from "29° north latitude" to "27° north latitude" to permit the return of Amami Islands.[113] Eventually, that is what would happen, but it would take a couple more years.

In order to prepare this petition and their other activities, the Emergency Measures Committee was meeting every other day that summer, either in the office space they acquired within the Sanshu Club, a social association for people from Kyushu then located in Minato-ku, or at the offices and meeting rooms of individual Diet members.[114] These actions reached a peak when the eleven representatives from Amami arrived in Tokyo in mid-August. Led by Kagoshima Diet members, the representatives were taken to the Diet and met with the Speaker of the House as well as numerous media organizations who had begun to cover their story.[115] Breaking up into smaller groups, they were subsequently taken around by former diplomat Ito, who interpreted on their behalf, to meet with officials from GHQ, the Allied Council of Japan, and the embassies of the Allied countries to make their final appeals.

At the same time, the representatives and their sponsors in Tokyo hoped to have the Diet pass a resolution (eventually prepared by the Democratic Party and the Right and Left Socialist Parties), specifically dealing with Amami and/or a resolution stating the Diet's "desire to see the return of territory."[116] The Secretariat of the House of Representatives, however, stated that such a resolution should not be submitted while the current Diet session was meeting specifically to approve the Peace Treaty, and thus the actions of the plenipotentiary delegation and the Diet, when meeting to ratify the treaty, would be hindered. After consultations between representatives of the Liberal Party and the three listed above, it was decided that instead of a Diet resolution, Nikaido, who had just visited Amami and Okinawa and was very much aware of the situation there, would pose "an emergency question (*kinkyu shitsumon*)" on the reversion of Amami to Japan.[117] This was done on August 18 and Nikaido's question and speech were reportedly highly received.[118] Due to illness, however, Yoshida was absent and Fukuoka-born Kusaba Ryuen, parliamentary vice minister for Foreign Affairs, answered the question in Yoshida's place.[119] Despite the oppressive heat that day, many from Okinawa and Amami-related groups turned out to watch from the spectators' seats above the main floor.

Also in Amami, around this time, Nakae quietly, but in an official manner, made an appeal in his own way, sending a memo to Brig. Gen. James M. Lewis, civil administrator for the Ryukyu Islands, who had visited the islands recently. In it, Nakae explained that

> The most important problem at present is [the] Reversion-to-Japan Movement. The Movement is not by any means an anti-U.S. campaign, but is rather the manifestation of the intention to co-operate with the United States more actively. Naturally these islands formed a Gun or county of Kagoshima Prefecture and we, people, are Japanese to the bone. Therefore, the Movement means the instinctive manifestation of the feeling and intention of the people themselves regardless of the theory.[120]

As seen in the last chapter, Nakae had made similar appeals (that were sympathetically received it seems) during a trip to Washington a few months before.

In essence, action was being taken at every level to raise awareness and try to force a change in the terms of the Peace Treaty. In the end, however, their efforts did not immediately bear fruit and only seemed to aggravate the situation. In San Francisco Dulles vented his anger at Yoshida for what he described as "demonstrative movements" in the Amami Islands and elsewhere, feeling "it shocking that there is a hunger strike when it has already been said that the islands would be considered as part of Japanese territory. America is to administer the Nansei Islands because of their strategic necessity—they are not to become our territory. It is exactly as I have often told you."[121]

In any case, the reversion movement did not give up following the Peace Treaty conference and, in fact, after a short spell of despair, decided to continue its activities and stepped up its efforts as Japan and the other signatories deliberated the treaty in order to ratify it.[122] With the fate of the islands still unknown, *Amami Rengo* visited the Foreign Ministry to inquire about the trusteeship arrangements and to request that the "implementation of

Article 3 through the trusteeship be postponed," with the rights of travel and relocation liberalized. They also visited the Diet to keep up their requests and insure that the issue of the islands was taken up in Diet questioning.[123] Later, on December 14, *Amami Rengo* petitioned Dulles to make the following appeal—quite similar to that raised by the Foreign Ministry in its December 10 memo to Dulles (as seen in the last chapter)—with regard to the islands:

1. The nationality of the Amami Gunto islanders shall be Japanese.
2. The Amami Gunto islanders shall be called Japanese and treated as Japanese.
3. The Amami Gunto islanders, being Japanese citizens, shall be allowed to display the Japanese national flag (*Nihon Kokki*) and play the national anthem (*Kokka*).
4. Free trade will be allowed with the mainland, with no duties applied.
5. Transportation will be allowed.
6. The use of Japanese currency will be permitted.
7. Uninhibited money transfers will be permitted.
8. An education system compatible with the mainland will be established with continued study on the mainland to be permitted.
9. Funds frozen in the mainland of islanders shall be unfrozen, and islanders will be allowed to receive pensions and other benefits like their fellow Japanese.[124]

It was not only those in Tokyo who were unsure of the island's fate. In Naze, Izumi (who had resigned two days before as chair of the Social Democratic Party to devote all of his time to the nonpartisan reversion movement) also had petitioned Dulles on October 15. Dulles' response came in the middle of December, during his visit to Japan to secure agreement with the Japanese government over the question of the recognition of China. In his reply, Dulles called attention to a speech he gave at a joint luncheon meeting of the American Chamber of Commerce and the Japanese Chamber of Commerce and Industry on December 15 in which he stated, "We hope and believe that a future administration of these islands can be worked out in a friendly way which will combine the natural desires of the inhabitants with the requirements of international peace and security."[125] Dulles added that Izumi's concerns would "receive careful consideration," suggesting that perhaps the Council's actions during the spring and summer had in fact paid off.[126] Indeed, as is discussed in latter chapters and in more detail in my *The Origins of the Bilateral Okinawa Problem*, the State Department continued with its policy review regarding the Nansei Islands, but a final decision was not reached as Japan was preparing for independence again in April 1952 due to the continued clash between the State Department and the military over strategic requirements and political considerations.

Interestingly, however, during this time, the reversion movement was significant enough to warrant great attention in the U.S. government, as seen not only in the Overton memo described earlier and Dulles' comments above, but by the fact that the military government launched an intensive, academic study of the reversion movement in September 1951.[127] While there were limits on the resources and time available to write the report, it nevertheless clearly found that "an overwhelming majority of Amamians are in favor of reversion to Japan, and are opposed to U.S. trusteeship or Ryukyuan independence" and was able to observe that "this attitude has been given considerable support by a well-organized and high emotional reversion movement."[128] Significantly, the report found the percentage of respondents favoring reversion to Japan at 99 percent in its own survey, a figure identical to that of the signature drive. This high percentage would not significantly decrease over the coming year, although there was some division over tactics in bringing about reversion, as is discussed in the next section.

The Third Stage of the Reversion Movement, 1952–1953: The Debate over Calling for the Abrogation of Article 3

With the Peace Treaty coming into force and Japan rejoining the community of nations, debate over whether to call for the abrogation of Article 3 became particularly intense within the reversion movement. Calls for the abrogation of Article 3 would mean, in essence, outright opposition to the Peace Treaty, formally agreed to by the Allies and signed by the Japanese government, and would put the movement against the official, albeit unpopular, policy of the government.

Such debate, namely reversion by *wakunai* (within the framework of Article 3) or *teppai* (abrogating the treaty), in fact had existed before following the announcement of the draft treaty and in the wake of the Peace Conference in San Francisco, with Kanai and other reversion leaders on the mainland calling for a more moderate approach, and more desperate groups (and in some cases, factions ideologically opposed to the Japanese and U.S. governments' such as the Communist-dominated groups) seeing an abrogation of an "unfair (*futo na*)" treaty—in their eyes—to be the only hope.

Locally, the moderate Amami United Teachers' Union (*Amami Rengo Kyoshokuin Kumiai*) argued that outright opposition to Article 3 would damage the movement and even began to challenge the long-standing basic policy of the movement as supported by the radical Amami Youth League and Government Employees Labor Union (*Kankocho Shokuin Kumiai*), which argued for the need to continue with outright opposition to a trusteeship and an immediate and complete return to Japan.[129] In the end, after several days of heated debate during which time Izumi offered to tender his resignation, *Fukkyo* reaffirmed on September 23 the traditional policy of opposing trusteeship and calling for a complete return to Japan.[130] This temporary agreement would not mean an end to the debate over *teppai* vs. *wakunai*, however, as events below show.

During the summer of the previous year, former lawyer and parliamentarian Kanai and others from the Tokyo-based Amami residents' groups, encouraged by the distinction between the renunciation of territories in Article 2 (Taiwan, Korea, etc.) and Article 3, which did not require of Japan renunciation of the Nansei and Nanpo Islands, began to doubt whether in fact the U.S. government would place the Nansei Islands under a trusteeship, having consulted with Foreign Ministry officials (who in turn were in regular contact with the sympathetic Office of the Political Advisor at GHQ, led by Sebald). On August 19, Kanai, having concluded (correctly) that the islands would not be placed under trusteeship, sent a telegram to Izumi in Naze stating that "America will not go ahead with a trusteeship. It looks like in two or three years like [the islands] will be returned."[131]

Pronouncements by the Japanese government, Dulles, and Sebald during the fall seemed to confirm this statement. For example, during a speech at the U.S.–Japan Society in Tokyo on September 28, Sebald pointed out the difference between Articles 2 and 3 and stated that he believed the U.S. government would resolve the issue in a way that the interests of the islanders and Japan would be taken into consideration.[132] Likewise, Dulles, as mentioned above, expressed his belief on December 15 in Tokyo that an arrangement could be worked out over the islands in which the "natural desires" of the residents would be reflected. The Japanese government, in particular Yoshida and the Foreign Ministry, also gave favorable interpretations. On October 15, at a session of the Upper House, Yoshida stated that the "United States would probably give up its rights once the military need was gone."[133] The Foreign Ministry added that they believed there was a strong probability that the United States would not request a trusteeship over the islands and thus there was still hope.[134] As a result, Kanai and his associates were encouraged by these events.

This did not prevent the passage of a near unanimous resolution in Okinawa at the Ryukyu Legislature on April 29, 1952, calling for reversion or the flying of the flag at half-mast at an *Amami Rengo*-sponsored event in Tokyo on May 28 and declaring April 28 (the day the Peace Treaty went into effect) "Amami Oshima's Day of Regret (*Amami Oshima Tsukon no Hi*)."[135] The latter incident suggested that there was still a great deal of concern over the fate of the islands among the former residents.

Within the reversion movement, members, including those on the mainland, began to lose hope. The Kobe chapter of the Committee on Emergency Measures for the Reversion of Amami Oshima to Japan voted to disband itself, seeing "No prospects for early reversion after the Peace Treaty," and instead elected to work gradually at outstanding issues, such as unrestricted travel and improvements in education.[136] This led to a visible rise in infighting over future tactics, with the optimistic forces (such as Kanai) not wishing to do anything to unnecessarily aggravate the situation, and others, more impatient, urging a more radical approach (such as calling for the abrogation of Article 3 and denouncing the Peace Treaty).[137] One meeting of the National Committee on Emergency Measures for the Reversion of Amami Oshima (*Amami Rengo Fukki Taisaku Iinkai Zenkoku Taikai*), held on November 14–15, 1951, in Tokyo, saw this debate come to a head, but the traditional policy of "opposition to trusteeship; complete reversion" was reaffirmed, as it had been in Amami two months before.[138] (Eventually, however, the movement in the spring of 1952 would come to adopt calls for abrogating Article 3.) These examples of infighting shed light on the fundamental ideological differences within the movement that had existed but became more dramatic with the passage of time. In a particularly ugly scene, communists and other radicals, for example, tried to physically prevent speeches by Tokonami and Kanbayashi at the rally at Shimbashi Station, embarrassing the movement.[139]

Witnessing these cracks, seventy-three-year-old Nobori made his way to Tokyo from Kamakura on August 10 to attend a special two-day meeting of *Amami Rengo*, held because of concerns about the future of the reversion movement. Nobori told the members that, while it seemed as if the movement was losing steam following the signing of the Peace Treaty, "our determination remains as strong as ever."[140] As the "core of a movement of 800,000 of our countrymen," *Amami Rengo* had to focus or else the movement would not succeed. While the incident at Shinbashi was regrettable, a movement without differences of opinion was a dead movement," Nobori explained, and, in one of the more dramatic and important moments, he appealed to the members to "Overcome your differences for the sake of the larger objective."

During this time, the reversion movement in Naze sought in late June (1952) to make its intentions clearer at its first mass rally after the treaty came into effect. At the June 28 gathering, the following demands were passed: 1) the abrogation of Article 3 and the complete return to Japan; and 2) the abrogation of all military government laws and the introduction of Japanese laws.[141] The following day, *Fukkyo* called another special meeting of its leadership and decided to initiate a second signature drive beginning in July, which included the new stance of calling for the abolition of Article 3.

Figure 2.6. *Fukkyo*-sponsored Rally at Naze Elementary School, June 28, 1952

By November, some 99.9 percent of Amami residents over the age of four-teen had again signed their names in favor of reversion, and, on November 24, Izumi, who had since been elected Mayor of Naze, Murayama, and Haraguchi Sumiji, director of the Amami branch of the Commerce and Industry Bureau of the government of the Ryukyus, left for Tokyo as representatives of *Fukkyo* to deliver the latest signatures to government officials and members of the Diet. Stopping first in Kagoshima, Izumi and his group sought to raise con-sciousness regarding Amami before departing for Tokyo (on November 27).[142]

After holding a rally in Tokyo on November 30, at which Izumi described the situation of Amami being separated from Japan as a "body that had lost its limb," the first several days in Tokyo were spent coordinating their efforts with the Tokyo-based groups; visiting the offices of newspaper editors to explain the situation in Amami and their trip to the mainland; and meeting with members of the ruling and opposition parties, Sato Naotake and Ono Banboku (leaders of the Upper and Lower Houses respectively), government officials, including Ogata Taketora (then Vice-Premier), Foreign Minister Okazaki Katsuo, and eventually U.S. Ambassador Robert D. Murphy and Prime Minister Yoshida. While in Tokyo, interestingly, former Maj. Gen. Takada heard of the group's trip and visited the delegation at their lodging in Takanawa to wish them well.[143]

Initially, the appointment with Murphy was scheduled for only five minutes. However, Murphy, intrigued by the discussion—likely because he was at that very point recommending to Washington the return of the islands—eventually

Figure 2.7. Izumi Horo (first row, second from left) and Other Representatives from Amami with representatives of *Amami Rengo* in Tokyo, November 1952

gave the group some forty minutes. Izumi and his associates went into a long explanation of Amami's history and situation, using maps and the collection of signatures they brought with them. According to Murayama's account of the December 15 meeting, it appeared to be the first time Murphy heard this "unbelievable story."[144] Ending the interview by stating that the "international situation made it necessary," Murphy told the group that he would do his best to see their wishes fulfilled.

The group wanted to meet with Prime Minister Yoshida next, a task that proved difficult but was made possible through the intervention of Kagoshima Governor Shigenari, who had recently returned from a trip to Amami in late October.[145] Finally able to meet with Yoshida on the 23rd, Yoshida requested that only Shigenari and two of the representatives come to the Prime Minister's residence.

Despite having set up the *Sorifu Nanpo Renraku Jimukyoku* (Prime Minister's Office Liaison Bureau for the Southern Areas) with an office in Naze that summer, Yoshida, according to Murayama's account, was completely in the dark about the situation in Amami, much like Murphy.[146] After expressing their gratitude for remarks by Yoshida on November 24 at the 15th Session of the

Figure 2.8.   Izumi Horo and Other Reversion Movement Representatives in Front of the U.S. Chancellery, Tokyo, with John J. Conroy, Who Later Would be Involved in the Reversion Negotiations

Diet that he would work hard to realize the return of Amami, the group opened up the same map that they used with Murphy and then launched into an explanation of the situation in Amami. Yoshida, according to Murayama, "sat in his Japanese dress with his famous cigar, looking incredulous and asking a lot of questions."[147] He explained the difficulty he had at the signing of the Peace Treaty, saying that "from the beginning, reversion has been a question of time. . . . I thought that being under the control of a first class country like America, people would be living a much better life than on the mainland, but America seems to be doing some terrible things there, it is now time that the islands be returned. I will try to speed up the negotiations." The group was relieved to hear this because just shortly before that, on December 17, the prime minister, in response to a question from Saigo Yoshinosuke of the Green Breeze Society at the Upper House Budget Meeting, had only weakly stated that "it will be a problem to be solved when the time comes." A step forward had been made, Murayama declared.

Yoshida also told the group that "from the beginning of negotiations with Dulles, I have been emphasizing Amami. With the exception of the military, American leaders understand. The problem is military. There is a fear of spies. Care has to be taken that the movement does not become anti-American. I want to give full consideration to your requests that a special disposition agency be set up."[148] On leaving, Yoshida added that with the U.S. administration would be changing in the next year from Truman to Eisenhower, a new path in the negotiations could open up. Yoshida was correct; a new era was indeed beginning. Before we look at that, however, it is necessary to examine the Japanese government's movements toward a solution to a territorial problem.

One final hurdle was waiting for the group while in Tokyo—seeing that the Diet pass a resolution regarding the Amami Islands. Importantly, this would be the first resolution dealing solely with Amami. On December 12, the group had met in the office of Representative Tokonami with other leaders from the Tokyo-based Federation to discuss the contents of a resolution and the timing.[149] After gaining the concurrence of the leadership of the ruling Liberal Party and other parties, the resolution, entitled "Amami Oshima ni Kansuru Ketsugi An (Proposed Resolution Regarding Amami Oshima)," was introduced on the agenda on December 25 and passed unanimously that same day.[150] Calling upon the government to take the necessary measures to see that the "people of Oshima Gun in Kagoshima Prefecture" have the same access to lifestyle, education, transportation, welfare, etc. as those on the mainland, the resolution sought a "*de facto* reversion," and, of note was the first one that focused exclusively on the Amami Islands, reflecting more realistic voices in the reversion movement that feared linking Amami to the fate of Okinawa would prevent the return of Amami.[151] Little did those proposing and voting on the resolution know that exactly one year later to the day, the islands would be returned. A year before Dulles' "Christmas present," the Diet had given the Amami islanders a "Christmas present" of its own.

It was around the same time in Amami that a similar debate was exposing the divisions that existed within the reversion movement as highlighted in a clash that took place on December 24 at the meeting room of the Naze City Office.[152] Moderates in the movement had been bothered for some time by the radicalism of the Communist members and feared that the movement was being used to serve the agenda of the outlawed Amami Communist Party and not the other way around. Indeed, the Communist Party of Japan, according to Kanai and others, seemed to be running with the issue (*warikomi senjutsu*), a prospect that worried them tremendously.[153] If the movement became identified as an anti-American, Communist one, the return of the islands would become very difficult, if not impossible. The moderates, in favor of a "*de facto* reversion*" through increasing political, administrative, economic, and cultural links with the mainland, moreover felt that as long as the movement continued to call for the abolition of Article 3 in the Peace Treaty—which was an international agreement honored by Japan and would require the concurrence of all signatory nations—reversion would be nearly impossible. A final decision about future strategy and organizational structure was put off until the New Year when Izumi was expected to return from Tokyo.

At the next meeting on January 15, the day after his return from the mainland, Izumi reported on the delegation's trip and activities. Following this, discussions moved to the question sponsored by the *Amami Oshima Nihon Fukki Kakushin Doshikai* (Progressive Brotherhood for the Return of Amami Oshima to Japan)—a group formed at the end of the previous year within the movement to block the influence of the Communists—of whether to ban "political parties," specifically the local Communist Party, from the movement. After heated debate, the Communist members left the meeting, in effect being purged from the movement as long as their agenda appeared in controlled along party lines. Discussions continued over the coming weeks and months to restructure *Fukkyo*, but it took nearly a couple of months for the issues of membership and funding to be finally worked out.

Symbolizing that their appeals were now being heard, during a rally held on February 28, 1953, *Fukkyo* received a telegram from Prime Minister Yoshida stating that the government was aware of the situation and doing its best to realize the return of the islands.[154] Furthermore, at the end of April 1953, *Fukkyo* was able to sponsor a "Realization of the Return to Japan Week," appealing for the return of the islands at events such as the rally at Naze Elementary School on April 21.[155] At the end of the week on April 28, the one-year anniversary of the coming into effect of the Peace Treaty, another hunger strike was held at Takachiho Shrine led by Izumi, who was not in good health.

Meanwhile, leaders in the Tokyo-based group were also actively pressing their requests, as seen for example by the their meeting with Ambassador Murphy, about to leave his post after one year, on April 27, 1952.[156] Likewise, on May 9, the new chairman of the National Committee on Emergency Measures, Okuyama Hachiro, met with John J. Conroy, first secretary of the U.S. Embassy, to relay the desire for both a *de facto* as well as a *de jure* reversion.[157] Two weeks later, on May 22, members representing delegations of Amami, Okinawa, and Ogasawara jointly petitioned the Embassy in an important show of unity despite their very different situations.[158] And on May 31, Kagoshima Governor Shigenari met with former U.S. First Lady, Eleanor M. Roosevelt, during her trip to Japan to attend a conference in Fukuoka as chairwoman of the International Committee for the Preservation of Human Rights, and presented to her a twenty-two-page "Petition for Return of the Amami Oshima Islands," which argued that "unless the return of the Islands is realized, there will be absolutely no means to help the Islanders out of [their] sad plight."[159] Roosevelt responded that she would be sure to inform the new ambassador, John M. Allison, of its contents.[160] Little did she, Shigenari, or the reversion movement know that it was through Allison's efforts, both as assistant secretary of state, and later as ambassador, that the U.S. government was at that very moment reaching a decision on the return of the islands. Continuing its appeals, the reversion movement awaited anxiously for a response. It would come, somewhat unexpectedly, that summer.

Before we look at the U.S. decision to return the islands (officially made that June), it is necessary to examine in detail the efforts of the Japanese government to seek the return of the islands.

Notes

1. This situation differed greatly from the one that confronted Okinawa, which had been its own prefecture, and thus not being part of another prefecture, lacked a high official in the Japanese governing body such as a governor who could argue on its behalf, like Shigenari did for Amami, a historic part of Kagoshima.

2. Nakamura, *Sokoku e no Michi*, pp. 62–63.

3. *Ibid.*

4. *Ibid.*

5. *Ibid.*, pp. 63–64. Elections, with voting done by both males and females over the age of twenty, were subsequently held on July 1. Naze was incorporated with city status on that day.

6. Saneshima, *Ano Hi, Ano Toki*, pp. 172–174. Technically speaking the newspapers were not new, just reincorporated with new names under new ownership by individuals from Amami, Murayama Iekuni in the case of *Nankai Nichinichi Shimbun*, and Nakamura Yasutaro in the case of *Amami Taimusu*.

7. *Ibid.*, p. 173. Also see Satohara Akira, *RyukyukoAmami no Sengo Seishinshi: Amerika Gunseika no Shiso-Bunka no Kiseki* (*The Postwar Psychological History of Amami-Ryukyu: Thought and Culture During the American Military Occupation*), (Tokyo: Satsuki Shobo, 1994), pp. 42–108.

8. It was Nakamura who described the proclamation as an *omiage*, or present, in his memoirs. He also notes the holding of an election in Amami, two years before Okinawa, makes it all the more meaningful and suggestive of the foresight and leadership of Porter. Indeed, although the occupation had just started and the military government team limited in personnel, the elections took place and were quite successful.

9. "Interview with Press Correspondents, Primarily Concerning Plan for United Nations Administration of Japan," in Government Section, Supreme Commander for the Allied Powers, ed., *Political Reorientation of Japan, September 1945 to September 1948*, Vol. 2 (Washington, D.C.: Government Printing Office, 1949; reprinted edition, Westport, Conn.: Greenwood Press, 1970), pp. 765–766.

10. Nankai Nichinichi Shimbun, ed., *Gojunenshi*, p. 116.

11. Ashida was foreign minister in the Katayama Tetsu cabinet (May 1947–March 1948), becoming prime minister himself (as well as his own foreign minister) from March 1948 to October 1948.

12. "Okinawa, Kuriles Asked by Japan, Ashida Declares," *Pacific Stars and Stripes*, June 6, 1947; "Japan Not Rearming, Says Ashida; Seeks Return of Okinawa, Kuriles," *Nippon Times*, June 7, 1947. For local coverage, see "Ryukyu no Ichibu Henkan Yokyu ([Ashida] Desires Return of Part of Ryukyus)," *Nankai Nichinichi Shimbun*, June 8, 1947. For a fuller discussion on Ashida's statements and the impact it would have, see Eldridge, *The Origins of the Bilateral Okinawa Problem*, chapter 5.

13. Kanai Masao, a former Diet member, governor of Wakayama, and influential member of the reversion movement in Tokyo, relates that Ashida was very sympathetic to the goals of the movement and would help them considerably in later years, introducing them to advisors of Yoshida, such as the influential House of Representatives member Kojima Kazuo, in order to impress upon the prime minister the importance of the Amami issue. See Kanai Masao, ed., *Amami Oshima Fukki Undo Kaikoroku* (*Recollections on the Amami Oshima Reversion Movement*), (Tokyo: Yamamotosha, 1966), esp. pp. 57–58.

14. "General MacArthur Foresees Japan Peace Within 18 Months," *Pacific Stars and Stripes*, June 29, 1947. This was reported locally in the Uruma Shimpo (predecessor to the Ryukyu Shimpo) as "Beikoku no Okinawa Senryo ni Nihon wa Hantai Sezu, Ryukyujin wa Nihonjin ni wa Hizu (Japan Does not Object to U.S. Occupation of Okinawa, 'Ryukyuans are Not Japanese')," *Uruma Shimpo*, July 4, 1947.

15. Kaitei Nazeshishi Hensan Iinkai, ed., *Kaitei Nazeshishi* (*Revised History of Naze City*), Vol. 1 (Naze: Nazeshiyakusho, 1996), pp. 780–781.

16. Nankai Nichinichi Shimbun, ed., *Gojunenshi*, p. 117. One of the issues of great concern was that of education. The school buildings were in a poor state, lack-

ing floors and windows. Classrooms lacked desks and textbooks, and students lacked notebooks and pencils. In desperation, two teachers—Morita Tadamitsu, of the Amami Elementary School, and Fukasa Genzo, of the Naze Middle School, secretly went to the mainland by boat to raise awareness there and to smuggle back textbooks and other teaching supplies. Having to risking their lives and possible imprisonment for what was seen as an inhuman situation on the island caused great bitterness among the islanders. For more on this, see the special edition of the local journal devoted primarily to women's issues entitled "Kanejumaru to Kyokasho Mikko (The Kanejumaru and Smuggling Textbooks)," *Sanenbana*, No. 3 (March 1995), pp. 12–31, and Saneshima, *Ano Hi, Ano Toki*, pp. 175–176. I would like to thank the editors of Sanenbana, particularly Satake Kyoko, for sharing copies of their journal. Recently, the interviews on the smuggling of textbooks and other subjects conducted by the editors of Sanenbana were published in Satake Kyoko, *Gunseika Amami no Mikko-Mitsu Boeki* (*Smuggling and Secret Travels in Amami During the Occupation*), (Kagoshima: Nanpo Shinsha, 2003).

17. Nankai Nichinichi Shimbun, ed., *Gojunenshi*, p. 117.

18. *Ibid.*, pp. 117–118.

19. Kanai notes that the wording "Northern Ryukyus" was translated in Japanese as "*Hokubu Nansei Shoto*," or "Northern Nansei Islands," in order to reflect the fact that the islands wanted to distinguish Amami from the Ryukyu Islands and to avoid repeating the incident at the time of the signing of the surrender document in September 1945 between Takada and U.S. forces. See Kanai, ed., *Fukki Undo Kaikoroku*, p. 40.

20. *Ibid.*; and Nankai Nichinichi Shimbun, ed., *Gojunenshi*, p. 118.

21. Labree was not replaced due to his actions. Rather, it seems, he had been promoted to director of administrative affairs in the Okinawa command. See Murayama, *Amami Fukkishi*, p. 149.

22. *Ibid.*, p. 149. Nankai Nichinichi Shimbun, ed., *Gojunenshi*, pp. 105–106.

23. A Directive on Political Parties (*Seitorei*), Special Proclamation No. 23, was also announced on October 5 that year. See Nihon Kyosanto Amami Chiku Iinkai, ed., *Amami no Noroshi: Amami Kyosantoshi, 1947–1953* (*The Beacon of Amami: A History of the Amami Communist Party, 1947–1953*), (Naze: Nihon Kyosanto Amami Chiku Iinkai, 1984), pp. 43–46.

24. Nankai Nichinichi Shimbun, ed., *Gojunenshi*, p. 119.

25. According to Kanai, the federation sent a message to local newspapers and mayors urging that a signature drive be started calling for reversion, but this was not realized at the time due to local conditions, including the still repressive atmosphere and the fact that a reversion movement organization was not in existence yet. See Kanai, ed., *Fukki Undo Kaikoroku*, p. 42.

26. Symbolic of this harsher environment, suspected (and actual) Communist activist, Nakamura Yasutaro, who had helped form the underground Amami Communist Party (Amami Kyosanto) on April 10, 1947, was prevented from resuming a lectureship at a school having been accused of teaching Communism later that summer and,

in August 1948, was arrested for being in possession of Communist party journals and materials that he had had smuggled in. See Nihon Kyosanto Amami Chiku Iinkai, ed., *Amami no Noroshi*, pp. 67–68; and Nakamura, *Sokoku e no Michi*, p. 105.

27. The labor union for public officials, Kankocho Shokuin Kumiai, came into being in May 1948, with an increase of their base salary and other benefits being one of their main issues. See Murayama, *Amami Fukkishi*, p. 160.

28. There had been reports, reported locally in the newspapers, of a similar policy being discussed in Okinawa in which prices would be raised to 60 percent of market value at the end of December 1948. Moreover, in the early part of the 1949, the military government in Okinawa went ahead and announced the implementation of this new policy in Okinawa itself. See Nankai Nichinichi Shimbun, ed., *Gojunenshi*, p. 120. Nevertheless, its adoption in Amami, some three months later, did in fact come as a surprise to the islanders.

29. Saneshima, *Ano Hi, Ano Toki*, p. 182. One of the newspapers reports that, symbolic of the dire straits at the time, public officials, whose salaries had not been raised, resigned and joined the black market, and some police officers left their work to become captains of smuggling boats. See Nankai Nichinichi Shimbun, ed., *Gojunenshi*, p. 109.

30. Nankai Nichinichi Shimbun, ed., *Gojunenshi*, p. 121. Nakae was then away touring one of the islands and thus Kasai seems to have commented in his place. Nakae made it back, however, to participate in deliberations about responses. See Murayama, *Amami Fukkishi*, p. 176.

31. Saneshima, *Ano Hi, Ano Toki*, p. 184.

32. *Ibid.*, pp. 184–185. Saneshima was a participant in the delegation, representing the Nazeshi Rengo Seinendan (Naze City Federation of Youth Groups).

33. *Ibid.*, p. 185. It seems that some in the delegation wanted to negotiate a deal.

34. *Ibid.*, pp. 185–186.

35. Sakida Saneyoshi, *Beigunsei no Teppeki o Koete: Watashi no Shogen to Kiroku de Tsuzuru Amami no Fukki Undoshi* (*Overcoming the Iron Curtain of the U.S. Military Occupation: A History of the Reversion Movement based on My Testimony and Records*), (Naze: Amami Rurikakesu no Kai, 1997), p. 38.

36. Saneshima, *Ano Hi, Ano Toki*, p. 186.

36. *Ibid.*, p. 186.

38. Added to these problems, a major typhoon, Della, hit the Nansei Islands, including a direct hit on Amami, just about this time in June 1949, damaging more than 1600 structures and devastating the islands' agricultural production. See Murayama, *Amami Fukkishi*, p. 180; and Arnold G. Fisch Jr., *Military Government in the Ryukyu Islands, 1945–1950* (Washington, D.C.: Center of Military History, 1988), p. 88.

39. Saneshima, *Ano Hi, Ano Toki*, p. 186; Sakida, *Beigunsei no Teppeki o Koete*, p. 38; and Murayama, *Amami Fukkishi*, p. 182.

40. Sakida, *Beigunsei no Teppeki o Koete*, p. 38; and Nankai Nichinichi Shimbun, ed., *Gojunenshi*, p. 122.

41. In fact, the organization did include members of the underground Amami Communist Party, which had been formed in April 1947, as one of the members of the council relates. See Sakida, *Beigun no Teppeki o Koete*, p. 38. For more on the Communist Party in Amami, see Nihon Kyosanto Amami Chiku Iinkai, ed., *Amami no Noroshi*, esp. pp. 72–77.

42. Sakida, *Beigunsei no Teppeki o Koete*, pp. 38–39.

43. Nankai Nichinichi Shimbun, ed., *Gojunenshi*, p. 122; and Murayama, *Amami Fukkishi*, p. 192.

44. Nankai Nichinichi Shimbun, ed., *Gojunenshi*, pp. 122–123. Also see Murayama, *Amami Fukkishi*, pp. 195–196.

45. Nankai Nichinichi Shimbun, ed., *Gojunenshi*, pp. 122–123.

46. *Ibid.*, p. 123.

47. Nihon Kyosanto Amami Chiku Iinkai, ed., *Amami no Noroshi*, pp. 82–83; and Murayama, *Amami Fukkishi*, pp. 196–197.

48. Murayama, *Amami Fukkishi*, pp. 196–197.

49. Nankai Nichinichi Shimbun, ed., *Gojunenshi*, p. 123. Limited trade was restored between Amami and Kagoshima in the early fall of 1949, but it was initially not enough to dramatically effect the economy. In addition, passenger ship lines were opened up between the Ryukyu Islands and the mainland in October 1949. See Murayama, *Amami Fukkishi*, pp. 189–190. In February 1950, Nakae went to Okinawa to make his appeal. This was followed by a four-month trip to the mainland by Vice Gov. Kasai to promote trade and increasing transportation links. See *Ibid.*, pp. 199–200. Duties and currency still remained a problem and trade did not grow that much.

50. Kaitei Nazeshishi Hensan Iinkai, ed., *Kaitei Nazeshishi*, p. 119. At a session of the Lower House Foreign Affairs Committee, Foreign Ministry Political Affairs Bureau Chief Shimazu Hisanaga, for example, stated in response to a question from Liberal Party member Sasaki Morio that "it was natural for Japan to claim its territorial rights to Okinawa and Ogasawara and other islands close to Japan as they were not taken by Japan out of violence or greed."

51. *Ibid.*, pp. 123–124; and Murayama, *Amami Fukkishi*, p. 218.

52. Nankai Nichinichi Shimbun, ed., *Gojunenshi*, p. 124. Also see Nankai Nichinichi Shimbun, "Amami Oshima no Kizoku Mondai Rekishi, Jinshu o Kangaeru Daro (Amami Oshima's Territorial Problem History, Ethnicity Likely To Be Taken into Consideration)," February 2, 1950.

53. Nankai Nichinichi Shimbun, ed., *Gojunenshi*, p. 124.

54. *Ibid.* Also see Murayama, *Amami Fukkishi*, p. 218.

55. Kagoshima had 20,000 former islanders in the prefecture. In addition to Shigenari, Vice Gov. Yasuoka Takehisa, from Amami, played a critical role in both raising awareness in the prefecture and the rest of the mainland as well as advising the Okayama Prefecture-born Shigenari. See Murayama, *Amami Fukkishi*, p. 219.

56. Nankai Nichinichi Shimbun, ed., *Gojunenshi*, p. 124.

57. *Ibid.* Also see "Amami Gunto Henkan Keii [Background Details Regarding the Reversion of Amami Gunto] (January 1954)," Reel Number A'-0146, Flash

Number 14, Dai 6 kan, Amami Gunto, *Nichibeikan Henkan Kyotei Kankei* (*Materials Relating to the Reversion Agreement of Amami Gunto Between the United States and Japan*), *Nansei Shoto Kizoku Mondai* (*Territorial Problem of the Nansei Shoto*), DRO-MOFA, p. 48

58. Nankai Nichinichi Shimbun, ed., *Gojunenshi*, p. 124.

59. *Ibid.*, p. 126.

60. Murayama, *Amami Fukkishi*, p. 219. Copies of the resolution were sent to the prime minister, foreign minister (also Yoshida), leaders of both Houses, chairmen of the Foreign Affairs Committees of both Houses, etc.

61. Nankai Nichinichi Shimbun, ed., *Gojunenshi*, p. 125.

62. *Ibid.*

63. For a history of the group and its relationship with the Communist Party, see Sakida Saneyoshi, "Kanzen Sokoku Fukki e no Michi: Joyaku Sanjo Teppai no Hata o Agete (The Road to the Full Return to the Homeland: Calling for the Abolition of Article 3 of the Peace Treaty)," in Amami Kyodo Kenkyukai, ed., *Gunseika no Amami: Nihon Fukki Sanju Shunen Kinenshi* (*Amami Under the Military Occupation: Report on the 30th Anniversary of the Return to Japan*), (Naze: Amami Kyodo Kenkyukai, 1983), pp. 285–287. Also see Sakida's memoirs, *Beigunsei no Teppeki o Koete*, pp. 26–58.

64. Saneshima, *Ano Hi, Ano Toki*, p. 189. Saneshima served as secretary of the federation as well as the master of ceremony at the gathering.

65. It might be worthwhile to point out here the relationship of the Communist Party with the issue of reversion. The Communist Party in Japan was not in sync with the Amami Communist Party on this issue, because the central party continued to view Okinawa and the southern islands as an oppressed people and therefore should be set free. In fact, the Amami Communist Party and others wanted to return to Japan. Moreover, the Communist Party tended to avoid comment on territorial issues because the Soviet Union was occupying the Northern islands. It took some time and a change of central party line before the two were in line.

66. "Unsigned Memorandum Prepared in the Department of State (September 11, 1950)," *FRUS, 1950, Vol. 6, East Asia and the Pacific* (Washington, D.C.: Government Printing Office, 1976), pp. 1296–1297.

67. "Petition [to MacArthur] for the Reunion of the Island Group of Amami O-shima With Japan Proper (November 15, 1950)," to be found in a large collection of materials prepared by Matsuda Kiyoshi in 1968 known as *Amami Oshima Nihon Fukki Undo Shiryo* (hereafter cited as *Fukki Undo Shiryo*) donated to the Amami Branch of the Kagoshima Prefectural Library, Naze City, Amami County, Kagoshima Prefecture (hereafter cited as Kagoshima Prefectural Library, Amami Branch). For a Japanese language version of the petition, see Murayama, *Amami Fukkishi*, pp. 220–221. Nobori sent a similar but shorter petition to Dulles the following February prior to the latter's leaving Japan. See "Petition [to Dulles] for the Reunion of the Island Group of Amami O-shima with Japan Proper (February 8, 1951)," *Fukki Undo Shiryo*, Kagoshima Prefectural Library, Amami Branch. A second petition was sent on May 25, 1951. See Kanai, ed., *Fukki Undo Kaikoroku*, p. 50.

68. "Petition [to MacArthur] for the Reunion of the Island Group of Amami O-shima With Japan Proper."

69. Migita Shoshin, *Tokyo ni Okeru Amami no Fukki Undo* (*The Reversion Movement in Tokyo*), (Tokyo: Shinko Sendensha, 1966), pp. 5–6; and Tokyo Amami Kai 100 Shunen Henshu Iinkai, ed., *Tokyo Amami Kai 100 Nen no Ayumi* (*100 Years of the Tokyo Amami Kai*), (Tokyo: Tokyo Amami Kai, 1999), pp. 72–73.

70. Migita, *Tokyo ni Okeru Amami no Fukki Undo*, pp. 5–6; and Tokyo Amami Kai, ed., *Tokyo Amami Kai 100 Nen no Ayumi*, pp. 72–73. Also see Kanai, ed., *Fukki Undo Kaikoroku*, p. 53.

71. Initially, Tokyo Amami Kai President Okuyama Hachiro acted as temporary chairman of Amami Rengo, but, in June 1947, Masatani Tada was elected to the chairmanship, as well as of the Tokyo Honbu. In early December 1947, however, Masatani had to resign for health reasons. After an appeal from Kanai and Soga Shiro, a Tokyo-based council member of Amami Rengo originally from Koniya, who visited his home in Kamakura, Nobori agreed to assume the chairmanship of Amami Rengo. Tanimura Tadaichiro agreed to head the Tokyo chapter. For more on this, see Tokyo Amami Kai, ed., *Tokyo Amami Kai 100 Nen no Ayumi*, p. 73; and Kanai, ed., *Fukki Undo Kaikoroku*, p. 56.

72. For more on the movement in the mainland, see, in addition to the work cited above by Migita, Tokyo Amami Kai 100 Nen Shunen Kinenshi Henshu Iinkai, ed., *Tokyo Amami Kai 100 Nen no Ayumi* (*100 Years of the Tokyo Amami Kai*), (Tokyo: Tokyo Amami Kai, 1999), esp. pp. 69–159; and Tokyo Amami Kai 80 Shunen Henshu Iinkai, ed., *Tokyo Amami Kai 80 Nen no Ayumi* (*80 Years of the Tokyo Amami Kai*), (Tokyo: Tokyo Amami Kai, 1984), pp. 307–392. I am grateful to Migita Shoshin and Nobori Amiko for sharing copies of these association journals with me.

73. This body of working knowledge, it should be noted, was also applied to later efforts on the mainland by private and semi-government organizations to seek the return of Okinawa and Ogasawara. Indeed, as Kanai notes in the foreword to his book, that is why he compiled the edited volume on the Amami reversion movement. See Kanai, ed., *Fukki Undo Kaikoroku*, pp. 9–22.

74. Migita, *Tokyo ni Okeru Amami no Fukki Undo*, p. 7.

75. Kanai Masao, "Amami Oshima no Sokoku Fukki Naru (What Would Become Amami Oshima's Return to the Homeland)," in Terebi Tokyo, ed., *Shogen: Watashino Showashi* (*Testimony: My Showa History*), Vol. 6. (Tokyo: Gakugei Shorin, 1969), p. 220.

76. Migita, *Tokyo ni Okeru Amami no Fukki Undo*, p. 8; and Tokyo Amami Kai, ed., *Tokyo Amami Kai 100 Nen no Ayumi*, pp. 75–76.

77. "Ryukyu wa Mukashi Kara Nihonryo" ("Ryukyus are Japanese Territory From Long Ago"), Nankai Nichinichi Shimbun, January 7, 1950. Also see "Despatch 936, Territorial Provisions of the Japanese Peace Treaty (January 15, 1951)," *Central Decimal File, 1950–1954* (694.001/1–1551), RG 59.

78. "Islands Seen Delicate Point in Treaty Work," *Pacific Stars and Stripes*, January 23, 1951.

79. "Ryodo Yokyu wa Muri (Territorial Demands Impossible)," *Asahi Shimbun*, February 1, 1951. In addition to the strong efforts of the Yoshida government to impress upon Dulles the significance of the territorial issues at the time during their talks, the political parties also delivered appeals to leave the Nansei Islands with Japan. For more on this, see Eldridge, *The Origins of the Bilateral Okinawa Problem*, esp. chapter 7.

80. Nankai Nichinichi Shimbun, ed., *Gojunenshi*, pp. 129–130. "Kizoku Mondai ni Tsuite (Regarding the Problem of Reversion)," Nankai Nichinichi Shimbun, February 8, 1951.

81. Murayama Iekuni, "Fukkyo Hossoku no Zengo (Before and After the Start of the Reversion Council)," in Kaitei Nazeshishi Hensan Iinkai, ed., *Kaitei Nazeshishi*, Vol. 1, p. 863.

82. Murayama, *Amami Fukkishi*, p. 234.

83. Nankai Nichinichi Shimbun, ed., *Gojunenshi*, p. 130.

84. Murayama, *Amami Fukkishi*, pp. 235–236.

85. *Ibid.*, p. 234. The Amami Oshima Social Democratic Party came into being on August 23, 1950, with Toyokura Tomohide, a lawyer and former police chief, as chairman in preparation for elections held that fall. Izumi was at the time one of its founders and became secretary general. By prior arrangement, the two switched positions later that year. According to Nakamura Yasutaro, a Communist member of the Ryukyu Legislature and leading influence behind the creation of the new party, there were three reasons why Izumi was later named chairman: "First and foremost, he was not a communist. As a pro-American, he would not be subject to pressure from America. Second, he was a simple poet who was not tainted in any way. He was strong in his determination, not vulnerable to the prevailing winds, and possessed a deep love for his country and people that went to the heart of his being. Finally, having had long experience in the education world, he was trusted by the people of the entire island. To be able to bring together all of the people of the Amami Islands was the most important condition [for leadership]." Cited in Nankai Nichinichi Shimbun, ed., *Gojunenshi*, p. 131. Nakamura and the Communists had for a while recognized the need to operate through legitimate organizations. This is one example, but it seems they were not able to actually control the party, and within the reversion movement itself, they began to lose influence.

86. Translated from Murayama, *Amami Fukkishi*, p. 236. The declaration was prepared by Nakamura Yasutaro. See Nankai Nichinichi Shimbun, ed., *Gojunenshi*, p. 131.

87. Kanai, ed., *Fukki Undo Kaikoroku*, pp. 48–49; and Murayama, *Amami Fukkishi*, pp. 239–240.

88. Murayama, *Amami Fukkishi*, p. 248. This figure reportedly represented 99 percent of the "entire" island population—"except for those outside of the islands and the 56 who refused to sign"—a figure, that while probably exaggerated, nevertheless shows the large extent that the residents desired the return of the islands to Japan. Nishimura provides a chart with a breakdown by community of the number of those

signing the petition. See Nishimura Tomiaki, *Amami Gunto no Kingendaishi* (*A Modern History of the Amami Islands*), (Tokyo: Kaifusha, 1993), p. 292.

89. Murayama, *Amami Fukkishi*, p. 249.

90. *Ibid.*, pp. 240–242.

91. *Ibid.*, p. 245. The Japanese version of the Amami Legislature resolution can be found on pages 247–248 of Murayama's work. Also see Nankai Nichinichi Shimbun, ed., *Gojunenshi*, pp. 132–133; and Kanai, ed., *Fukki Undo Kaikoroku*, p. 90. It was sent to the deputy governor, the commander for the Amami District, President Truman, General MacArthur, Prime Minister Yoshida, and the heads of both Houses. The Naze City Assembly resolution was sent to MacArthur, the United Nations, the Far Eastern Commission, the Allied Council for Japan, Prime Minister Yoshida, and the heads of both Houses. As an interesting side note, Maj. Gen. Robert B. McClure, Military Governor and Commanding General of RYCOM, attended the ceremony at the time of the creation of the Amami Legislature. The following day (November 26, 1950), McClure, on a tour of the islands, asked Nakae if the "people of Oshima wish to return to Japan." Nakae responded that "while perhaps not quite 100 percent do, about 99 percent wish to." See Nankai Nichinichi Shimbun, ed., *Gojunenshi*, p. 127. McClure reportedly told his staff later—"That guy's got guts to say that." See Murayama, *Amami Fukkishi*, p. 215.

92. Kanai, ed., *Fukki Undo Kaikoroku*, pp. 108–112; 121–126. Kanai had been purged as G-Class war criminal by GHQ in June 1946 for having been a high official in the Ministry of Railways in the first Konoe Fumimaro Cabinet (1937–1939) and was depurged on November 13, 1950. During that time he could not assume any official positions and had acted essentially as an unofficial liaison and advisor. Following his depurging, he assumed the chairmanship of the Tokyo Chapter.

93. *Ibid.*, p. 222. See also Murayama, *Amami Fukkishi*, p. 254. The 10 Diet members were: Tokonami Tokuji, Kanbayashiyama Eikichi, Nikaido Susumu, Chuman Tatsui, Inoue Tomoharu, Ishihara Noboru, Mitsuo Ryokichi, Iwakawa Yosuke, Maeda Iku, Ozaki Suekichi. Following this successful petition and recognizing the need to strengthen the movement, Amami residents living in the Tokyo area formed the Tokyo Fukki Taisaku Iinkai (Emergency Measures Committee for the Reversion of Amami Oshima to Japan) on May 26, with Kanai becoming chairman. The following month on June 24, at a national meeting of the Amami Federation groups, a new organization was created within the Federation with Nobori as chair—Amami Oshima Nihon Fukki Zenkoku Taisaku Iinkai (National Committee on Emergency Measures for the Reversion of Amami Oshima to Japan). For the membership of both of these groups and guiding principles, see Kanai, ed., *Fukki Undo Kaikoroku*, pp. 113–120; and Murayama, *Amami Fukkishi*, p. 257.

94. Kanai, ed., *Fukki Undo Kaikoroku*, pp. 123–125.

95. Murayama, *Amami Fukkishi*, p. 254. Also see Hoshijima Niro, "Jobun (Preface)," in Kanai, ed., *Fukki Undo Kaikoroku*, pp. 1–2. Four different drafts of the resolution were prepared. The first one was entitled "Resolution Concerning the Return of the Amami Islands." The second one was "Resolution Concerning the Return of Territory," and the

third one was "Resolution Concerning the Reversion of Territory." The fourth one, "Resolution on the Territorial Problem" was the one finally adopted after discussions with Foreign Ministry Officials. Because the territorial problem was a "delicate" one and there were fears of negatively influencing the status of other territories, such as Okinawa, Ogasawara, and the Northern Islands, Amami was not listed by name.

96. Tokyo Amami Kai, ed., *Tokyo Amami Kai 100 Nen no Ayumi*, pp. 92–93; and Kanai, ed., *Fukki Undo Kaikoroku*, pp. 113–120.

97. Nankai Nichinichi Shimbun, ed., *Gojunenshi*, p. 134.

98. Saneshima, *Ano Hi, Ano Toki*, p. 196. The following week, on July 16, Fukkyo sent a telegram to the Emperor asking him to intervene on their behalf with Yoshida to have the Prime Minister more strongly request to the Allies that the islands be left with Japan. Nankai Nichinichi Shimbun, ed., *Gojunenshi*, p. 136.

99. Murayama, *Amami Fukkishi*, pp. 263–264.

100. Saneshima, *Ano Hi, Ano Toki*, p. 197. A gathering on July 18, organized by the Amami Seinen Rengo (Amami Federation of Youth Groups) and attended by some 3,000 representatives of the youth associations in all nineteen cities, towns, and villages around the islands, was also ordered stopped by military government personnel who had showed up at it, but the organizers, including Saneshima, argued that a "Reversion rally is not a political rally. This is an inappropriate intervention in our affairs." Eventually, a compromise was worked out, with the name of the sponsor being changed to the youth division (Seinenbu) of the Social Democratic Party (see *Ibid.*, pp. 199–201).

101. *Ibid.*, p. 197.

102. *Ibid.*, p. 198.

103. *Ibid.* The rally passed the following resolution: "We, 240,000 Amamians, had expressed to the world our earnest desire to revert to Japan and relied upon the fair play of democratic nations that the status of a territory cannot be changed without the people's will. However, according to the final draft of the peace treaty published on July 10, not only were our opinions not respected in the draft at all, but also the Ryukyu Islands south of 29°north latitude will be put under the trusteeship without mercy. We will carry on to the last, our struggle against the unfair draft which overrides the wishes of we, the people." Reported in the *Okinawa Times*, July 15, 1951.

104. "Memorandum from Izumi Horo to Chief, Amami Civil Administration Team on Report of the Opening of Mass Meeting of all the People in Favor of Reversion to Japan (July 13, 1951)," *Fukki Undo Shiryo*, Kagoshima Prefectural Library, Amami Branch. Also see Nankai Nichinichi Shimbun, ed., *Gojunenshi*, p. 136.

105. Kanai, ed., *Fukki Undo Kaikoroku*, pp. 177–180. According to Kanai's account, which includes the full record of the proceedings, originally a resolution was planned calling for the restoration of territories, but as the Diet session was called to recognize the contents of the draft treaty, a passing of the resolution at that point would conflict with the later procedures to ratify the treaty and thus have the effect of restricting the Diet. After discussions between the Liberal Party and the opposition Democratic and Left and Right Socialist parties, a *kinkyu shitsumon*, or "emergency

question," format was adopted whereby Nikaido presented questions on the issue (see *Ibid.*, pp. 180–181).

106. Nankai Nichinichi Shimbun, ed., *Gojunenshi*, pp. 136–137. The rally passed the following the resolution: "The draft of the Japanese peace treaty firmly acknowledges that the Ryukyu Islands below south of 29 degrees north latitude will be a trust territory, irregardless of whether the 220,000 inhabitants of Amami–Oshima gunto desire it or not. This draft not only ignores the wishes and the freedom of the two hundred twenty thousand inhabitants of the Amami–Oshima gunto, but it is also a threat to the firm establishment of peace in the world. Therefore, we, two hundred twenty thousand inhabitants of Amami–Oshima gunto, in order to achieve our aim, will struggle to the last moment. We resolve, as one corporate body, to: 1) Definitely oppose trusteeship; 2) Achieve a perfect reversion to Japan."

107. *Ibid.*, pp. 136–137.

108. Their story is told in "Mikko Chinjodan (The Secret Mission to Appeal [for Reversion])," *Sanenbana*, No. 3 (March 1995), pp. 32–41. Also see Satake, *Gunseika Amami*, esp. chapter 3.

109. Saneshima, *Ano Hi, Ano Toki*, pp. 203–205; and Murayama, *Amami Fukkishi*, pp. 273–275.

110. Saneshima, *Ano Hi, Ano Toki*, p. 205.

111. Kanai, ed., *Fukki Undo Kaikoroku*, pp. 161–162; and Migita, *Tokyo ni Okeru Amami no Fukki Undo*, pp. 10–11.

112. Tokyo Amami Kai, ed., *Tokyo Amami Kai 100 Nen no Ayumi*, pp. 97–98.

113. *Ibid.*, pp. 94–97. Also see Kanai, ed., *Fukki Undo Kaikoroku*, pp. 157–161.

114. Kanai, ed., *Fukki Undo Kaikoroku*, pp. 114–116.

115. Murayama, *Amami Fukkishi*, pp. 284–287.

116. *Ibid.*, pp. 283–284; and Kanai, ed., *Fukki Undo Kaikoroku*, pp. 126–141.

117. Hoshijima, "Jobun," p. 2.

118. Not everyone was pleased, however. Yamamoto Kamejiro, a council member of Amami Rengo who had just returned from a visit to Okinawa with Nikaido, repeatedly fought with the secretariat of the Lower House saying a "question had no meaning" and stormed out of the meeting, perhaps reflecting feelings pent up following his trip. Kanai took Yamamoto to task in his memoirs as he probably did at their next meeting. See Kanai, ed., *Fukki Undo Kaikoroku*, p. 182.

119. *Ibid.*, p. 181.

120. "Memo from Governor, Amami Gunto, Ryukyu Islands to Brig. Gen. James M. Lewis with Regard to the Present Conditions in Amami O'Shima (August 11, 1951)," in *Status of the Ryukyus, 1950–1952* Folder, Papers of Edward O. Freimuth (shared with author).

121. Nishimura, *San Furanshisuko Heiwa Joyaku*, pp. 190–191. Also see Nishimura, "Okinawa Kizoku no Kimaru Made," p. 20.

122. Nankai Nichinichi Shimbun, ed., *Gojunenshi*, p. 141.

123. Tokyo Amami Kai, ed., *Tokyo Amami Kai 100 Nen no Ayumi*, p. 101; and Murayama, *Amami Fukkishi*, pp. 315–316.

124. Tokyo Amami Kai, ed., *Tokyo Amami Kai 100 Nen no Ayumi*, pp. 102–107; and Murayama, *Amami Fukkishi*, pp. 315–317.

125. "Letter from Dulles to Izumi Horo (December 18, 1951)," *JFD–JMA Chronological Series*, Eisenhower Library. Dulles' letter, received by Izumi on January 21, 1952, was published in the Nankai Nichinichi Shimbun on January 22.

126. *Ibid.* Shortly before Dulles' December trip to Japan, the northern part of the Nansei Islands, comprising Toshima-mura and seven other islands north of 29 degrees North Latitude, were returned to Japanese administration, news that encouraged Izumi and the movement (see figure I.1).

127. "The Reversion Movement on Amami Oshima, Final Report," *SIRI*, Pacific Science Board, National Research Council, CI&E Department, USCAR, March 1952. I am grateful to Professor Iwao Ishino, who coauthored the report, for discussing the background to the preparation of it. "Letter from Iwao Ishino to Author (August 21, 2002)."

128. "The Reversion Movement on Amami Oshima, Final Report," p. 23.

129. Nankai Nichinichi Shimbun, ed., *Gojunenshi*, pp. 141–142.

130. Murayama, *Amami Fukkishi*, pp. 296–297.

131. Kanai, "Amami Oshima no Sokoku Fukki Naru," p. 225. For a fuller discussion of the "Kanai Shokan (Kanai Letter)," see Kanai, ed., *Fukki Undo Kaikoroku*, pp. 183–185; and Murayama, *Amami Fukkishi*, pp. 298–300.

132. Murayama, *Amami Fukkishi*, pp. 299–300.

133. *Ibid.*, p. 299.

134. *Ibid.*

135. Murayama, *Amami Fukkishi*, pp. 353–358; and Kanai, ed., *Fukki Undo Kaikoroku*, pp. 250–257.

136. Tokyo Amami Kai, ed., *Tokyo Amami Kai 100 Nen no Ayumi*, pp. 101–102; and Migita, *Tokyo ni Okeru Amami Fukki Undo*, p. 15.

137. Murayama, *Amami Fukkishi*, pp. 313–314.

138. *Ibid.*

139. Migita, *Tokyo ni Okeru Amami no Fukki Undo*, p. 10; and Tokyo Amami Kai, ed., *Tokyo Amami Kai 100 Nen no Ayumi*, p. 112.

140. Tokyo Amami Kai, ed., *Tokyo Amami Kai 100 Nen no Ayumi*, p. 112.

141. Nankai Nichinichi Shimbun, ed., *Gojunenshi*, p. 146.

142. Murayama, *Amami Fukkishi*, pp. 411–415; and Kanai, ed., *Fukki Undo Kaikoroku*, pp. 306–311.

143. Murayama, *Amami Fukkishi*, p. 422.

144. *Ibid.*, p. 424.

145. *Ibid.*, p. 425. Nankai Nichinichi Shimbun, ed., *Gojunenshi*, p. 149. Also see "People of Amami–Oshima Cry For Return to Japan Gov. Shigenari Coveys Islanders Feeling," *The Mainichi*, November 18, 1952.

146. Murayama, *Amami Fukkishi*, pp. 411–415. The Sorifu Nanpo Renraku Jimukyoku, or Nanren, was established by law on July 1, 1952, with the main office being established in Naha, Okinawa, on August 13 and a branch office in Naze on

October 9. Importantly, the Nanren office was established as a part of the central government as a whole, and, in this case, the Prime Minister's Office, rather than within the Foreign Ministry alone, which would make it appear as if it were a consulate in a foreign country rather than a regular office of the central government established locally. See Sorifu Nanpo Renraku Jimukyoku, ed., *Nanpo Renraku Jiho* (*Report of the Southern Areas Liaison Office*), Vol. 1, No. 1 (August 1953), pp. 3–10 (published by the Sorifu Nanpo Renraku Jimukyoku and in the special magazines collections room [2f] of the National Diet Library's new wing). On July 19, 1952, a liaison council (Amami Oshima Bokoku Seifu Renraku Kai) was formed, headed by Vice Governor Otsu Tetsuji, with Murayama as vice chair, to coordinate the establishment of the office. See Nankai Nichinichi Shimbun, ed., *Gojunenshi*, p. 147; and Murayama, *Amami Fukkishi*, pp. 367–370. For more on Nanren, see Kanai, ed., *Fukki Undo Kaikoroku*, pp. 275–282; and Yoshida Shien Tsuito Bunshu Kanko Iinkai, ed., *Kaiso Yoshida Shien* (*Remembering Yoshida Shien*), (Tokyo: Yoshida Shien Tuito Bunshu Kanko Iinkai Honbu, 1990), pp. 113–143. The two-person Naze Branch office was headed by Tagami Shigemi, a fourteen-year veteran of the Foreign Ministry, and Kawabata Yoshiji, an official of the Kagoshima Prefectural government, under him. During a meeting at the prime minister's office on July 26, 1952, to launch Nanren, Nobori asked the director, Ishii Michinori, to consider having the Naze Branch made into a full office like the one in Naha, but, in the end, this was not done. See Kanai, ed., *Fukki Undo Kaikoroku*, p. 280.

147. Murayama, *Amami Fukkishi*, p. 426.

148. *Ibid.* Murayama records that Yoshida also called Gen. Mark W. Clark—who was actually sympathetic to the need to return the islands as the discussion below will show—to introduce the group to him. The group met with him later that afternoon.

149. *Ibid.*, p. 427; and Kanai, ed., *Fukki Undo Kaikoroku*, pp. 316–322. An eleven-part petition on which the resolution was based was given to Yoshida on November 25, 1952. See Migita, *Tokyo ni Okeru Amami Fukki Undo*, p. 15.

150. Murayama, *Amami Fukkishi*, p. 427. The resolution can be found on page 428 of Murayama's account.

151. Nankai Nichinichi Shimbun, ed., *Gojunenshi*, p. 150.

152. "Zengun Daigiinkai Gijiroku (Proceedings from the All [Amami Oshima] County Representatives Meeting), December 24, 1952," *Fukki Undo Shiryo*, Kagoshima Prefectural Library, Amami Branch. I wish to express my gratitude to Yamashita Fumitake, who made a copy of the proceedings available to me. Also see Sakida, "Kanzen Sokoku Fukki e no Michi," pp. 293–295.

153. Kanai, ed., *Fukki Undo Kaikoroku*, pp. 167–169. Their concerns were further peaked when the Communist Party tried to block a resolution on territorial issues because of its including the northern territories in it and calling upon the Soviet Union to return them.

154. Murayama, *Amami Fukkishi*, p. 585.

155. Nankai Nichinichi Shimbun, ed., *Gojunenshi*, p. 157.

156. Tokyo Amami Kai, ed., *Tokyo Amami Kai 100 Nen no Ayumi*, pp. 121–123.

157. *Ibid.*, p. 158. Okuyama had replaced Nobori the previous summer due to the latter's illness.

158. Migita, *Tokyo ni Okeru Amami Fukki Undo*, p. 16; and Tokyo Amami Kai, ed., *Tokyo Amami Kai 100 Nen no Ayumi*, p. 124.

159. Nankai Nichinichi Shimbun, ed., *Gojunenshi*, pp. 159–160. Also see "Petition for Return of the Amami Oshima Islands," in Flash Number 4, Reel Number A'-0146, Nihon Kizoku Seigan Kankei, Amami Gunto, Nansei Shoto Kizoku Mondai, *DROMOFA*, pp. 64–86. Although found in the Foreign Ministry materials, the petition was drafted by Nishida. For Roosevelt's discussion of her trip to Japan, see Eleanor Roosevelt, *The Autobiography of Eleanor Roosevelt* (New York: Harper and Brothers Publishers, 1958), pp. 333–341. On Roosevelt, see Joseph P. Lash, *Eleanor: The Years Alone* (New York: W. W. Norton and Co., 1972), pp. 224–229; and Tamara K. Hareven, *Eleanor Roosevelt: An American Conscience* (New York: Da Capo Press, 1975).

160. I have not located any actual records of her conversation with Ambassador Allison on this subject, but, according to a letter she sent to Murayama Iekuni, she did speak with Allison but "was afraid she did no more than that." In fact, according to Murayama's account, Roosevelt spoke of the plight on Amami in her many meetings in Japan. See Murayama, *Amami Fukkishi*, pp. 454–457.

~

CHAPTER THREE

The Japanese Government and the "Amami–Okinawa Problem"

"Control over the Ryukyus must be turned back to Japan soon!"

—Araki Eikichi, Japanese ambassador to the United States,
to Jeff Graham Parsons, July 7, 1953, Japanese Embassy

Although the representatives of the reversion movement found Prime Minister Yoshida surprisingly ignorant about the local conditions in Amami when they met with him in late December 1952 as described in the preceding chapter, Yoshida and the Japanese government had in fact taken a major interest in seeking to have the islands restored to Japanese control. These actions, while not known to the public then, began well before the start of the reversion movement.[1] Importantly, the Japanese government undertook these efforts in the pre-Peace Treaty years despite not technically possessing diplomatic rights, having lost them to the Allies in September 1945 as part of the surrender.

Preparing for the Peace Treaty

Beginning in November 1945, the Japanese government, specifically the Foreign Ministry, started planning for the future Peace Treaty, with the territorial problem being one of the biggest concerns.[2] In early 1947, after much study, the Foreign Ministry relayed a territorial study done on the Nansei Islands (including Amami) to GHQ through Political Advisor, George A. Atcheson, Jr. This study portrayed the islands as being "minor islands" to be left with Japan and noted that "the northern half of the Nansei Islands which constitutes a part of Kagoshima Prefecture, was historically bound with closer ties with Japan proper than the Ryukyu Group."[3] Shortly after this during a press interview in early June 1947, as discussed in chapter 2, Foreign Minister Ashida called for the Nansei Islands and the Northern Territories to be returned to Japan based on the understanding that they were originally Japanese islands. The Allies, however, were not receptive to these calls—and, in fact, quite critical—and, as a result, the Foreign Ministry had to keep quiet for some time. Indeed, when a story about their internal studies on the future shape of the Peace Treaty was written up in *World Report*, Vice Minister Okazaki Katsuo was forced to resign due to the outcry from the Allies.[4]

Some six months prior to his resignation, around the time that Ashida took office, Okazaki had prepared a secret position paper, which I have named the "Okazaki Memo" in another study.[5] In addition to calling for a base-leasing arrangement by which Japan would be allowed to keep not only sovereignty but also "common affairs of administration" over the islands, Okazaki's memo included the following description regarding the Amami Islands:

> Among the Nansei Islands, while the Osumi Islands which lie north of 30° N. remain, in accordance with the Memorandum of the Supreme Commander for the Allied Powers dated January 29, 1946, under the Japanese administration as part of Kagoshima Prefecture, the Tokara Islands which lie immediately to the south have, same as the Osumi Islands, long been Japanese territory and formed part of Kagoshima Prefecture. The Amami Islands which lie further south, although they were for a time under the influence of the Ryukyu Dynasty when it was in its prime, are an integral part of Japan from the ethnological, historical and any other point of view. Their inhabitants are Japanese and they had been part of Kagoshima Prefecture until the surrender of Japan.[6]

Although the memorandum was prepared in both Japanese and English, suggesting that it would be relayed to the Allies, it does not seem to have been presented to GHQ at this point likely because of the strong reaction of the Allies to Ashida's June comments, as well as the later "scoop" regarding Japan's planning for a peace treaty that further aggravated feelings among the Allies.

Upon taking control of the government again in late 1948 (with the resignation of the Ashida Cabinet), Yoshida and the Foreign Ministry began relaying once again to the United States and the Allies its requests regarding a peace treaty based on its inhouse evaluation of Japan's desires and the international situation. Yoshida was told that the United States found the studies to be valuable reference materials.[7]

In the latter half of 1950, following the outbreak of the Korean War and signals that the Allied Powers were moving toward a peace treaty with Japan (as publicly stated by Truman in September), the Japanese government stepped up its own studies of the Peace Treaty, and had a formal position on the territorial problem worked out in time for Dulles' second trip to Japan in January 1951 for "consultations," but which were in many ways "negotiations."[8]

The Japanese government's position on the territorial issue was made known in what has been called the "S.Y. Memo" because Yoshida's initials were written on the document. The Japanese government was very much afraid that the United States was going to put the islands under a trusteeship, and Japan sought to have the Americans reconsider. However, if that were impossible, Yoshida called upon the United States to return the islands as soon as possible once a trusteeship were no longer needed. He also suggested a "joint authority" arrangement in which Japan would take part in such a trusteeship. Dulles, however, did not wish to negotiate at this time on the territorial provisions, a position pushed on him by the JCS before he departed for Japan and MacArthur after he arrived. Indeed, meeting with MacArthur on January 25, Dulles was told by the General in no uncertain terms that he should tell Yoshida that the question of the islands "simply was not open for discussion."[9] As a result, Dulles took a strict, somewhat cold stance toward Yoshida later at the meetings, although personally he was very much moved by the strong Japanese reactions.[10] John M. Allison, Dulles' assistant during the preparations for the Peace Treaty, even went so far as to note his boss's reaction in his memoirs, *Allison Wonderland*:

> We were deeply impressed by the Japanese plea for the restoration of the Ryukyus and Bonin Islands. While we could not grant their wishes at the time, I believe it was then that Mr. Dulles conceived the idea, which he later announced at the San Francisco Peace Conference, that Japan should retain residual Sovereignty over the islands but that they would be administered by the United States.[11]

The Japanese government, however, did not give up and pleaded with the United States to keep sovereignty. Eventually, Dulles was able to convince the U.S. military and the Allies to support Japan's desires to be allowed to keep the islands and developed the "residual sovereignty" formula toward the treaty islands. Yoshida was informed of this in early August prior to his speech at the Diet. As a result, Yoshida stated at the August 16 Diet Session regarding the proposed treaty:

> The wording of Article 3 is deemed not without significance in that residual sovereignty remains. The flexible provisions of Article 3 leave room for us to hope that subject to strategic control by the United States in the interest of

international peace and security, some practicable arrangements might be worked out to meet the desires of the inhabitants of these islands concerning intercourse with the homeland of Japan, nationality status of inhabitants and other matters.[12]

In other words, Yoshida sensed correctly that there was room for maneuver in the interpretation of Article 3 and, in many cases, received such signals from Dulles and the State Department staff at GHQ in Tokyo. With the expected arrival of Dulles, who was in favor of seeking a workable solution, and a delegation of senators and other officials in mid-December, Yoshida and the Foreign Ministry set out to prepare a proposal for a "practicable arrangement."[13] On December 10, the same day Dulles arrived, the Foreign Ministry completed its memorandum, and, on December 13, Vice Minister Iguchi Sadao presented it to Sebald for Dulles' attention.[14]

In submitting the memorandum, the Foreign Ministry also attached a two-point, one-page introductory statement in which it was written that Japan was "most grateful that the Peace Treaty leaves the Nansei Islands as Japanese territory and their inhabitants as Japanese nationals. We understand that the reason America wants to administer these islands lies in the military necessity for safeguarding the peace and security of the Far East. We earnestly hope that as far as this military necessity permits, the desire of the inhabitants will be considered" in the final disposition of the islands.[15]

According to the complementary and more detailed memorandum, the Japanese Government sought the "sympathetic consideration by the United States Government" with regard to a "practicable arrangement" on the following six points:

1. The United States confirms that the Southern Islands remain under Japanese sovereignty and thus the inhabitants remain Japanese nationals.
2. The United States agrees to restoring the previous relationship between Japan proper and the Southern Islands as far as military requirements allow; in particular, the United States recognizes that the islands will be treated as a part of Japan with regard to moving and travelling between Japan proper and the islands, trade (no custom or duty imposed), financial transactions, fishing, monetary (the Japanese yen is to be the legal tender in the Southern Islands).
3. The United States admits that the Southern Islands are to be treated by Japan as a part of its territory in any economic, social, and cultural agreements or treaties the Japanese Government enters into. Japan will exercise its protective authority over the inhabitants of the islands who reside abroad or are to travel abroad and issue passports for them.

4. The United States declares its intention to permit self-rule of the inhabitants in matters of civil administration and to allow complete self rule in educational matters and juridical jurisdiction over civil and criminal cases among the inhabitants themselves.

5. The United States recognizes the property rights in those islands which belong to Japanese nationals in Japan proper and will facilitate the resumption of their business activities.

6. The United States abstains in favor of Japan from exercising administrative, legislative, or juridical powers over the inhabitants of islands which it does not presently see any military necessity to administer.[16]

Dulles apparently welcomed receiving it, implying he would give it his consideration.[17] Indeed, the special ambassador, in his speech the following day (December 14) at the Union Club for a joint meeting of the American Chamber of Commerce and the Japanese Chamber of Commerce, reemphasized his hope to work out a fair arrangement.

> The result of the provisions relating to the Nansei Islands in the Treaty of Peace make it that the United States becomes a neighbor of Japan. Residual sovereignty in the islands was left with Japan due to the strong desire of Japan. I hope that the form of administration for the islands that takes shape will be one which allows the desires of the islands' inhabitants to be taken into consideration with the needs of international peace and security.[18]

The State Department's two highest representatives in Japan, Sebald and Niles W. Bond, both of whom had visited Okinawa in the past (but not Amami itself), likewise found the Japanese government's memorandum "to be of great interest" and "further evidence of the strong pressure in Japan for action which will clarify the relations of the Nansei and Nanpo Islands to Japan and clear the way for eventual restoration of the islands to Japan."[19] Just what shape a "practicable arrangement" would take would remain undecided for quite a while however, (as discussed earlier) while the U.S. government came to grips with other more pressing problems related to the Peace Treaty and the Security Treaty.

In the meantime, the Japanese government had hoped to send a delegation to Amami and Okinawa to observe the situation first hand and to explain to the islanders the somewhat unclear situation they faced.[20] The delegation was to be headed by Hoshijima Niro, who had participated in the San Francisco conference as a member of the Plenipotentiary delegation and was originally from neighboring Kyushu. The delegation was to be comprised of fellow Diet member Iwakawa Yosuke of the Liberal Party (from Yakushima, who formerly had been president of Kagoshima Shosen, a ferry line and shipping company based out of Kagoshima City) and two officials from the Foreign Ministry, Ushiroku Torao, director of the ministry's administration bureau, and Yoshida Shien, chief of the Okinawa Division of the same bureau and himself from Okinawa. In addition, Kanai was to be sent down earlier to prepare for the arrival of the delegation and to stay for one month, based on discussions with Prime Minister Yoshida and Liberal Party Secretary General Masuda Kaneshichi. The group was scheduled to leave on October 12, but, unfortunately and for reasons unclear, U.S. military authorities did not give them permission to travel to the islands and the trip was postponed indefinitely. Observers critical of the government's decision to agree to the terms of the Peace Treaty, including Article 3, wrote (without evidence) later to the effect that the "government simply got cold feet knowing that it would not be able to convince the people to be patient with the situation and might actually end up inflaming the issue."[21]

Amami as a Bilateral Issue

Although the U.S. government had not come to a decision on the fate of the islands by April 28, 1952, the day the occupation ended and Japan returned to the community of nations again, the Japanese government continued to be concerned about the fate of the Nansei Islands and anxiously awaited word of the result of its request for the return of the islands or on the establishment of a "practicable arrangement." Having received permission (in fact a request from U.S. officials) to set up a liaison office in Okinawa, the Diet passed a law on July 1 establishing (that August) the Liaison Bureau for the Southern Areas in Naha (*Nanpo Renraku Jimukyoku*), with an office (*shucchosho*) in Naze (opened on October 9) in order to handle the consular-like affairs of Japanese there as well as to gather and relay information.[22]

This bureau would play an important symbolic as well as practical role in that it was able to hear opinions directly and was also a *mado-guchi*, or window, for *Amami Rengo* to relay and receive information. The bureau's director, Ishii Michinori, visited Amami in October 1952 and would take the lead in both organizing a trip to Amami in September 1953, after the announcement of the return of the islands, and in drafting the special legislation to accommodate the return of the islands.[23]

In the meantime, Yoshida continued to await word on a U.S. decision on the fate of the islands, although little did he know that while the State Department took the matter seriously, the military was not willing to review its requirements. American Ambassador Robert D. Murphy, who had arrived on April 29 and had, as described earlier, been involved in the last-minute discussions between the State Department and the Defense Department on the territorial problem, was surprised at first to find an "absence of public agitation" on the question of the return of the islands, adding that he had not "been approached by people like Prime Minister Yoshida, Foreign Minister Okazaki, or any one else in the Japanese Government with a plea for the return of the Ryukyus to Japanese administration. The Embassy receives an occasional letter or petition, usually from private individuals or interested organizations."[24] In an attempt to explain this situation, Murphy suggested that "Perhaps the Japanese feel that it would be simply a waste of time on their part, or perhaps now that the issue of ultimate sovereignty is no longer at stake they have simply lost interest in the lesser question of administrative control, but the fact remains they have raised the question urgently."

Murphy's letter only half explains the situation, however, and would be out of date by the time it reached Washington. For example, showing the interest of the Diet in this issue, earlier on July 31, the Lower House had passed a resolution sponsored jointly by the Liberal Party, the Progressive Party (*Kaishinto*), and the Right and Left Socialist parties which stated that "the territorial problem was extremely important to the feelings of the people of Japan."[25] It called on the government to "respect the wishes of the people of Amami Oshima and other parts formerly of Kagoshima Prefecture and make special efforts to have some administrative responsibilities returned to Japan, especially for Amami Oshima, whose circumstances are different from the rest of the Okinawa islands." In response to this, Foreign Minister Okazaki stated that "The Japanese Government will try to effect the return of the islands to Japan, as it has done in the past, and in light of this resolution, make even stronger efforts." Okazaki added that the government was in the process of establishing a liaison office and, as a result, "will be able to be in greater contact with the residents there and believe that it will be possible to fulfill your expectations. Along these lines, I understand that the policy of the American Government is to accede to the hopes and desires of the people so long as they do not conflict with the military aims."[26]

In short, it seems that the lack of official "agitation" that Murphy observed at the time was due to the fact that Yoshida had placed his trust in the U.S. government to come up with, in a timely manner, a workable solution along the lines of a base-leasing arrangement in which not only sovereignty but also administrative control would be returned to Japan. The Japanese government probably chose not to apply pressure to give the U.S. government time to make up its mind.

With nothing to show for his decision to wait for a positive sign from the U.S. side and stung by the resolution in the Diet, Yoshida was forced to begin raising the issue again, however. At the end of August, Okazaki, having heard reports from the U.S. Embassy about Murphy's optimistic letter to the Amami Teachers' Association, met with Murphy to tell him of Japan's desires about Amami and that he hoped the U.S. government would look favorably on Japan's requests.[27] Murphy, according to newspaper reports (later found to be incorrect) that came out a month later, responded that the United States was favorably reviewing the situation and was considering the return of administrative rights for the Amami Islands north of 27° north latitude.[28]

Okazaki followed up on this shortly after the respective meetings between the delegation from Amami and Murphy, Yoshida, and Gen. Mark W. Clark in December. In early January 1953, Okazaki gave Murphy a petition dated November 20 that he had received from the National Council of Superintendents of Education (*Todofuken Kyoikucho Kyogikai*) calling for the "realization of [the] reunion of the Amami–Oshima Islands with Japan at the earliest possible moment" and asked again that consideration be given for the return of the islands.[29] With no response forthcoming, Yoshida and Okazaki decided to pursue the issue more seriously.

Amami as an Election Issue

In March, Okazaki began more actively pushing the issue in his meetings with Murphy due to the desperateness of the situation itself and the fact that an election was just around the corner. After a lunch meeting between the two on March 23 in which Okazaki raised the issue again, Murphy informed Robert J. G. McClurkin, deputy director of the Office of Northeast Asian Affairs, that "as you know, Okazaki is activating the Amami Oshima question right now because of the electoral campaign. He has mentioned the matter to me three times in the past week . . . [and] urges that some encouraging word be said at this time. He obviously wishes to demonstrate that the Japanese Foreign Office is not being negligent or dilatory regarding this important question."[30] Murphy understood, however, that Okazaki's requests were not just political, writing "Quite apart from the electoral campaign the issue is an important one in the eyes of the Japanese. It will undoubtedly be agitated persistently." The Ambassador lamented that he could not help with a final decision from Washington: "As much as I would like to be helpful to him in view of the apparently adamant position of the Joint Chiefs of Staff, I am at a loss to suggest what we could do. In my conversations with Okazaki I am merely passing the buck to you gentlemen in the Department."

The electoral campaign Murphy alluded to in his March 24 letter to the State Department was the elections that were called as a result of the dissolution of the Diet in March. This came about due to Yoshida's having made an inappropriate comment (*bakayaro*, or "You damned fool!") during an interpel-

lation on February 28 by Nishimura Eiichi, a Right Socialist Party Representative. Although Nishimura did not pursue the issue further after the cantanker-
ous seventy-five-year-old Yoshida retracted the remark, an unprecedented motion of disciplinary action was voted on and passed by the Diet (due to the
absence of anti-Yoshida factions of the Liberal Party who used the opportunity
to weaken him).[31] Yoshida, in turn, punished those individuals in the anti-
Yoshida groupings of his party, who, in turn, further rebelled and supported a
motion of no-confidence on March 18 (by a vote of 229 to 218). Rather than
having the Cabinet resign *en masse*, Yoshida dissolved the Diet, as per Article
69 of the Constitution. As a result, the dissolution that took place in March
1953 came to be ignominiously known as the "*Bakayaro* dissolution."

The incident was symbolic, on the one hand, of Yoshida's dislike of the
opposition (and perhaps of politics in general), and, on the other, of frustration within the Liberal Party and the general public with his sometimes ar-
rogant "one-man" style of doing things. In fact, beginning in the fall of 1952,
a movement of sorts had grown within the Liberal Party centered on dissatisfied elements (led by the rival Hatoyama Ichiro faction) to democratize the
party and make the president's decisions more transparent. Many within the
party, several of whom had been depurged and were rejoining politics and
other places of influence, felt that Yoshida had usurped Hatoyama's rightful
place as president.[32] Others just felt Yoshida had been in power too long.
This feeling was shared obviously by members of the opposition. The April
1953 elections would necessarily be one of Yoshida's toughest fights, particularly as the politically hot issues of recovering lost territory, such as Amami,
Okinawa, and Ogasawara, and the problem of rearmament and discussions
on the related Mutual Security Act (MSA) were widely reported.

In light of this, the resolving of the Amami–Okinawa issue in order to
benefit in the upcoming Lower House elections—scheduled for April 19—
became all the more important to Yoshida politically over the next several
weeks. On March 24, the same day Murphy sent his message to the State Department, Yoshida wrote to Murphy requesting that consideration be given
to the reversion of the Nansei Islands to Japanese administration.[33] Yoshida
raised this issue with Murphy again over lunch at Yoshida's home in Oiso,
Kanagawa Prefecture, on Thursday, April 2, handing him a copy of a "confidential *aide-memoire*," which also cited such questions of World Bank loans
and war criminals.[34] Regarding the Nansei Islands, Yoshida requested consideration of the following three points:

> Return of civil administrative jurisdiction is desired over the entire archipel-
> ago, including Okinawa and Amami Oshima. If this is difficult of realization
> [sic], we ask that the civil administration of the Amami Oshima Group be

turned over as the first step to [sic] that direction. As for Okinawa, we earnestly hope for the return of educational jurisdiction (for carrying on language instruction).[35]

Murphy wrote to the State Department for instructions that Sunday (April 5), explaining that he "express[ed] sympathy for these issues which are of obvious importance in the electoral campaign" and "promis[ed] to pass" the list to the State Department "for whatever consideration might be possible."[36]

The next morning, immediately after Murphy left for the Philippines, Vice Minister of Foreign Affairs Okumura Katsuzo called the Embassy to "ascertain as soon as possible" the reaction in Washington to Yoshida's request for the "gradual restoration of administrative rights by the Japanese government over the Amami and Ryukyu Islands."[37] Okumura said that the Prime Minister had "ask[ed] him to ask the Ambassador" and explained that "it would be of great assistance if it could be given out that steps to resolve this question were being discussed between the two countries." William T. Turner, chargé d'affaires *ad interim*, echoed Murphy's political assessment in a letter to Kenneth T. Young, director of the Office of Northeast Asian Affairs, that "Mr. Yoshida obviously has his eye upon the coming electoral campaign," and added that "the Prime Minister considers the Amami–Ryukyu issue to be the most important from a campaign point of view." Turner urged that the views of Washington be sent "by telegram in time to serve Mr. Yoshida's purposes."

At the same time, Yoshida also directed his ambassador to the United States, Araki Eikichi, to raise the same question directly with the State Department.[38] On April 9, Araki met with the new assistant secretary of state, Walter S. Robertson, who had officially assumed his position the day before.[39] Araki handed him a copy of the *aide-memoire* given to Murphy (and Gen. Clark) on April 2. After introducing the contents of the memorandum, Araki read a prepared statement which said that "the question of Amami Oshima and [the] other Nansei Islands . . . should not be left long unsolved. Petitions have been pouring in from the inhabitants who are in a quandary about the future of their status and dissatisfied with the present administration. It is obvious that this dissatisfaction will grow stronger as days go by."[40] Acting Secretary of State W. Bedell Smith replied that the U.S. government "would do everything it could to expedite" the requests of the Japanese government.

At lunch on April 11, a little more than one week before the election, Okumura again asked Turner if there had been any reactions from Washington to the Japanese government's request and explained that "Mr. Yoshida was very anxious to obtain something that would be usable as ammunition in his electoral campaign."[41] Turner explained that the Embassy had not received an official response from Washington other than a general report about Araki's meeting with Assistant Secretary Robertson.

At that point, Okumura made a "suggestion" to Turner that Amami and Okinawa be "placed in a status similar to that of Japan under the Occupation." In other words, Okumura explained, "in such [an] arrangement . . . the ultimate authority over these islands would remain in the hands of the U.S. authorities, but this authority would be exercised through the local Japanese agencies." Turner noted that Okumura said he believed that this "would go a long way toward satisfying the Japanese and Okinawan aspirations, and to make it possible to meet the needs of the islanders in education and other fields that are now much neglected." Although Okumura emphasized that the suggestion was "his own and did not necessarily represent the views of the Japanese government," it is highly unlikely that he did not have the approval of Foreign Minister Okazaki or Yoshida in doing so. Indeed, such a proposal was not too different from other proposals the Japanese government had made in the past. Turner was in no position to comment (particularly in light of the fact that a reexamination of policy was taking place in Washington), and instead immediately prepared a memorandum of conversation and circulated it in the Embassy. A copy does not appear to have been forwarded immediately to the State Department, however.

As expected, Yoshida's Liberals lost seats in both Houses in the elections held on April 19. The damage was all the greater because of the revolt that took place in March (which led to the creation of a forty-person Separatist Liberal Party, or *Buntoha Jiyuto*, on March 16 under Hatoyama's leadership). The Liberal Party going into 1953 had 240 seats, but with the split, Yoshida's Liberals emerged with only 199 in the elections for the Lower House.[42] Despite the shake-ups, the conservatives (Liberal parties and Progressive Party) essentially retained the same number of seats, but the Left and Right Socialist parties, which opposed rearmament and also strongly called for the return of Okinawa, made gains. In the Diet interpellations following the start of the Fifth Yoshida Cabinet (on May 21), the Amami–Okinawa issue would get special attention.

On June 17, just as the NSC was about to make a decision on the Amami Islands, Right Socialist Party representative Sone Eki, considered an authority on diplomatic affairs and a strong critic of Yoshida, raised the territorial issue in his questioning of the new Yoshida cabinet's policies.[43] For Sone and Yoshida, it was not only policy matters that divided the two. There was a personal rivalry as well. Sone had been a career diplomat, joining the Foreign Ministry in 1925 and serving in China and France. Following the end of World War II, Sone worked as the director of Political Affairs in the Central Liaison Office in Tokyo, but he clashed with Yoshida when the latter was Foreign

Minister in the Shidehara Cabinet and was sent to Kyushu to work in a liaison office. In 1949, Sone joined the Socialist Party and the following year was elected to the Lower House from Kanagawa (and would later be instrumental in forming the Democratic Socialist Party, or *Minshato*, in 1960).[44]

Sone, in his questioning, called for the "immediate return of Amami, Okinawa, and Ogasawara" and asked Yoshida what he thought about the recent critical comments in the United States of the Yalta accords (permitting the expansion of Soviet influence in Eastern Europe and the Far East). Yoshida, repeating earlier statements, responded that the "United States did not desire territory and that it was only administering the islands due to strategic needs, and when the international environment permitted it, the islands would be likely be returned." Yoshida added that his government was "continually making efforts at creating the situation in which the islands could be returned."

The next day, Suma Yakichiro, a member of the Progressive Party and a former diplomat himself, followed up on the territorial issue by asking Yoshida point blank (to the delight of those in the observation deck) if "he had the guts to try and see the Amami Islands returned" and argued that with the ceasefire on the Korean peninsula, the timing was particularly appropriate.[45] Okazaki responded on Yoshida's behalf, emphasizing that the government was making every effort it could.

As Kanai records in his memoirs, the preparation of this question had been aided by the numerous groups from Amami who had presented documents containing the latest information on the situation in the islands.[46] Leaders of *Amami Rengo* were also instrumental in helping to prepare a bipartisan resolution calling for the return of Amami, Okinawa, Ogasawara, and the Northern Islands, passed by the Diet on July 7.[47]

The resolution, entitled "Resolution on Territory (*Ryodo ni Kansuru Ketsugian*)," was read by Uetsuka Tsukasa, a Liberal Party member from Kumamoto in Kyushu. It called upon the government to "adopt the best measures to see that the islands are returned as quickly as possible."[48] It argued that "territory is inherently the historical and spiritual spring of the people of that country," and it went "without saying" that territorial issues "exercise a major effect on national sentiment." Moreover, the resolution continued, "the islands are important for the continued existence and the economy of Japan, limited in population and size as it is," and thus, the return of the islands is "appropriate." With regard to Amami, Okinawa, and Ogasawara specifically, the resolution went on to state:

In the Peace Treaty, our country approved of placing these islands under a U.N. Trusteeship with the United States as the administering authority, and until that time, recognizes that the United States would exercise all rights of administration, legislation, and judicial matters. However, the U.S. trusteeship of these islands has not been realized due to the current international situation, and in line with Article [3] of the Peace Treaty, the U.S. continues to exercise its rights. These islands however for many years have been a part of our country and historically, geographically, economically have had an integral relationship with the mainland. Our people strongly desire that the administration of these islands be united with the mainland as quickly as possible, and the islanders have all felt the inconveniences and pains of the islands being separated from the mainland and sent on occasion petitioners to the mainland as well as participating in signature drives and employing other means. If the early and complete return of these islands is difficult, we call upon the government to make every effort to see that these islands participate in the educational, industrial, administrative aspects of our country to the widest degree possible. In particular, regarding the Amami Islands which are the closest to Japan and were a part of Kagoshima Prefecture, the desires of islanders, many of whom have extremely close blood relations with people on the mainland, are strongest, and we ask the Government to give special consideration.

After the resolution passed unanimously by standing vote, Foreign Minister Okazaki spoke.

> The Government is in complete agreement with the need for the islands to revert. . . . In the Peace Treaty, it is clear that our country has sovereignty, but in line with the very strong desires of the islanders, we have repeatedly approached the U.S. side. As a result, the United States has stated that as long as there is no interference with military objectives, it has no problem with normalization of economic and cultural relations between these areas and the mainland, and we are currently attempting to take measures along those lines . . . With regard to the Amami Islands. . . . we are proceeding along the lines raised in the resolution and are prepared to make even more efforts.[49]

Okazaki was quite serious when he made the above statement. That same day in Washington, having heard no response from the U.S. government, Ambassador Araki, after a luncheon at the Japanese embassy on July 7, stressed "quite bluntly" to J. Graham Parsons that "control over the Ryukyus must be turned back to Japan soon" as the territorial problem "was becoming most difficult" for the Japanese government.[50] Araki added that the United States "could, of course, arrange to use what it needed for defense purposes but it was important to settle the Ryukyu problem." Parsons, about to leave for Japan himself as deputy chief of mission, acknowledged he was quite aware of the "importance of the problem" and urged patience.

Indeed, it was not only Parsons who was aware of the problem. The State Department as a whole had been giving it particular consideration. The next time that Araki would meet with a State Department representative on this issue, it was to thank him for the announcement to return the islands. It is to this decision within the new Eisenhower Administration and an announcement by Dulles that we turn next.

Notes

1. For more on the views of the Japanese government with regard to the territorial issue at the time of the Peace Treaty, see Eldridge, *The Origins of the Bilateral Okinawa Problem*, particularly chapters 5, 7, and 8.

2. *Ibid.*, chapter 5. Also see Eldridge, "The Japanese Government, the San Francisco Peace Treaty, and the Disposition of Okinawa, 1945–1952," pp. 123–141; and Eldridge, "Showa Tenno to Okinawa," pp. 153–154.

3. Eldridge, "Showa Tenno," p. 155. "Minor Islands Adjacent to Japan Proper, Part II. Ryukyu and Other Nansei Islands (March 1947)," Beigawa ni Teishutsu Shiryo (Eibun), Dai Ikkan, Tainichi Kowani Kansuru Honpo no Junbi Taisaku Kankei, Reel No. B'0012, Flash No. 1, DRO-MOFA, pp. 65–84. The phrase "minor islands" was a reference to Point 8 of the Potsdam Declaration, which stated "The terms of the Cairo Declaration shall be carried out and Japanese sovereignty shall be limited to the islands of Honshu, Hokkaido, Kyushu, Shikoku and such minor islands as we determine."

4. For the "scoop" reporting that the Japanese Government hoped to see the islands returned to Japan, see "Tokyo's Secret Plans for Peace," *World Report*, Vol. 3, No. 24 (December 9, 1947), pp. 18–19, 33–36.

5. Eldridge, *The Origins of the Bilateral Okinawa Problem*, chapter 5.

6. "Nihon no Ryodo Mondai ni Kansuru Ippanteki Kosatsu," Heiwa Joyaku Tokushu Mondai ni Taisuru Iken Oyobi Nihon no Genjo ni Kansuru Shiryo, Tainichi Heiwa Joyaku Kankei Junbi Kenkyu Kankei, Dai Nikan, Reel No. B'0008, Flash No. 2, DRO-MOFA, pp. 143–167.

7. Shigeru Yoshida, *The Yoshida Memoirs: The Story of Japan in Crisis* (Westport, Conn.: Greenwood Press, 1961), pp. 247–248.

8. Eldridge, *The Origins of the Bilateral Okinawa Problem*, pp. 301–306.

9. *Ibid.*, p. 302. MacArthur voiced his "strong impatience with Japanese pleas that the Ryukyu Islands be left with Japan . . . When all that the United States asked in a treaty, in every other respect a model of generosity, was a chain of islands which had been an economic drain on Japan and whose population was not Japanese."

10. *Ibid.*

11. John M. Allison, *Ambassador from the Prairie or Allison Wonderland* (Boston: Houghton Mifflin Co., 1973), p. 157.

12. "(Draft of) Prime Minister's Address (August 7, 1951)," Flash Number 8, Reel Number B'0009, Tainichi Heiwa Joyaku Oyobi Nichibei Anzen Hosho Joy-

aku Teiketsu Kosho Kankei (Files Relating to the Negotiations on the Conclusion of a Treaty of Peace With Japan and the U.S.-Japan Security Treaty), DRO-MOFA, p. 95.

13. Nishimura, "Okinawa Kizoku no Kimaru Made," p. 21. This was Dulles' fourth trip to Japan after assuming the responsibility of negotiating the Peace Treaty. It was a trip made out of U.S. domestic conditions in order to secure from Yoshida an agreement that Japan would not recognize mainland China (the People's Republic of China). The agreement reached became known as the "Yoshida Letter," although the contents were in fact drafted by Dulles.

14. "Memorandum Submitted by the Japanese Vice Minister for Foreign Affairs to the United States Political Adviser for Japan on a 'Practicable Arrangement' for the Southern Islands," Roll 7, Microfilm C0043, ONA Records, 1943–1956, RG 59. Also see "Nanpo Shoto ni Kansuru Jissaiteki Sochi Dures e no Teishutsu (Practicable Arrangements for the Southern Islands), December 10, 1951," Flash Number 9, Reel Number B'0009, Daisanji Dares Raiho Kankei (Documents Relating to Dulles' Third Visit), DRO-MOFA, pp. 29–41. (As noted above, it was in fact Dulles' fourth visit; the first one in June 1950 not being for negotiations per se but more in the nature of a fact-finding mission.) The memorandum labels the islands under question the Nanpo Shoto, or "Southern Islands;" however from the context of the memorandum, as well as a clarifying paragraph, it is clear that the Ryukyu/Nansei Islands are included in the discussion.

15. "Nanpo Shoto ni Kansuru Jissaiteki Sochi." Perhaps written in a great hurry, this introductory memorandum does not appear to have a corresponding Japanese version unlike the other enclosed memorandum.

16. Ibid.

17. Nishimura, "Okinawa Kizoku no Kimaru Made," p. 21. A similar petition on Amami was given to Dulles' party on December 14, 1951. See Kanai, ed., Fukki Undo Kaikoroku, pp. 231–236.

18. Quoted in Japanese in Nishimura, San Furanshisuko Heiwa Joyaku, p. 322; Diary entry for December 14, 1951, Sebald Diaries.

19. "Dispatch No. 1021 from the USPOLAD to SCAP (Sebald) to the Department of State (January 17, 1952)," FRUS 1952–1954, Vol. 14, Part 2, pp. 1089–1091.

20. Kanai, ed., Fukki Undo Kaikoroku, pp. 3, 216–217.

21. Sakida, Beigunsei no Teppeki o Koete, pp. 155–156.

22. For background on this bureau, see Nanpo Renraku Jiho, pp. 6–7.

23. Ibid., p. 8.

24. "Letter from the Ambassador in Japan (Murphy) to the Assistant Secretary of State for Far Eastern Affairs Allison (August 11, 1952)," FRUS 1952–1954, Vol. 14, Part 2, p. 1312. One of the petitions that Murphy was likely referring to was one dated June 4 from the Amami Teachers' United Union calling for the return of education rights (kyoiku ken) to Japan. Murphy responded on June 20, explaining that the U.S. government was carefully studying the issue. See Murayama, Amami Fukkishi, p. 583.

25. Murayama, *Amami Fukkishi*, p. 373.

26. *Ibid.*, p. 375.

27. "Amami Gunto Henkan Keii," p. 17.

28. *Ibid.*, pp. 17–18; "Ogasawara Jumin no Kito, Bei, Koiteki ni Koryochu, Ma Taishi, Gaisho ni Genmei Amami no Gyoseiken Henkan mo (U.S., Favorably Looking Into Allowing Ogasawara Residents to Return, Ambassador Murphy Tells Foreign Minister That Administrative Rights for Amami Islands May be Returned Too)," *Mainichi Shimbun*, September 27, 1952.

29. "Amami Gunto Henkan Keii," p. 18.

30. "Letter from Murphy to McClurkin (March 24, 1953)," Office of Northeast Asian Affairs—Records Relating to Foreign Policy Decisions, 1950–1956, Microfilm C-0044, RG 59.

31. For more on this see Masumi, *Postwar Politics in Japan, 1945–1955* (Berkeley: Institute of East Asian Studies, 1985), pp. 286–293.

32. Apparently when Hatoyama resigned as president of the party in 1946, due to his being purged by GHQ officials, and turned the presidency over to Yoshida, it was done on the understanding that Yoshida would permit him to "take over right away" after Hatoyama was depurged. See Masumi, *Postwar Politics in Japan*, pp. 104–108.

33. "Letter from Murphy to the Director of the Office of Northeast Asian Affairs Young (April 5, 1953)," *FRUS 1952–1954, Vol. 14, Part 2*, p. 1405.

34. *Ibid.* At the end of the letter, Yoshida wrote: "Declaration of policy by the United States along the lines I have indicated, will go a long way toward ensuring the victory of my party in the elections. And that declaration, to be effective [in the elections], must come around the end of next week (April 10). Can you help me?" For the letter, not printed in *FRUS*, see "Copy of the Letter Handed on April 2, 1953, to Mr. Robert D. Murphy, Ambassador of the United States, and General Mark W. Clark, Commander in Chief of the American Security Forces in Japan," Tab D to "Memorandum of Conversation with Ambassador Araki on Various Matters Relating to Japan (May 14, 1953)," Box 5, Bureau of Far Eastern Affairs, Miscellaneous Subject Files, 1953, RG 59. Murphy's Deputy Chief of Mission, William T. Turner, strongly advised against intervention in the election, arguing that "1) there was not sufficient time to take effective action; 2) any successor government would likely be pro-United States [anyway] (whether or not headed by Yoshida); 3) intervention might be a liability rather than an asset." Cited in fn. 4, *FRUS 1952–1954, Vol. 14, No. 2*, p. 1405. It seems that Turner would change his mind after this, however.

35. "Copy of the Letter Handed on April 2, 1953, to Mr. Robert D. Murphy."

36. "Letter from Murphy to Young (April 5, 1953)."

37. "Letter from Charge d'Affaires ad interim to Kenneth T. Young (April 6, 1953)," Folder 322.3 Ryukyus, Box 25, RG 84, NA. Turner, who was born in Kobe and served in posts in prewar Japan, arrived in Tokyo as counselor of Embassy just one year before that on April 10, 1952.

38. Araki Eikichi (1891–1959), then governor of the Bank of Japan, was appointed ambassador to the United States in mid-1952 and served until 1954.

Yoshida's nomination of him was unusual in that Araki was not a diplomat by background, unlike most former and all succeeding Japanese ambassadors to the United States. I am indebted to the family of Araki for their many insights and materials on the late Ambassador.

39. See fn. 1, *FRUS 1952–1954, Vol. 14, No. 2,* p. 1409.

40. "Statement of Ambassador Araki Regarding Letter of April 2, 1953, from Prime Minister Yoshida to Ambassador Murphy (undated)," attachment to "Memorandum of Conversation with Ambassador Araki on Various Matters."

41. "Memorandum of Conversation between Okumura and Turner (April 11, 1953)," Folder 350 Japan, Jan.–Dec. 1953, Box 25, RG 84.

42. See Masumi, *Postwar Politics in Japan,* pp. 293–295, for the results of the elections.

43. Kanai, ed., *Fukki Undo Kaikoroku,* p. 333.

44. For more on this relationship and Sone's background, see Sone Eki, *Watashi no Memoaaru: Kasumigaseki Kara Nagatacho e* (*My Memoirs: From Kasumigaseki to Nagatacho*), (Tokyo: Nikkan Kogyo Shinbunsha, 1974).

45. Kanai, ed., *Fukki Undo Kaikoroku,* pp. 335–337; and Murayama, *Amami Fukkishi,* p. 462.

46. Kanai, ed., *Fukki Undo Kaikoroku,* p. 335.

47. *Ibid.,* p. 338.

48. *Ibid.,* p. 339.

49. *Ibid.,* pp. 343–344.

50. "Memorandum of Conversation with Eikichi Araki by J. Graham Parsons (July 7, 1953)," Box 6, Bureau of Far Eastern Affairs, Miscellaneous Subject Files, 1953, RG 59.

~

CHAPTER FOUR

The Eisenhower Administration and the Decision to Return the Amami Islands

"To insist on controlling this little group of islands, which obviously meant a lot to Japan, amounted to risking the loss of our main objective, which was to assure ourselves of Japan's friendship and loyalty over the long run."

—President Dwight D. Eisenhower, at the June 25, 1953 meeting of the National Security Council

In mid-March, after receiving the views of Ambassador Murphy in Tokyo in a March 13 telegram, Allison decided to raise the issue of the stalemate in Okinawa policy with the new secretary of state, John Foster Dulles, his former boss during the Peace Treaty negotiations.[1] Allison found that his own conclusions, that the Amami Islands could *and should* be returned as early as possible, were "reinforced" by Murphy's telegram.[2]

The conclusions, which were based on reporting from the Embassy and after detailed discussions with the Defense Department on the limited strategic importance of the islands, were as follows:

1. It would be undesirable to apply for trusteeship (problems in the United Nations as well was with the Japanese who would feel it was a turn away from sovereignty);
2. Status of islands acute political issue, particularly as little had been done for inhabitants in such important areas as education;
3. Okinawa is of such major strategic importance that we should retain it in its present status while tensions in the Far East continue. This may

have political advantage for Japan as well in that it would enable Japan to disclaim responsibility if the United States were to use bases for operations against Indochina and mainland China;

4. Strategic necessity for retention of Bonins is weaker than Okinawa and question of return of approximately 7,000 former inhabitants constitute a political problem;
5. Strategic reasons are least important with regard to Amami group;
6. Urgent necessity for improved civil affairs directive in order to make possible more adequate administration as well as increased degree of self-government.

As a result, Allison recommended that he either be allowed to request his predecessor, Dean Rusk, who was now president of the Rockefeller Foundation,[3] to arrange for financing of a four-month study by the Council on Foreign Relations of the situation in the Ryukyu and Bonin islands, or that he be allowed to develop a paper for presentation either to the Defense or the National Security Council, making specific suggestions with respect to the disposition of the Ryukyu and Bonin Islands along the following lines:

1. Okinawa should be retained in its present status while the international tensions in the Far East continue.
2. The Bonin Islands should be returned to Japan, or arrangements made to allow the repatriation of those inhabitants who want to return.
3. The Amami group should be returned to Japan at an early date, after agreement with Japan on the necessary rights there for military purposes, the precise timing to be determined with a view to obtaining the greatest possible political advantage.
4. The civil affairs directive for the retained islands should be modified to provide increased self-government for the inhabitants and improved administration.
5. After the decisions have been made, a public announcement should be made by the president of our intentions.

After reading through Allison's memorandum, Dulles handwrote the following message in the margin: "Mr. Allison—please follow No. 2. JFD."[4]

Allison and his staff began working on the position paper immediately, with the task being turned gradually over to the staff as Allison had been named ambassador to Japan by this point.[5] It would be up to Allison's successor, Walter S. Robertson, to guide the study through the bureaucracy after taking up his duties on April 8.[6]

Robertson, a banker from Virginia known for his hard-line views on China, was, it seems, well versed on the issue prior to his assumption of duties, as a March 27 briefing paper showed.[7] Over the coming weeks, the Division of Northeast Asian Affairs worked on its position paper (outlining the views above), which Robertson brought to Dulles' attention on June 2.[8] Dulles subsequently approved it on June 11.[9] This paper, as well as that of the Defense Department, were subsequently submitted to the NSC Planning Board, chaired by Brig. Gen. Robert M. Cutler. The Planning Board completed its thirty-page paper on June 15 for submission to the NSC, scheduled to meet on the 18th.[10]

In the meantime, a meeting was held in the State Department on the afternoon of June 17 in order to prepare for the NSC meeting scheduled the following day. In a one-page brief, Robertson notes the status of the State Department's policy on the islands:

> The NSC is presented with a basic difference in political judgment. Nothing in the Defense paper indicates that the Amami group has any strategic importance which could not be adequately protected by securing appropriate base rights from the Japanese. The Defense case is therefore predicated upon the theory that relinquishing control over the Amami group would whet the enthusiasm of the Japanese to regain control over the rest of the islands and would increase irredentist sentiment among the islanders. Our own judgment is that we can ease a serious and increasing source of friction by relinquishing control over the Amami group. The Japanese Government desires reversion of the islands and formally told us so. They know that the strategic case for our retention of Amami is weak, whereas the strategic case for the retention of the other islands is strong. In order to enable us, without alienating the Japanese, to retain control over the islands where we need it for our strategic interest, we should relinquish the control we do not need.

For reasons that are unclear, the NSC did not take up discussion on the treaty islands' question until June 25.[11] Although some time was lost, in the end it was probably a good thing in that it gave the participants a chance to fully digest the thick report they had received. While the report itself was dense, its recommendations were clear and to the point:

a. Decide whether the United States should:
   (1) As recommended by the Department of Defense, maintain the degree of control and authority now exercised, pursuant to Article 3 of the Peace Treaty with Japan, over all the islands in Article 3, until conditions of peace and stability prevail in the Far East.

Or

>   (2) As recommended by the Department of State, relinquish civil administration over the Amami group to Japan, subject to agreement with Japan on U.S. military rights in this group, but maintain the degree of control and authority now exercised pursuant to Article 3 of the Peace Treaty with Japan, over all the other islands mentioned in Article 3, during the present international tensions in the Far East.
>
> b. Decide that the United States should, at an appropriate time to be determined in the light of the international situation, make a public announcement of its intentions with respect to the Japanese Treaty Islands, as determined under (a) above.
>
> c. Direct the Department of Defense, in coordination with other interested agencies to (1) expedite revision of the present civil affairs directive providing for continued improvement of the civil administration of those Ryukyu Islands under U.S. jurisdiction, and (2) prepare any other necessary instrument defining the basic authority for administration of these islands.[12]

While unambiguous and to the point, the recommendations were anything but easy to implement.

The National Security Council and its 151st Meeting

It was Eisenhower's Special Assistant for National Security Affairs, Cutler, who began the discussion of point 5 on the agenda, "The Japanese Treaty Islands," pointing out the difference between the policies of the State Department and the Defense Department with respect to the return of the Amami group to Japan and noting the above recommendations to be decided upon.[13] Cutler asked Secretary of State Dulles to speak first.

Cutler, enjoying Eisenhower's full confidence, prepared for and managed the meetings, although the president himself formally chaired the NSC meetings on almost every occasion.[14] The council, which became "a valuable tool for [the President's] constant use," was used for policy recommendations, not decisions.[15] Only the president could make decisions on national policy. Eisenhower, observed Cutler, "was the central focus of a council meeting. All remarks were addressed to him."[16] Importantly, "Those who sat at the Council table," Cutler noted in his memoirs, "had a right to speak; none was denied a chance. . . . As long as the managing hand was mine, people whose responsibilities entitled them to be heard by the Council were to be heard if they so requested, and nothing was to be swept under the rug or compromised or glossed over."[17] Indeed, Eisenhower liked a "good debate" and it was Cutler's responsibility as planning board chairman and national security advisor "to assure debate by presenting differences which had not been resolved at a lower level sharply and precisely in the draft document before the Council."[18] "You could see the President," Cutler continued, "at times holding himself back from joining in too early." He wished to hear frank assertions of differing views, if they existed, "for from such interchanges might emerge a resolution which reasonable men could support."[19] And "when he spoke, everyone listened."[20] This is precisely what happened that day.

On Cutler's cue, the drafter of the San Francisco Peace Treaty, Dulles, began his presentation on the Amami Islands, observing that "it seemed to him perfectly possible to maintain the necessary U.S. bases in these treaty islands without assumption by the U.S. of civil administration in them." Dulles pointed out that he had drawn up the peace treaty in such a way as to permit the United States to retain "all that was needed by way of authority to protect vital security interests" but did not believe that "we needed to annex all these islands to achieve our military objectives." Okinawa, however, "was an exception to his general thinking" because it was such a large military base and such an important one, and that it would likely have to remain wholly under U.S. administration. Dulles felt the administration should be made more "civilian-minded," adding his warning that "the extraordinary legal rights which had been secured to the United States . . . would eventually prove quite worthless unless we exercised these rights in a manner designed to secure the support and loyalty of the Japanese. This was true both in Japan and in the islands."

After this preface, Dulles in conclusion stressed "his complete inability to grasp why . . . it was necessary to take over the entire administration of these islands" in order to maintain a radar and radio station. "This makes no sense," Dulles announced. At the same time, Dulles cautioned that in light of current developments in Korea, he strongly questioned whether it was the right moment to decide on the return of any of the islands to Japan and said he would not mind if the NSC deferred decision until it was known whether "there is to be more war or more peace in Korea."

After Dulles spoke, Cutler briefly interjected that costs to the United States to administer the Amami group ran at approximately two million dollars. Interestingly, when Eisenhower inquired about the size of the population of the Amami Islands, no one had the answer. The fate of islands with a large population of nationals of an ally, Japan, was being debated without all the facts being known, it seems.

Secretary of Defense Charles E. Wilson then spoke. According to Cutler, council members tended to "be concise" in their exchanges "in the realization of the fair allotment of opportunities to speak," but Wilson often spoke on and on, although "he learned in time [to be concise], occasionally prompted by direct Presidential intervention."[21] Fortunately, Wilson was brief this time, stating that "if we could be sure that the Japanese would 'stay with us' over the long term, he would be glad to give up administration of the islands" and expressed agreement with the secretary of state's position that it was "not necessary to rule over all the people of the Amami Islands" in order to maintain a radio and radar station.

President Eisenhower argued that it was necessary to recognize Japan and its potential strength of "vital importance to our own security interests. Accordingly," the president continued, "to insist [as the military had done to date] on controlling this little group of islands, which obviously meant a lot to Japan, amounted to risking the loss of our main objective, which was to assure ourselves of Japan's friendship and loyalty over the long run." This was "silly," he said, and felt that "the Army was taking a little too narrow view if its opposition to the return of these islands was only to secure a radar station."

Wilson said that while Okinawa was becoming a very real problem for the United States, he was prepared to agree to the return of the Amami Islands. Essentially, Wilson seemed to hope that returning the Amami Islands would help to lower pressure on calls for the return of Okinawa, both in Okinawa and Japan, as well as in U.S. government circles. In agreeing to do so, Wilson was overriding the views of those in the military and the Pentagon who feared that the return of Amami would be the first step in more calls for the return of the other islands. (Indeed this is what would happen.)

Interestingly at this point, Dulles—the ultimate, cautious, power politics statesman—reemphasized his concern about the timing. He suddenly stated that now "was not the moment to return the Amamis," adding, as his assistant secretaries Allison and Robertson had suggested, that the "return should be timed to extract the utmost advantage from it." (Later on, Dulles recommended the return be calculated and timed in ways that would tend to hasten the process of Japanese rearmament.)

When a staff aide came into the meeting to report that the islands had a population of 219,000, the president spoke up and said "emphatically that to him it was a 'must' to return" them to Japan. "Maybe," the president said, "the time is actually approaching for the return of some, at least, of these islands." Eisenhower added that while it was impossible to return all of the islands, he could see "no objections to turning over the small Amami group."

These views of Eisenhower were very much in line with earlier opinions he held back in the late 1940s when he was Army chief-of-staff. In discussions with Secretary of War Robert P. Patterson on "the wisdom of planning to retain Okinawa as a permanent base," in March 1947, Eisenhower explained that while he did not agree with Patterson's discounting of Okinawa's strategic importance, he did recognize the "great cost to which the U.S. would be put, economically, politically, and socially, by an assumption of permanent administration" over the affairs of the islands.[22] Eisenhower instead suggested that "what we need is the use of naval and air installations which would probably be located, for the most part, only in the southern third of Okinawa. These installations would represent as [sic] an asset. Any other U.S. commitments in the Ryukyus would constitute a liability. I believe," Eisenhower wrote to Patterson, "[that] it should be possible to work out arrangements to keep the asset and lose the liability." Eisenhower continued to hold these views some six years later when he was presiding at the Council meeting.[23]

With the president's views known, Cutler suggested that the council might agree to accept the State Department recommendation to return the islands and leave the implementation of this policy to a future joint decision of the secretaries of state and defense. Eisenhower, however, felt the issue was too important to be decided in that way and stated that the question should be brought before the Council in not more than ninety days. He added his emphasis that it was important to relate the return of these islands to the development of Japan's military strength.

As a result, the Council decided the following:

a. Adopted the recommendation of the Department of State, contained in paragraph 18-a-(2) of the reference memorandum, to relinquish civil administration over the Amami group to Japan as a matter of policy; subject to the understanding that, in view of the current situation in the Far East, implementation of this policy and any public announcement as proposed in paragraph 18-b will be deferred pending review of the situation by the National Security Council on the recommendation of the Secretaries of State and Defense within 90 days.

b. Agreed that the Secretary of Defense, in collaboration with the Department of State, the Bureau of the Budget, and other interested agencies, should recommend for Council consideration a policy on the civil administration of those Ryukyu Islands remaining under U.S. jurisdiction, which would reduce U.S. responsibility for such civil administration as rapidly as compatible with U.S. military requirements.

With this decision made, Eisenhower approved the statement contained in NSC 125/5, as amended and adopted by the Council, and the action of the

Council with respect to the Japanese treaty islands. On June 29, the acting executive secretary of the NSC prepared the new version of the NSC document, which became NSC 125/6, and included the following report about the islands:

> The United States should relinquish civil administration over the Amami group to Japan, subject to agreement with Japan on U.S. military rights in this group, but to maintain the degree of control and authority now exercised pursuant to Article 3 of the Peace Treaty with Japan, over all the other islands mentioned in Article 3, during the present international tensions in the Far East.[24]

Although the above decision sought a response within ninety days, it would be a mere six weeks before the U.S. government would be pressed by circumstances to make a decision. The announcement of that decision, as discussed in the next section, would come when Dulles made an unplanned stopover in Japan in early August.

The Dulles Trip to Japan and the Announcement to Return the Amami Islands

Dulles did not originally plan to stop in Japan during his trip to Asia, focusing instead primarily on his visit to Korea to deal with the armistice agreement. But when U.S. ambassador to Japan John M. Allison read about Dulles' planned trip in the newspapers, he quickly sent off a telegram to the State Department stating that "it was most important that the Secretary stop in Tokyo for a day or two on his return from Korea."[25] It is a good thing that Dulles did in fact agree to pay a visit to Japan; while in Tokyo, Dulles announced on August 8 that the United States would return the Amami Islands following an agreement.

After arriving at Tokyo's Haneda Airport, Dulles and Allison met with Yoshida and Okazaki in the afternoon at the Embassy where Dulles surprised his guests with the announcement.[26] According to Okazaki, Dulles told Yoshida that he "brought a little early Christmas present for him," and then searched his pockets for it.[27] When nothing turned up, Dulles asked Allison to go upstairs to look for it. When Allison returned with a piece of paper and asked him "whether this was what he meant by the Christmas present," Dulles said, "Oh, yes. Yes it was." On it was written the announcement to return Amami.

That evening at 7:30 P.M., Dulles made the following announcement to the press gathered outside the Embassy building (with the message being simultaneously released in Washington):

I am pleased to make in Tokyo the following announcement which I have just communicated to His Excellency the Prime Minister on behalf of the United States Government.

The Government of the United States desires to relinquish its rights under Article 3 of the Peace Treaty over the Amami Oshima Group in favor of the resumption by Japan of authority over these islands as soon as necessary arrangements can be concluded with the Government of Japan.

With respect to the other islands included under Article 3 of the Japanese Peace Treaty, it will be necessary during the present international tensions in the Far East for the United States to maintain the degree of control and authority now exercised. The United States will thus be able to carry out more effectively its responsibilities under the Security Treaty between the United States and Japan to contribute to the maintenance of peace and security in the area. Meanwhile the United States will make increased efforts to promote the welfare of the inhabitants of those islands.

The prospective reunion of the Amami Oshima group with Japan, reuniting its inhabitants with their homeland, is a source of gratification and pleasure to the Government of the United States.

Although one participant in the reversion movement wrote, in what is by far the best account of the movement, that Allison did not know beforehand of the announcement, we now know it was in fact the Ambassador himself who had recommended to Dulles that he make the statement while in Japan to "demonstrate that [Dulles] had [an] important mission to carry out in Japan as well as in Korea."[28] Allison even went so far as to lay out a scenario for informing Yoshida and, on August 6, had his staff at the Embassy draw up a draft text for an announcement after having consulted with the State Department that day.[29] Acquiring the concurrence of Dulles and the responsible offices in the State Department and Defense Department for the Secretary's statement, as well as of course the contents of the announcement, had to be done quickly. This was made more problematic in that Dulles was at this point in Korea, which meant communications were going back and forth between Tokyo, Seoul, and Washington. It may be good to describe in more detail exactly what took place in the four days before Dulles' arrival in Japan.

On the afternoon of August 4, Allison sent a top secret, priority telegram to the U.S. embassy in Korea for the attention of Dulles, who had arrived that day in Seoul to meet with President Syngman Rhee, urging that he announce the return of the Amami Islands while in Japan.[30] Allison in fact, in response to a request by Dulles for his opinions, had recommended one month earlier, on July 6, that "promptest action [be taken on NSC decision to return Amami] in view [of] danger that any leak would deprive us of immense psychological advantage which we may expect to derive from this decision."[31] Allison's urging even prompter action on the eve of Dulles' visit seems to have been based on informal reports from an unidentified official at the Japanese Foreign Ministry that the Soviet Union was "preparing [to] make [a] bid any day to improve relations with Japan," adding that "our contact thinks [the] Russians may soon want to talk [about a] peace treaty."[32] Allison took the reports seriously, warning that the "possibility of some overt friendly gesture by Russians is yet another important reason for us to announce NSC decision regarding Amami group soonest. If announcement were made only after Russian move, it would look like hasty defensive action on our part rather than genuine initiative by us. Under such circumstances psychological benefit to us would be nil." With Stalin's death in March and the Soviet Union's call for "peaceful coexistence," a Soviet move to conclude a peace treaty with Japan, in which the Northern Islands would be returned, could not be ruled out.[33]

After conferring with Admiral Felix B. Stump, Admiral Arthur W. Radford's replacement as CINCPAC, and Vice Admiral Robert P. Briscoe, who agreed with necessity to "move quickly," Allison sent his telegram to Dulles in Seoul and the State Department.

Upon receipt of the telegram, Allison's former colleague, U. Alexis Johnson, the deputy assistant secretary of state for Far Eastern Affairs, and Robert J. G. McClurkin, deputy director of the Office of Northeast Asian Affairs, quickly sought the agreement of Acting Secretary of State Smith.[34] Smith, Eisenhower's former European chief-of-staff and an efficient administrator, quickly concurred. The State Department went about getting the consent of the Defense Department, followed by the president.

After receiving the agreement of Secretary of Defense Wilson and President Eisenhower on August 5, Smith sent a telegram to Dulles later that day informing him that all concerned had concurred in Allison's recommendation to make the announcement in Tokyo at Dulles' discretion.[35] Smith also included the following suggested text for the announcement, drafted by Alexis Johnson:

> The U.S. intends to relinquish civil administration over the Amami Islands to the Government of Japan as soon as agreement is reached on the necessary understandings involved.
>
> With respect to the other islands included under Article 3 of the Japanese Peace Treaty it will be necessary for the U.S. to continue its civil administration while present conditions of insecurity and instability in the Far East continue. The U.S. will thus be able to carry out more effectively its responsibili-

ties under the security treaty between the U.S. and Japan to contribute to the maintenance of peace and security in the area. Meanwhile the U.S. is reviewing present arrangements for the civil administration of the Ryukyu Islands.[36]

Finally, Smith also suggested that Dulles might want to "make [the] point that the turning back of [the] Amami group increases [the] area of Japanese defense responsibility and thus emphasizes desirability [of] increased Japanese efforts to fulfill expectations expressed in security treaty that Japan will increasingly assume responsibility for its own defense."[37] This was a point that Dulles did not need any convincing on whatsoever, as we saw in the NSC discussion in the previous section in which Dulles echoed this view in an August 6 telegram from Seoul that "If [the] statement [is] made, [it] will emphasize importance [that] Japan make increased security effort, as intimated by Yoshida at [the] San Francisco conference."[38]

However, Allison, while in basic agreement with Smith's recommendation that the "announcement should help in promoting Japanese awareness that they are increasingly on their own and therefore must develop capacity for self-defense," argued in his earlier August 4 telegram that he "continues to believe it is neither practical nor advantageous to attempt to tie this decision to some specific concessions from [the] Japanese."[39] Allison likely was referring here to the question of the Mutual Security Act talks which had received bad press play in the run up to Dulles' visit and would get even more negative commentary.[40] Likewise, in a follow-up telegram, dated August 7, Allison strongly recommended that the "formal statement not contain anything which would make it appear that [the] return of [the] islands [was] contingent on increased Japanese defense effort," noting that he was "in favor of emphasizing privately to Yoshida [the] importance of increased security effort by Japan, but [was] certain any public statement to this effect by [the] Secretary at this time would be counterproductive."[41] Dulles eventually Allison's advice, as the official statement above reflects.

In any case, the draft text sent by Smith was reviewed by Allison and his staff in Tokyo, who had also been working on their own version when the State Department's draft arrived. One problem they found with the draft text, which was pointed out by the chief-of-staff of the Far Eastern Command, Admiral B. Hall Hanlon, was the last sentence, which the embassy and the FEC believed "could give too much encouragement to irredentist activity."[42] Having already consulted with Gen. Otto P. Weyland, the commanding general of the Far East Air Force and the U.N. Air Forces in Tokyo (and someone known as the "Father of the New Japanese Air Force" for his efforts to reorganize air defenses and aviation in Japan), Allison suggested the following text:

> I am pleased to make in Tokyo the following announcement which I have just communicated to His Excellency the Prime Minister on behalf of the United States Government.
>
> The Government of the United States desires to relinquish its rights under Article 3 of the Peace Treaty over the Amami Oshima Group in favor of the resumption by Japan of authority over these islands as soon as necessary arrangements can be concluded with the Government of Japan.
>
> With respect to the other islands included under Article 3 of the Japanese Peace Treaty, it will be necessary during the present international tensions in the Far East for the United States to maintain the degree of control and authority now exercised. The United States will thus be able to carry out more effectively its responsibilities under the Security Treaty between the United States and Japan to contribute to the maintenance of peace and security in the area. Meanwhile, the United States will make increased efforts to promote the welfare of the inhabitants both locally and in their relationship to Japan.
>
> The prospective reunion of the Amami Oshima group with Japan, reuniting its inhabitants with their homeland, is a source of gratification and pleasure to the Government of the United States.[43]

Allison's suggested text, sent to Washington on August 6, was in turn amended by the State Department when Frank C. Nash, the assistant secretary of defense, objected to the last part of the third paragraph which read "both locally and in their relationship to Japan."[44] Nash's objection, to which the State Department later admitted it was "inclined to agree," was that this phrase was "more susceptible of giving rise to irredentist sentiment than [the] last sentence contained [in the State] Department draft."[45] Eventually the statement adopted this recommendation as well, becoming a combined version of the efforts of the embassy, State Department, and Defense Department, with the biggest contribution having come from the embassy and Allison.

With this announcement made, Dulles departed for Washington the following afternoon. Symbolic of how well the announcement was received, as Dulles was preparing to board his plane, someone in the crowd gathered at Haneda Airport yelled out "Amami Oshima Island, Thank You!"[46] Dulles reportedly threw a smile and waved to the group gathered from Amami, and then went over to meet them personally. Okuyama Hachiro, the leader of *Amami Rengo* introduced in chapter 2, stepped forward and shook hands with the secretary. In response to Okuyama's words of thanks, Dulles, speaking into a microphone, stated, "I am very pleased that you all came all the way out here to the airport on my behalf. I will be very glad to report about the return of Amami and your happiness when I return to Washington. I hope that with this opportunity, you will all work hard to make relations between Japan and the United States even stronger." Dulles was given a bouquet of roses from two twelve-year-old girls, Oyama Kazuko and Seda Kazuko, and boarded the plane. Upon arriving in Washington, Dulles told reporters, "The thing that left the greatest impression in Tokyo was the group of dozens of people from the Amami Islands who saw me off with flowers and signs with their gratitude written on them expressing their happiness and deep gratitude for the return of the islands to Japan."

The Japanese press in general was equally satisfied with Dulles' announcement, and reaction in Amami and mainland-based reversion groups was, of course, ecstatic.[47] At the same time, some problems were pointed out. The *Asahi Shimbun*, for example, noted that issues both big and small remained, including the return of Okinawa and the delineation of the territorial limits of the Amami Islands. Likewise, as historian Watanabe Akio writes, "the suddenness of the U.S. decision made some people wonder what its real intention was."[48] Many viewed the true U.S. aim as a request for Japanese rearmament and wondered what sort of *quid pro quo* had been worked out. Ironically there was none, but the suspicious environment at the time during the Cold War and domestic criticism of the U.S.–Japan alliance led to a great deal of speculation.

Immediately prior to this, a major controversy had emerged over the question of Mutual Security Act (MSA) discussions and Japanese rearmament when the opposition accused Yoshida and Okazaki of "secret diplomacy," leading to calls on July 29 for a vote of no-confidence in Okazaki by the Socialist Party.[49] Thus, in this environment, there were fears that Yoshida had agreed to rearmament in exchange for the return of the islands, a fear not put to rest when the text of an off-the-record interview given by Dulles to James Reston of the *New York Times* (as reported by the *Asahi Shimbun*) was made public in which Dulles "expressed extreme dissatisfaction with the passive attitude of the Japanese Government toward the defense of Asia."[50] Allison, who had been against Dulles granting the interview in the first place, was "amazed and shocked" to see the off-the-record interview carried in the newspaper, fearing that "much of the good impression created by Dulles's announcement about the return of the Amami Oshima group would be wiped out by this story," which Allison noted in his memoirs had been "repeated and played up" by all of the Japanese newspapers in their afternoon editions.[51] Allison warned in a subsequent telegram that the "political situation in Japan is so delicate that in [his] opinion there should be no public statements by American officials regarding [U.S.] desires for rearmament no matter how carefully phrased. . . . Any public statement by United States officials is only taken as interference and is used by opposition and by Communists with which to beat government."[52] He added that "it would have been hard for Reston to have published anything that could have done more harm to American–Japanese relations," a point not too far off base in the context of the times.[53] But that is exactly the point Dulles was trying to make, in public if necessary—by returning the Amami Islands, the United States expected Japan to take a larger role in defense and expanding its military capacity. The link between the return of the Amami Islands and Dulles' desire for Japan's rearmament (and eventual frustration with its slow pace) became clearer in the follow-up discussions and negotiations over the return of the Amami Islands, taken up next.

Notes

1. Dulles was, in general, a figure that was feared, but according to Jeff Graham Parsons, the deputy chief of mission at the U.S. embassy in Tokyo, Allison, when he was ambassador, "minced no words in disagreeing sharply with his old chief" on occasion. See "Unpublished Manuscript" (chapter 11, page 8), Folder 16, Box 13, Papers of Jeff Graham Parsons, Special Collections and Archives Division, Lauinger Library, Georgetown University, Washington, D.C.

2. "Memorandum by the Assistant Secretary of State for Far Eastern Affairs Allison to the Secretary of State (March 18, 1953)," FRUS, 1952–1954, Vol. 14, Part 2, p. 1398.

3. It is not clear where this particular suggestion arose, but I did locate a letter to Allison from Harold J. Coolidge, executive director of the Washington, D.C.-based National Research Council, which supported the activities of the Pacific Science Board, mentioning the Council's activities, its cooperation with the Civil Administration in the Ryukyu Islands in a joint scientific research project known as SIRI, and the fact that he planned to make his fourth visit to Okinawa in March. Coolidge also mentioned that they were interested in getting outside funding, including from the Rockefeller Foundation, and that the foundation's Dr. Charles B. Fahs had visited Okinawa a couple of years before. See "Letter from Harold J. Coolidge to Assistant Secretary Allison (January 16, 1953)," Central Decimal File, 1950–1954 (794c.0221/1-1653), RG 59. Allison may have gotten a hint from this letter about encouraging a study by the Rockefeller Foundation.

4. See fn. 5, FRUS, 1952–1954, Vol. 14, Part 2, p. 1400.

5. According to his memoirs, Allison was told by Dulles shortly before Christmas 1952 that he was to succeed Murphy as Ambassador to Japan, with Murphy to take up "an important position back in Washington." However it was not until early March 1953 before Allison learned that the White House was going to officially announce his appointment. This was done shortly thereafter and reported in the March 7, 1953 edition of the Washington Post, although he still needed to be confirmed by the Senate. See Allison, Ambassador from the Prairie, pp. 213–221.

6. See fn. 1, *FRUS, 1952–1954, Vol. 14, Part 2*, p. 1409.

7. "Memorandum on Major Political and Economic Problems in Our Relations with Japan (March 27, 1953)," Far East–General folder, Box 5, Bureau of Far Eastern Affairs, Miscellaneous Subject Files, 1953, Lot File 55D388, RG 59. Robertson did not leave memoirs unfortunately, but his papers have been recently opened after having been sealed for twenty-five years following his passing in 1971. The papers are housed in the Virginia Historical Society in Richmond, Virginia, his hometown. Robertson also conducted two oral history interviews, one for The John Foster Dulles Oral History Project at Princeton University Library in 1965 and the other for the Eisenhower Library in 1967.

8. See fn. 4, *FRUS, 1952–1954, Vol. 14, Part 2*, p. 1435. Robertson explained to Dulles in an accompanying memorandum that "In all but one respect this [position] is consistent with the position you approved as the result of a memorandum of March 18 to you from Mr. Allison. This one respect is the implicit recommendation that the Bonin Islands should be retained and that the islanders should not be permitted to return during present international tensions in the Far East. At the conference in Honolulu with Admiral Radford and Frank Nash, Mr. Allison agreed that he would be willing to present this position to the Japanese Government and to recommend it to you. FE concurs."

9. "Memorandum from Robertson to Dulles on NSC Consideration of the Japanese Treaty Islands (June 16, 1953)," Box 29a, PPS Records, RG 59. Also see *FRUS, 1952–1954, Vol. 14, Part 2*, pp. 1435–1436.

10. "Memorandum for the National Security Council on the Japanese Treaty Islands (June 15, 1953)," Box 29a, PPS Records, RG 59. The paper can also be found in Box 3, NSC Series, Policy Papers Subseries, White House Office, Office of the Special Assistant for National Security Affairs Records, 1952–1961, Dwight D. Eisenhower Presidential Library, Abilene, Kansas.

11. See fn. 1, *FRUS, 1952–1954, Vol. 14, Part 2*, p. 1435.

12. These recommendations, found on page 10 of the report, can also be seen on page 1433 of *Ibid.*

13. "Memorandum of Discussion at the 151st Meeting of the National Security Council, Washington, June 25, 1953," *FRUS, 1952–1954, Vol. 14, Part 2*, pp. 1438–1445.

14. Robert Cutler, *No Time for Rest* (Boston: Little, Brown, and Co., 1965), p. 303.

15. *Ibid.*, p. 295. On the Eisenhower Administration and the NSC in addition to Cutler, see for example, Robert H. Johnson, "The National Security Council: The Relevance of its Past to Its Future," *Orbis*, Vol. 13, No. 3 (Fall 1969), esp. pp. 714–717.

16. Cutler, *No Time for Rest*, p. 303.

17. *Ibid.*, p. 305.

18. *Ibid.*, p. 305.

19. *Ibid.*, p. 305.

20. *Ibid.*, p. 303.

21. *Ibid.*, pp. 303–304.

22. Eldridge, *The Origins of the Bilateral Okinawa Problem*, pp. 174–175.

23. Importantly, not only at the time of the decision to return Amami but also in 1958, Eisenhower considered returning Okinawa for precisely the same reasons. For a detailed study, see Robert D. Eldridge, "40 Nenmae Togo Keikaku ni Manabu" ("Learning from the Consolidation Plans of 40 Years Ago"), *Ryukyu Shimpo*, January 19–February 2, 2001 series. Also see Nicholas E. Sarantakes, *Keystone: The American Occupation of Okinawa and U.S.–Japanese Relations* (College Station: Texas A & M University Press, 2000), p. 108.

24. "Statement of Policy by the National Security Council on United States Objectives and Courses of Action with Respect to Japan," enclosure to "Note by the Acting Executive Secretary S. Everett Gleason to the National Security Council on NSC 125/6, United States Objectives and Courses of Action with Respect to Japan (June 29, 1953)," *FRUS, 1952–1954, Vol. 14, Part 2*, pp. 1448–1452.

25. Allison, *Ambassador from the Prairie*, p. 240.

26. *Ibid.*, p. 241.

27. Interview with Katsuo Okazaki, October 2, 1964, Tokyo, The John Foster Dulles Oral History Project, Seeley G. Mudd Library, Princeton University, Princeton, New Jersey, p. 14.

28. Murayama, *Amami Fukkishi*, p. 471. For Allison's correspondence on this subject to Dulles, see "The Ambassador in Japan (Allison) to the Embassy in Korea (August 4, 1953)," *FRUS 1952–1954, Vol. 14, Part 2*, pp. 1468–1469.

29. "The Ambassador in Japan (Allison) to the Embassy in Korea (August 6, 1953)," *FRUS, 1952–1954, Vol. 14, Part 2*, pp. 1472–1473.

30. "The Ambassador in Japan (Allison) to the Embassy in Korea (August 4, 1953)." Here, Allison suggested that the demarcation line of the Amami Islands be set at 27° degrees north latitude to include Okino Erabu Shima and Yoronto, historically a part of the Amami Islands (and which protested in the fall of 1952 their possible separation from the rest of the islands). See figure I.1 in the introduction for reference.

31. "The Ambassador in Japan (Allison) to the Secretary of State (July 6, 1953)," Central Decimal Files, 1950–1954 (794C.0021/7-653), RG 59. Also see "Memorandum from Johnson to Secretary of State Dulles on Attached Letter to the Department of Defense Concerning the Japanese Treaty Islands," Box 29a, PPS Records, RG 59.

32. "The Ambassador in Japan (Allison) to the Embassy in Korea (August 4, 1953)." It is unclear from whom Allison got his information, or whether or not such information was actually received by the Foreign Ministry or if the ministry pretended to have such information in an effort to force the United States to move on the issue. In an exhaustive search, I failed to turn up any reports of such information on either the U.S. or Japanese side.

33. For more on the Russian factor in U.S. strategy on Okinawa and Amami, see Kajiura "Amami Shoto no Henkan o Meguru Beikoku no Tainichi/Taisokan," pp. 112–126.

34. By coincidence, each of the bosses of these men—Dulles, Robertson, and Young—were in Korea at the time, with decisions and actions having to be taken up by the deputies.

35. "The Acting Secretary of State to the Embassy in Korea (August 5, 1953)," *FRUS, 1952–1954, Vol. 14, Part 2*, pp. 1471–1472.

36. *Ibid.*, p. 1471.

37. *Ibid.*, pp. 1471–1472.

38. See fn. 3, *Ibid.*, p. 1477.

39. "The Ambassador in Japan (Allison) to the Embassy in Korea (August 4, 1953)."

40. See for example, Allison, *Ambassador from the Prairie*, pp. 231–241.

41. "The Ambassador in Japan (Allison) to the Embassy in Korea (August 7, 1953)." For more on Allison and the issue of rearmament, see Ikeda Shintaro, "Jon Arison to Nihon Saigunbi, 1952–1953" ("John Allison and Japanese Rearmament, 1952–1953"), *Gaiko Jiho* (*Diplomatique Revue*), No. 1343 (November–December, 1997), pp. 109–125.

42. "The Ambassador in Japan (Allison) to the Embassy in Korea (August 6, 1953)."

43. *Ibid.*

44. See, fn. 2, *Ibid.*, p. 1477.

45. *Ibid.*

46. Murayama, *Amami Fukkishi*, p. 474.

47. See for example, *Ibid.*, pp. 470–478.

48. Watanabe, *The Okinawa Problem*, p. 34. For press reaction, see, for example, the editorial "Amami Oshima no Henkan ni Saishite" ("On the Occasion of the Return of the Amami Oshima Islands"), *Asahi Shimbun*, August 11, 1953.

49. Allison, *Ambassador from the Prairie*, p. 234. Also see Kono, *Okinawa Henkan o Meguru Seiji to Gaiko*, p. 93.

50. "Dulles Complains to Yoshida on Lag in Japan's Defense," *New York Times*, August 10, 1953. Also see Allison, *Ambassador from the Prairie*, pp. 241–242.

51. Allison, *Ambassador from the Prairie*, p. 242.

52. "The Ambassador in Japan (Allison) to the Department of State (August 14, 1953)," *FRUS, 1952–1954, Vol. 14, Part 2*, p. 1485.

53. Allison, *Ambassador from the Prairie*, p. 242.

CHAPTER FIVE

~

The Amami Reversion Negotiations and Bilateral Agreement

The reunion of the Amami archipelago with the mainland of Japan has been long and eagerly awaited for not only by the 200,000 islanders but by the entire people of our country. To this fervent national aspiration of the Japanese people the American government has happily responded.

—Okazaki Katsuo, Minister of Foreign Affairs,
Remarks at Ceremony of the Signing of the Reversion Agreement,
December 24, 1953

The implementation of the final decision to return the Amami Islands taken at the NSC meeting in June, and the subsequent agreement to announce the decision in August, went fairly smoothly and were helped along by the summer signing of the ceasefire agreement on the Korean peninsula.[1] This was primarily because of Amami's relatively limited strategic importance (as compared to Okinawa) and the increased political sensitivities of the Japanese government and public.

At the same time, however, the issue of the reversion of Amami Oshima was also one closely intertwined with that of America's Okinawa policy as well as its views on Japanese rearmament, namely the need for a U.S. presence in the region and concurrent increase in Japanese military and political contributions to the Western alliance. These aspects were most visibly demonstrated in a meeting held shortly after Dulles' return to Washington with Araki, the Japanese ambassador to the United States.

Araki and Ushiroku Torao, first secretary of the Japanese embassy, called on Dulles and Director of the Office of Northeast Asian Affairs Young in the afternoon of August 13 to thank the secretary of state for the U.S. decision to return the Amami group to Japan and to hand him a letter of appreciation from Foreign Minister Okazaki.[2] Dulles explained that he felt the decision to relinquish control of the Amami group "was the right one" since the islands have "little strategic value" and because the United States "as a matter of policy does not wish to retain control over alien peoples any longer than necessary."[3]

Araki, concerned about the incident in late September 1952 when there were reports of only some of the Amami Islands being returned (discussed in chapter 4), then asked about the exact geographical designation of the islands concerned. Using a map, the ambassador asked specifically about Okino Erabu and the Yoronto stating it was his government's view that the delineation between the Amami group and the Okinawa group was just south of the Yoron Islands. Although Dulles acknowledged that his announcement had been made before all the details had been worked out between the Defense and State Dpartments, Young explained that they would probably use "the general formula" that the islands which had formerly been part of Kagoshima Prefecture would be relinquished and the islands that formerly had been part of Okinawa Prefecture would not.[4] Young added that his office was carefully analyzing this question and that they expected to complete their work within the next few weeks. In fact that answer came later that day, and the embassy informed Deputy Foreign Minister Okumura informally and confidentially shortly after that.[5]

Ambassador Araki next stated that it was the "strong hope" of his government that action regarding Okinawa and Ogasawara would also be taken now that the Amami Islands question had been solved. Dulles, who was afraid of precisely this sort of request, cautioned the ambassador "not to press immediately for the return of control over Okinawa and the Bonins" because such an action "would confirm the very suspicions of those who had argued against even the relinquishment of control" of the Amami Islands. Dulles probably included himself in that group.

Relating the issue to the lack of Japanese efforts for its own defense, Dulles stated that it would be impossible for the U.S. government to relinquish control over such strategic islands as the Okinawa and Ogasawara "as long as the government and people of Japan showed such little interest and were making such small efforts in the security of the area. It would not be right," he continued, "for the United States to let these islands fall into a 'vacuum of power' at the present time." Dulles expanded on this by stating that he was "very disappointed" over "the lack of effort and interest" in developing its own defense and contributing to the security of the region and likewise was disappointed that there had been "no revival in Japan of the spirit of sacrifice and discipline required to meet the conditions of the world as we all face them." Dulles also explained that he found the explanations given by Yoshida, during talks in Tokyo as to why Japan could not rearm, "quite unsatisfactory."

As this comment and the above conversation and following look at the reversion negotiations would show, the question of the return of the Amami, Okinawa, and Ogasawara Islands were very much interrelated, as well as being inherently connected with the issue of Japan assuming a larger regional role in defense matters.

Preparing for the Negotiations

With Dulles' announcement, Yoshida and Foreign Ministry officials immediately met on August 11 to discuss how to go about handling the transfer of the islands back to Japan—specifically the issues of corresponding legislation, budgets, reports, and the establishment of a liaison committee.[6] On August 14, the committee came into being when the Japanese government established the *Amami Gunto Jimu Hikitsugu Renraku Kyogikai* (Liaison Council for the Transition of Administration of the Amami Islands), having received Cabinet approval that day.[7]

The Liaison Council, administered by the *Nanpo Renraku Jimukyoku* (Southern Areas Liaison Office under the Prime Minister), was nominally headed by Chief Cabinet Secretary Fukunaga Kenji and was comprised of representatives from the Prime Minister's Office, the Foreign Ministry, the Finance Ministry, Justice Ministry, and other interested ministries and agencies, appointed by their respective directors. Within the Liaison Council, an executive committee (*kanjikai*) was also established for interagency coordination and decision-making purposes.[8]

The Liaison Council met for the first time on August 22, two weeks after Dulles' announcement, and decided to send a mission to the islands to develop a report on what needed to be accomplished prior to the transfer.[9] This was followed by a second meeting held on September 5, which further studied what needed to be done.[10]

Several days later, the thirty-five-member mission, led by Ishii Michinori, head of the prime minister's Southern Areas Liaison Office, left for Kagoshima and the Amami Islands to gather information during its two-week stay for its report.[11] The mission was enthusiastically received in Naze upon its arrival on the 13th.[12] Fortunately, preparations had been proceeding in Amami and Ishii's group was handed a study on local conditions upon its arrival to help in the writing of its report.[13]

By October, the mission's final report was ready and, in parallel with discussions in the Liaison Council on October 8, a revised version, "Amami Gunto no Fukki ni Tomonau Zantei Sochi ni Kansuru Kihon Hoshin (Fundamental Policy Regarding Temporary Measures Following the Return of the Amami Islands)," was approved by the Cabinet at its meeting on October 23.[14] The following month, at the 17th Extraordinary Session of the Diet, a related bill, the "Amami Gunto no Fukki ni Tomonau Horei no Tekiyo no Zantei Sochito ni Kansuru Horitsuan" ("Law Relating to Temporary Measures, etc. for the Application of Laws Following the Return of the Amami Islands"), submitted on October 29, was passed on November 7.[15] Likewise, a supplementary budget for Amami was approved at the same time. (In any interesting footnote to history, at the time this bill was passed, Sato Eisaku, later prime minister when Ogasawara (1968) and Okinawa (1972) were returned, proposed a resolution calling for the return of the remaining territories.) In this way, the domestic preparations on the Japanese side proceeded steadily.

The U.S. side, too, had begun its preparations immediately following Dulles' announcement. On August 13, Allison and Deputy Chief of Mission Parsons, who had just arrived in Japan, sent the State Department the embassy's basic recommendations for planning the reversion of Amami and requested Dulles' instructions.[16] In it, they suggested the following:

Figure 5.1.   Arrival of the Ishii Mission in Amami to a Large Reception, September 1953

1. Use the prewar Kagoshima Prefecture delineations;
2. Agree within U.S. government promptly on necessary security installations;
3. Communicate definite time limit to Far Eastern Command and Japanese Government for completion of all necessary technical adjustments (such as sixty-day period);
4. Use exchange of notes rather than protocol to treaty or separate agreement to minimize possible interference from other treaty powers; and
5. Work out details of ceremonies at time of transfer and other issues later.

Their telegraph followed one sent out earlier that day, describing the "tremendous [positive] psychological effect" of the announcement of the decision to return Amami.[17] "Its timing and manner of announcement were most satisfactory," Allison reported, "and we are receiving from every quarter indications that it has broken through prejudice barrier of Japanese intelligentsia and publicists as has no U.S. action since end of Occupation."[18] In order to "derive full value" from the announcement and to "properly exploit this decision" so that the Amami reversion can be later viewed as a "turning point in Japanese anti-Americanism which had gathered disturbing momentum over [the] past six months," Allison urged moving along speedily with arrangements for the return.

In order to learn better what arrangements would in fact need to be made for the transfer, John J. Conroy, counselor at the U.S. embassy in Tokyo, and two counterparts from the Far Eastern Command, Roderick M. Gillies (Political Division, J-5) and Phil C. Woodyatt (Division of Civil Affairs, Military Government, Department of Army), attended a conference in Okinawa the following week (August 17–21) that had been called by USCAR to discuss the issues involved in the reversion of Amami.[19] Conroy, who considered himself only an "observer," discovered that military officials in Okinawa still possessed "considerable apprehension . . . at times attempt[ing] to reopen the basic arguments against reversion." Nevertheless, he found their support helpful, with the "utmost cooperation" extended to him.

The eight conference participants discussed the economic considerations of reversion, such as currency conversion, the assumption of financial indebtedness by the Japanese, the transfer of credits, and future financing for public works already under progress; strategic considerations, such as the retention of existing military installations and provisions for construction of facilities required in future military plans; humanitarian issues, such as the repatriation of 40,000 to 50,000 Amami residents living in Okinawa; and, finally, the "full political significance" of the return. On occasion they also sought advice from the Chief Executive of the Ryukyu Islands, Higa Shuhei.

The participants of the four-day conference were able to draw up a report entitled "Recommended Basis for Agreement in Transfer of Administration of the Amami Islands to Japan" on the last day of the gathering to serve as the basis for understanding U.S. requirements when negotiating.[20] In fact, the Far East Command had received a joint State–Defense telegram from Washington that asked for the recommendation of General Clark's headquarters, and the document would serve as the basis on which Clark would respond.[21]

During these discussions, Conroy, as noted in his report to Samuel D. Berger, head of the political division of the embassy since August 1 and later ambassador to Korea, found that the military requested little in the way of actual facilities but desired that "provisions for their future needs be left as flexible as possible and that their rights of entry and restrictions on use of their installations be unlimited" and emphasized that "in their opinion an arrangement of future military rights under the Administrative Agreement would probably be unsatisfactory" because "it would place too many limitations on the types of operations contemplated in the Amami Islands, especially in the case of the outbreak of hostilities." This latter point was in direct contrast to the State Department's belief in the importance of applying the Security Treaty and related Administrative Agreement and would continue to be a point of contention in discussions both between State and military representatives within the U.S. government and between the U.S. and Japanese governments during negotiations that fall.[22]

In the meantime, on August 31 the Foreign Ministry had received word informally from the U.S. embassy that the U.S. government was shooting for October 5 for discussions to start and November 1 as the target date to return the islands, and the embassy and the Far Eastern Command were discussing what items needed to be decided upon.[23] In early September, the Foreign Ministry was told that the embassy would like to commence negotiations in the near future.

Initially there was an informal sense among representatives on the U.S. side that reversion would take place in early October. Shortly after this, a consensus was reached that reversion could take place on October 15, with November 1 as "an outside limit." Subsequently, as little progress was made in interagency discussions on the U.S. side due to differences on the question of the retention of military rights and other issues, as well as the fact that discussions were going on that time on the Mutual Security Act and U.S. requests for Japan's military build-up with Finance Minister Ikeda Hayato in Washington, the date of actual reversion became difficult to determine, as would the question about when to start formal negotiations with the Japanese side. Eventually, it was not until November 27 that formal talks actually began.

Essentially, prior to beginning negotiations with the Japanese side, the U.S. team had to come up with a unified position. In order to reach this consensus, several rounds of talks had to be held at different levels and venues to bring together the thinking from the different responsible parties. As looked at above, the first of these efforts was the USCAR-sponsored conference in Okinawa, attended by FEC officials and Conroy from the embassy. The result was the joint USCAR–FEC draft, which would then become the FEC draft. With this, the military and administrative requirements were essentially clarified, and it was now necessary to discuss the political consequences and diplomatic tactics to be taken, which involved FEC discussions with the embassy. When these talks were done, and a joint embassy–FEC draft appeared, it would then have to be approved in Washington by the secretary of state and concurred in by the JCS and the secretary of Defense.

The U.S. side established a joint embassy–FEC working group at the end of the summer and held its first meeting at the embassy in the afternoon of September 2 to consider the problems involved in the transfer of the islands.[24] Specifically the meeting, attended by Berger, Jules Bassin, legal attaché, Richard B. Finn, political officer, Conroy, Gillies, and Alfred C. Oppler, also of J-5, was held to discuss the timing of the actual transfer, the form and content of the transfer documents, and the degree of military rights to be guaranteed when transferring the islands.

As mentioned previously, these issues proved quite difficult to resolve. While there was general agreement on most of the issues, the question of the application of the Administrative Agreement saw fundamental differences highlighted. According to Conroy's memorandum of the meeting, he and his State Department colleagues emphasized that "it [was] impossible and most undesirable from a political standpoint to press the Japanese Government for different security arrangements in the Amami Islands than those granted in the rest of Japan." To this, the FEC representatives, echoing the view of their uniformed colleagues that Amami's geographical proximity to Okinawa placed it in a unique situation in which the military had special requirements, argued that the Amami Islands should be in a "separate status because use of military facilities there would be principally for the protection of, and in aid of military operations initiated on, Okinawa and other islands in the Pacific Far East." Finn, who had been serving in Tokyo since 1947 and was well acquainted with the security and diplomatic problems of such an approach, "refuted this argument" by observing that the Security Treaty "does not limit the use of Japanese bases and facilities," and its Article 1 clearly states that "such forces may be utilized to contribute to the maintenance of international peace and security *in the Far East*" (emphasized in original). According to Conroy, while the FEC representatives did not appear to be "fully convinced," they did agree that "at least a substantial portion of the demands for military rights contemplated could adequately be provided for" by applying the Security Treaty and Administrative Agreement.

In addition to the above working group, a Subcommittee on Financial Arrangements was also created, comprised of William Diehl, the treasury attaché, Conroy, Stuart H. Baron, and Ralph Phillips, J-5, FEC. This subcommittee held its first meeting the following day on September 3 at FEC headquarters and sought to work out the details of the financial issues in the transfer of the islands, taking up paragraphs 8 to 13 of the August 21 "Recommended Basis for Agreement" for discussion.

The embassy–FEC working group held its second meeting in the morning of September 10, with members of the above Subcommittee on Financial Arrangements also in attendance, followed by a third meeting the next day, starting at 2:00 P.M., adjourning at 5:30 P.M., and resuming the following morning (September 12) at 10:00 A.M.[25] These meetings were primarily devoted to reaching agreement on financial arrangements and the "joint economic message" to be sent to the Departments of State and Defense.[26]

Unfortunately, due to a bureaucratic miss by the Department of the Army, a joint embassy–FEC telegram of September 12 never made it to the State Department, and a critical ten days seem to have been lost.[27] However, in a telegram dated September 23, the State Department confirmed that, despite this loss in time, it still wished to go ahead with October 15 as the target date, although final instructions would have to await further discussion on the contents of the joint telegram and receive further recommendations from the embassy.

After a hiatus of almost three weeks, the embassy–FEC Joint Working Group met for its third meeting in the afternoon of September 29.[28] Symbolic of the fact that the issue of military rights had assumed greater importance in the discussions, more uniformed officers were represented, including Brig. Gen. M. C. McDaniel, the assistant chief-of-staff for the Air Force, Far East, Col. Donn Hart, J-3, FEC, and Col. Frank J. Holzapfel, also of J-3, and the embassy staff was fortified with Finn, who, as we saw above, did not hesitate to defend the State Department's position in earlier meetings.

Gen. McDaniel, who had been appointed Special Representative of CINCFE for the meeting, opened it by stating that CINCFE believed that the Amami Islands "must continue in some way to be 'controlled' for the defense of Okinawa itself" and that "future military rights in the Amami Islands must be divorced from plans for the rest of the Japanese archipelago.'" Essentially, according to the memorandum of conversation prepared by Berger and his staff, the FEC thought that the United States "should not be encumbered by the procedures of the Administrative Agreement and must consider the future when Japan may not be amenable to voluntarily granting us any rights."

Reviewing the FEC draft note on "Arrangements for Military Rights," the State Department representatives stated that the note did not "vary substantially from embassy thinking," but that the "heart of the question" appeared to be whether those requirements could be obtained through the application of the Security Treaty or necessitated an "additional guarantee of U.S. rights which go beyond" it. To this, the FEC representatives "indicated a strong desire to avoid the necessity of using machinery" such as the Joint Committee, established in 1952 as per Article 26 of the Administrative Agreement (see appendix 4), to secure future requirements. Berger argued that the machinery is "not nearly as cumbersome" as the military believed and pointed out that the Administrative Agreement includes all of the rights necessary and that "its use [was] greatly preferable to a new procedure for obtaining requirements."

As an example, Berger and his colleagues referred to paragraph 5, Article IV of the FEC-drafted note that requests the "unilateral right for the U.S. to take whatever land it desires." Gen. McDaniel interrupted to point out that "military interests" in Okinawa "require" the United States to "have the ability in the Amami Islands to take immediate action at any time and that such action would be impossible" under the Administrative Agreement. Berger shot back, arguing that the FEC note was "tantamount to a request for extraterritorial rights over a part of Japan," something that would be "wholly unacceptable" to the Japanese government and "deleterious to U.S.–Japan relations." Forcing the issue, he continued, it "could destroy the salutary effect of the original announcement of the Islands' return."

Berger then explained the embassy-drafted proposal, dated September 24. A one-paragraph note, it read:

It is recognized that on November 1, 1953, the Security Treaty between the United States and Japan and any implementing arrangements thereunder will apply to the Amami Islands in the Nansei Shoto. In Article II, paragraph 1 of the Administrative Agreement, it is stipulated that "agreements as to specific facilities and areas, not already reached by the two Governments by the effective date of this agreement, shall be concluded by the two Governments through the Joint Committee provided for in Article XXVI of this agreement." It is understood that consultation and agreement regarding facilities and areas in the Amami Islands to be used by the United States forces shall be on an urgent basis and at the earliest possible date. Pending the completion of such arrangements, it is understood that the Government of Japan agrees to grant the continued use of those particular facilities and areas presently retained or in use by the United States Armed Forces in the Amami Islands.

Berger explained that the draft recognized the application of the Administrative Agreement and provided for the retention of facilities, and he suggested that "FEC objections" could be met by "extending" the embassy draft or by including in the U.S. note "an understanding that Japan recognizes the special character of Okinawa and the close strategic relation of the Amami Islands to Okinawa." Legal attaché Bassin pointed out that even that proposal would be "difficult to sell" to the Japanese government "but could possibly be done, whereas the FEC approach would never be accepted."

After discussion of the question as to how to go about securing "all the FEC demands" without a direct statement in the official notes, embassy representatives suggested that if the military still believed that "specific concessions were required" from the Japanese side, "unpublished minutes" could possibly be used. Eventually this is the approach that would be taken some two months later, but Gen. McDaniel at this point "demurred," arguing that in "his opinion . . . Amami is different from any 'base situation' elsewhere in the world." In other places, he continued, "we negotiate with a sovereign nation for what we want, whereas here we are giving back something and are not required to negotiate for or to give back anything we desire to keep." In response, Berger "reiterated" that such a position would be "resisted to the utmost" by the Japanese government and even if it were successfully "driven through" as a condition for the return of the islands, "it would leave a 'festering sore' which would harm our longer-term relations with Japan" and would also open up the United States to accusations that it had "established extraterritoriality" over parts of Japan.

At the end of this heated and exhaustive exchange, the representatives agreed that the embassy and FEC would draft alternative proposals and seek an agreed method of securing military requirements "without giving the appearance of making unreasonable demands" upon Japan.

With the October 15 deadline rapidly approaching and with Washington "awaiting our joint recommendations," the Joint Working Group met again later in the week on October 1 for its fourth meeting.[29] The participants examined the embassy's proposed text of the "U.S. Note" to be included in the agreement explaining U.S. intentions to return the islands and its views on related issues. The embassy draft was adopted, with minor changes added and minus paragraph 4 of the note, which read:

> The United States will continue to maintain the degree of control and authority now exercised over the other islands of the Nansei Shoto under Article 3 of the Peace Treaty so as to permit the United States to continue to carry out effectively its responsibilities under the Security Treaty between the United States and Japan and to contribute to the maintenance of peace and security in the area.

The FEC representatives, on the other hand, suggested the following version of paragraph 4:

> The proposed relinquishment of governmental authority over the Amami Islands by the U.S. Government does not in any way alter or affect the powers of the U.S. of America under Article 3 of the Peace Treaty insofar as they apply to the other islands of the Nansei Shoto. The U.S. will continue to exercise these powers until the Pacific area is no longer threatened by any expanding imperialism and until enduring conditions of peace and stability prevail in the Far East.

The embassy representatives, who preferred simple wording, objected strongly to the phrasing of the second sentence because it, in their opinion, "subject[s] the U.S. retention of the remaining islands to more limited contingencies than those stated in Article 3, and open[s] the door to Japanese claims in the future that the stated conditions exist and that the U.S. is therefore committed to leave the islands."

In the end, the working group agreed to forward the proposed text on to Washington, with its internal disagreements on paragraph 4 clearly spelled out.

The working group then turned its attention to the FEC draft on military rights. The embassy side raised objections to all of the paragraphs in the first section, "Arrangements for Military Rights," because "neither the form nor the substance of these paragraphs had any place in the exchange of notes contemplated." The embassy representatives added that if these points were "deemed essential to the U.S. position," they could be included in the negotiations and recorded in the minutes.

Paragraph 4 was also found to be objectionable to the embassy. It read:

> Now therefore, the rights provided for in the following Special Arrangements are being reserved within the area specified . . . by the United States and will be retained as long as the United States continues to maintain military bases in the remaining Islands of the Nansei Shoto. This reservation will not lose its effect if, for any reason, the Security Treaty Between the United States of America and Japan and/or the Administrative Agreement under Article III thereof have expired while the United States continues to maintain aforementioned bases.

Because it "attached to the transfer of the islands a series of 'reservations,'" it would undoubtedly be "unacceptable" to the Japanese side, embassy officials argued. Bassin chimed in saying that it "in effect created a new Security Treaty with Japan with respect to these islands." After this exchange, the remainder of the afternoon was devoted to examining the rest of the FEC draft, which saw numerous other differences arise, as well as the embassy draft of the unpublished minutes.

In an attempt to overcome the "difference in approach" between the embassy and the FEC, Allison met with Gen. John E. Hull on October 14.[30] Allison found Hull "very cooperative," offering suggestions "to reconcile divergences." Nevertheless, further examination by the respective staffs had not "resolve[d] the fundamental point of difference," Allison noted. In the end, despite "long and amicable discussions" in the working group, the embassy, on October 14, telegrammed the department that it "regret[ted it was] unable [to] reach agreement due [to] fundamental difference[s] in approach to [the] problem."[31]

The different approaches to the problem on the question of military rights were essentially the ones examined above but were spelled out clearly in this telegram. "The heart of the difference," Allison pointed out, was that the FEC "seeks [to] reserve at time of transfer broad rights granted under peace treaty which may be exercised unilaterally in Amamis and their territorial waters. Secondly, FEC proposes [the] establish[ment of] joint machinery outside security treaty and administrative agreement through which United States would exercise these rights." The embassy position, on the other hand, was, as we have seen, "predicated on the application of the security treaty and administrative agreement to Amamis." It explained that its objections to the FEC position were based on the following considerations.

Firstly, the embassy believed it would be "impossible" to get the concurrence of Japan in the reservation by the United States of rights which "would be tantamount to retaining extraterritorial status" in the Amami Islands. "No Japanese Government," the embassy cautioned, "could survive such an arrangement and if it was our intention to relinquish [the] islands on this basis, we should have never made the announcement."

Secondly, the embassy argued that the Japanese government would "never accept" the return of the Amami Islands under conditions "substantially different" from those in the rest of Japan. "Any attempt," it warned, "to negotiate on [the] FEC basis [will] likely result in a long and bitter wrangle and [the] great psychological boon which accompanied [the] Secretary's announcement would be nullified."

Thirdly, the embassy pointed out that the FEC approach was based on the assumption that Okinawa "must be safeguarded by defense perimeter against future contingency when [the] security treaty may no longer be tenable," and American troops "may be forced to retire from Japan because of Japanese neutrality or unfriendliness." The embassy countered, however, that "under such circumstances . . . all basic . . . [U.S.] assumptions regarding this area would need to be re-examined" and stated that it failed to see "how [the] United States position in Amami would be secure if our position became untenable in the rest of Japan."

Finally, the embassy pointed out that an "inherent contradiction seemed to exist in the FEC approach. Essentially, "none" of the rights the FEC was seeking to reserve "could be effectively exercised in the absence of Japanese cooperation. This being the case," Allison continued, "we fail to see why [the] Security Pact and Administrative Agreement are not adequate."

By chance, on the next day, October 15—the initial internal deadline set for the return of the islands—the embassy received an informal visit by Tsurumi Kiyohiko, the chief of the 5th Section of the Asian Affairs Bureau of the Foreign Ministry, who would be one of those tasked with negotiating the terms of the reversion.[32] Tsurumi asked about the starting date of negotiations and noted that the respective ministries on the Japanese side had already "thoroughly investigated the problems" involved that would require negotiation. Conroy explained that the U.S. side had also "made a full study of the matter" and that negotiations could begin "as soon as" final instructions had been received.

As if to emphasize the concern on the Japanese side with the delay in the start of discussions, Foreign Minister Okazaki spoke with Allison the following week on the morning of October 20.[33] Okazaki explained that a special Diet session would convene at the end of the month and it would be necessary to submit the budget for the coming year's expenses for the islands. The foreign minister stated that while the exact date was not necessary for inclusion in the legislation itself, the government would have to mention the approximate date of return, and he "hoped it would be able to say the islands would be returned on or about December 1." Allison, who also wished to see the early and smooth return of the islands, explained that he could give no definite response but "hoped it would be possible to meet his desires."

The ambassador mentioned to Okazaki that it was necessary to reach agreement on the military facilities to be retained, and he revealed that "one of [the] difficulties" was the "close relationship which the Amami group bears to the security of Okinawa" and thus the necessity of "devising some method of insuring that future developments would not menace that security." Okazaki, according to Allison, "appeared most understanding," stating that "he was certain [his] government would go to great lengths to meet American desires." Okazaki added that if the U.S. military listed the "rights and facilities it might need in [the] future," he believed his government "would at any time be willing to negotiate . . . for such rights or facilities."

Allison was obviously moved by Okazaki's overture. "I believe," Allison wrote in a telegram to Dulles, "Okazaki reflects the true cooperative attitude of Japanese Government toward this question and that if we approach them on reasonable basis, we can obtain all our legitimate needs. However, if we demand everything in writing in first instance, thereby indicating to Japanese our distrust of their goodwill, I seriously doubt that [the] present cooperative attitude will be maintained." The State Department immediately responded, explaining that it "concur[red in the] inadvisab[ility of] initiat[ing] discussions with [the] Japanese [side] until resolution [of] military arrangements [issue]" and "intend[ed to] attempt [to] immediately narrow areas [of] disagreement" with the remaining issues to be submitted to the Operations Coordinating Board, a policy implementation body, or the NSC for "final determination."[34]

In the meantime, the JCS confirmed their views on military requirements in the Amami Islands in a letter to the secretary of Defense, dated October 16.[35] Specifically, the JCS, which had been studying this issue intensively since the summer, called for the necessity of "reserving military rights" in the islands for an "indefinite period after their return" to Japan "in view of the strategic importance of the Amami Islands in relation to our bases in Okinawa" and for "a clear statement of United States intentions with respect to the remainder of the islands enumerated in Article 3 of the Peace Treaty until enduring conditions of peace and stability prevail in the Far East," views with which Assistant Secretary of Defense Frank C. Nash informed Robertson he concurred.[36]

Discussions continued at the working level back in Washington through the remainder of October between the Departments of State, Defense, and Treasury, and, on October 29, Robertson informed Undersecretary of State Smith that agreement had been reached at the staff level on the text of the exchange of notes between the United States and Japan effecting the transfer.[37] The note was to contain a unilateral statement that "pending the establishment of enduring conditions of peace and stability in the Far East," the United Stated did not intend to modify the degree of control and authority it exercised in the remainder of the Ryukyus.

In addition, Robertson told Smith that his bureau had proposed to the Defense Department, in place of the FEC–JCS proposal for special arrangements, an enclosure to the exchange of notes which would apply the Security Treaty and Administrative Agreement to the Amami Islands while establishing "Japanese recognition of the unique strategic relationship" existing between the Amami group and Okinawa. In unpublished minutes, "certain of those special rights" in the Amami Islands, desired by the JCS to be viewed as "politically negotiable" and not clearly stated in the Administrative Agreement, would be spelled out. A second enclosure, Robertson explained, would provide for U.S. retention of the facilities now held and any additional ones the JCS, whose "primary concern [was] the effectiveness and protection of the . . . radar system" in the Amami Islands, think the U.S. military might need in the future.

According to Robertson, the Defense Department "liked" his bureau's proposal and was submitting it to the JCS. The embassy also approved the proposal, which was expected as the embassy had done much of the original work on it. In addition, Robertson relayed to Smith that Nash had told him that the JCS would consider the proposal "within the week." However, conscious of time, Robertson told Smith that "if further delay is encountered," he would ask him to take up the matter directly with the Defense Department.

Robertson had reason to be concerned about the increasing delay. The initial internal deadline of October 15 had long since passed, and the "outer limit" set in September of November 1 was just a couple of days around the corner. Moreover' in Tokyo, Tsurumi had told an embassy official that he was concerned over a message the Foreign Ministry had received from its embassy in Washington that a State Department official had indicated that negotiations on the return of the islands would not commence "until late December."[38] Tsurumi warned that the delay in the transfer of the islands until "sometime [in] 1954" would "result in adverse public reaction [in] Japan and Amami and arouse suspicion [of] U.S. intentions and conditions surrounding transfer." Although Conroy, in drafting the message sent out in Allison's name, added that he thought Tsurumi "exaggerate[d the] adverse effect on Japanese opinion," he did think it "would be unfortunate if this matter [were] delayed" and expressed his hope that the State Department would "press for [an] immediate decision."

Robertson and Dulles did not need any convincing and responded to the embassy's telegram with their own in which they wrote that they "expect[ed] reconciliation [of] State-Defense position[s] within 10 days."[39] Dulles also told the embassy that they had informed Ambassador Araki of their "hope [that the] transfer [could be] accomplished shortly before [the] end of year if not sooner."

When no response was heard from Defense as of November 10, Robertson recommended, as he had laid out in the October 29 memorandum, that Smith call Undersecretary of Defense Roger M. Kyes directly and urge an "immediate settlement . . . on the terms proposed" by the Bureau of Far Eastern Affairs and that Defense agree to informing the Japanese government that the transfer of the islands back to Japan would take place on December 1.

It is unclear whether Smith placed the call, but shortly after he submitted his memo to the undersecretary, Robertson also sent Nash a letter on November 13 requesting "a prompt indication as to whether" the State Department-prepared documents were "satisfactory" to Defense as the basis for negotiations with the Japanese government.[40]

During this time, pressure had been building from the Japanese side, as seen by the visit of Tsuchiya Jun, director of the Europe and North American Division of the Foreign Ministry, who called on the embassy on Sunday, November

130 ～ Chapter Five

8, to explain that the delay in the return of the islands was "becoming a matter of increasing concern," particularly in light of the "mounting pressure and criticism [of] U.S. inaction reflected" in the Diet session the week before. He informed the embassy that Okazaki was requesting Araki to propose December 1 as the "effective date [of] reversion."[41]

Conroy, who met with Tsuchiya, expressed his frustration in a telegram to the State Department the next day and urged consideration at the highest levels of unresolved issues:

> [the] US [is] in danger [of] creating needless irritation and suspicion and possible resentment which could impede other negotiations here unless we speedily conclude arrangements for Amami transfer. Fact we can neither sit down with Japanese to work out arrangements nor tell them what is delaying matters is obviously detrimental to our relations and is [a] source of embarrassment to Foreign Office in dealing with Diet and public. I would urge matters still unagreed between State and Defense be raised for resolution at NSC meeting this week if possible and that we or Department give Japanese definite date for opening negotiations.

With no answer forthcoming, Tsurumi of the Foreign Ministry visited the embassy later that week on November 12 to "determine" whether the embassy could agree to December 1 as the date for "actual transfer" of the islands and, if that were not possible, that the transfer date be the first piece of business during the negotiations.[42] Tsurumi explained, as had Tsuchiya before him, that the Japanese government was proceeding on the assumption that December 1 would be the target date and was hoping to send a Maritime Safety Agency ship carrying supplies, police, and government officials on November 20 to begin local preparations for the transfer. Conroy was not able to give a direct answer on the exact date but promised to fix the transfer date "as early as possible and far enough in advance" to insure a smooth transition.

Tsurumi's visit to the embassy was followed by one from Minister Takeuchi Ryuji to the State Department on the same day in Washington to meet with Deputy Assistant Secretary for the Far East Everett F. Drumright and McClurkin. Takeuchi, on instructions from the Foreign Ministry, asked that December 1 be the effective date of transfer of the islands, explaining that: 1) commercial transactions are "grinding to a halt" due to the uncertainty about the transfer date; 2) two week's prior notice was necessary to make arrangements for the transfer; 3) a second special Diet session was expected to begin in early December; and 4) the opposition parties were exploiting the fact that the transfer has yet to take place.[43] Drumright's answer, like that of Conroy, was sympathetic but noncommittal as the State Department was still waiting for a response from Defense.

The Japanese side nevertheless continued with its inquiries. Subjected to "thrice-daily pressure" from the Foreign Ministry, Ambassador Allison wrote on November 18 to the department explaining that he considered "the commencement [of the] Amami negotiations [a] matter of greatest urgency" and warned that the "situation here has reached [a] serious stage, and [the] Amami Oshima relinquishment is now beginning to boomerang against us."[44]

Allison's message hints that he may have become aware of the petitions, rallies, and hunger strikes that were taking place in Amami and elsewhere due to the "delay" in the return. The most recent rally was held on November 10 in Naze and was followed two days later by a symbolic twelve-hour hunger strike by 1,300 children in Amami on November 12.[45] Local leaders and their supporters in Japan were concerned about the fate of their islands. Just as they had been in a "vacuum" back in 1946, when the MacArthur's headquarters separated the islands from Japanese administration but had not begun the military occupation of the islands, the people once again found themselves in a state of "limbo" after the U.S. government had announced its intention to return the islands without a timeline.

Anticipating a decision by the Defense Department, Robertson drafted an order that same day for Dulles' signature, instructing him to inform Ambassador Allison to start negotiations as soon as he had received clearance from the Pentagon. Word came on November 20.

In a letter to Robertson, Assistant Secretary of Defense Nash approved going ahead with negotiations, but he cautioned the State Department's proposal as "the minimum position" acceptable to the Defense Department and urged that if it seemed those rights could not be obtained during the negotiations, "the entire matter should be reconsidered by our departments."[46] Nash promised, in any case, the full support and "necessary technical assistance" of the FEC in the conduct of negotiations, and he requested that the Department of Defense be kept abreast of the progress of the negotiations.

Robertson, based on the instructions Dulles had agreed to and signed two days before, immediately sent a telegram to Allison to inform him that he was authorized to "undertake negotiations [for the] Amami transfer."[47] Reflecting the difficult discussions the State and Defense had had, Robertson noted that "Defense concurs but considers position reflected in documents in following cable minimum acceptable." Three days later in the late afternoon of November 24, Allison sent word to the Foreign Ministry that the U.S. side would like to begin negotiations and submitted the U.S. text and enclosures for its consideration.[48]

Included among them was the problematic issue of military rights, which took the form, as suggested earlier, of "unpublished minutes."[49]

1. Article II, paragraph 1, of the Administrative Agreement is understood to constitute recognition that the unique relationship of the Amami Islands to the defense and security of both Japan and the United States may require that additional facilities and areas in the Amami Islands (including the sites for navigational aids, devices, and aircraft control and warning sites needed to insure complete radio and radar coverage) be granted to the United States.
2. Article II, paragraph 1, of the Administrative Agreement is understood to extend freedom of air space to all areas over the Amami Islands and their territorial waters.
3. Article II, paragraph 1, of the Administrative Agreement is understood to permit the United States to utilize in connection with the carrying out of the Security Treaty all territorial waters of the Amami Islands.
4. Article II, paragraph 1, of the Administrative Agreement is understood to permit authorized personnel of the United States, upon notification to the Government of Japan, to conduct site surveys in the Amami Islands in connection with the selection of land areas for additional facilities as may be requested in the future.
5. Articles II and III are understood to permit the entry of the Armed Forces of the United States into the land area of the Amami Islands, the air space above them, and their territorial waters for the purpose of removing or destroying any hostile or nuisance device such as, but not limited to, electronic-jamming facilities which might interfere with the effective operations of United States military forces and installations.
6. Article III, paragraph 1, is understood to provide for consultation between the United States and Japan concerning possible future Japanese plans for the establishment of defense facilities in the Amami Islands.
7. It is understood that the exchange of notes between the secretary of state and the prime minister, dated September 8, 1951, is applicable to the Amami Oshima group.

With the submission of these materials to the Japanese side, the first round of "negotiations" was over, among parties concerned within the U.S. government anyway.

The Reversion Negotiations

The First General Meeting on the transfer arrangements between representatives of the United States and Japan was held at 9:30 A.M. on November 27 at the Foreign Ministry.[50] The United States was represented primarily by those that had participated in the earlier interagency discussions, namely, Berger, Bassin, Conroy, Finn, Gillies, Baron, and Hart, now working as one team.[51] The Japanese negotiating team was made up of Nakagawa Toru, director of the Asian Affairs Bureau, Shigemitsu Ao of the Treaty Bureau, Tsurumi, Yasukawa Takeshi, Saeki Mamoru, and Sasaki Seiken, also of the 5th Section, Asian Affairs Bureau.

Nakagawa, anxious to have the negotiations concluded as early as possible, voiced his desire to set a date for the transfer of the islands.[52] Berger did not commit to a date but instead explained that the arrangements had been made to accommodate transfer as soon as notes were exchanged. He cautioned that the more changes in the draft agreement the Japanese side sought, the greater the potential for delay and difficulty in getting approval back in Washington, including Congress.

Despite this warning, the Japanese side stated that it did have some problems with "certain points" that "required modification"—points, in Nakagawa's view, "illegal if not unconstitutional." Tsurumi then expressed the views of the Japanese side with regard to financial arrangements, claims waivers, recognition of military court rulings, and other financial and administrative issues. These problems were referred to a Subcommittee on Financial Arrangements to meet later that day.

The discussions next turned to military arrangements. Yasukawa, later ambassador to the United States (1973–1976), delivered the following simple counter-proposal, meant to replace the first paragraph of the document "U.S. Enclosure I" and all of "U.S. Enclosure II" submitted on November 24.[53]

As from _____, 1953 the Security Treaty between Japan and the United States of America and any implementing arrangement thereunder will be applicable to the Amami Islands of the Nansei Shoto.

The Governments of the United States of America and of Japan have agreed that the two installations and sites precently [sic] utilized by the United States Government in the Amami Islands will be continuously used by the United States Armed Forces after _____, 1953 pending the decision through consultations by the Joint Committee as provided for in Article XXVI of the Administrative Agreement under Article III of the Security Treaty between Japan and the United States of America.

As Allison told the State Department, the embassy had "no objections" to the Japanese suggestion but was "reserving recommendation" to State "until picture of whole Japanese position . . . is clearer."[54] Berger told his Japanese counterparts that his team would study the draft and noted that the "unusual relationship" of Amami to Okinawa "required special recognition" by Japan.

Yasukawa stated that the Japanese side was aware of that but believed the "additional expression" of Japan's "recognition of this relationship" would be covered in the Agreed Official Minutes. The two sides decided to take up the issue in the Subcommittee on Military Rights.

Another problem that emerged was the use of the word "agreement" in the U.S. draft. The Japanese side argued that the word had a "formal denotation which would necessitate Diet approval" and requested that alternate phrasing (that they would submit) be considered. The Japanese side probably feared opening up a "Pandora's box," which could, depending on the contents, embarrass the government and, at the minimum, delay the return of the islands.

Symbolic of the fact that the two sides had agreed to carry out negotiations on "an urgent basis," a smaller Subcommittee on Military Rights was held on the afternoon of Saturday (November 28) at the Foreign Ministry.[55] Tsurumi and Yasukawa, representing the Foreign Ministry, attended, as did Conroy, Gillies, Hart, and Col. Harold A. Thompson, a member of the Joint Committee on Administrative Agreement, making up the U.S. team.

Yasukawa submitted a new proposal on Enclosure I, which was a revised version of the draft submitted the day before and shown above. He explained that in either case, the "main" Japanese objection to the U.S. draft was that it "removed" the agreement on existing facilities "from the hands" of the Joint Committee "where it properly belonged," and he stated that the Japanese side proposed referring the matter of facilities currently being used by the U.S. military to the Joint Committee for "immediate action" and that their "pick up" would be concluded before the notes were exchanged. Thompson objected to this due to the time constraints and inability to provide detailed information on the facilities on short notice. The Japanese side then suggested that it would be willing to include in its draft wording similar to that of the Rusk–Okazaki formula (of February 1952—see appendix 5) that would allow the United States to continue to use the facilities until the completion of consideration by the Joint Committee. The subcommittee agreed to refer the issue to the next General Meeting, scheduled for the 30th.

Discussion then turned to the phrase on Japanese recognition of the "unique relationship" of Amami to Okinawa, which was still missing from the second Japanese draft. Conroy pointed out that the issue was of "primary concern" to the U.S. government and that the U.S. side "would continue to insist" that it be specifically stated in the enclosure. This issue was also referred to the next General Meeting.

Yasukawa then turned to specific clauses in the U.S. draft of Agreed Official Minutes, which requested unusually broad rights. The two sides argued about each point, with Yasukawa suggesting that the concerns could be met by the existing Security Treaty and Administrative Agreement, and the U.S. side pointing out that narrow interpretations were also possible and thus, because the United States required "considerable freedom" in these matters, the U.S. government "would appreciate Japan's express understanding." These issues, too, were referred to the next General Meeting.

The Second General Meeting took place in the morning of November 30, again at the Foreign Ministry building and attended by the same members.[56] Berger opened the meeting by stressing the importance of a "specific reference" to the "unique relationship" of Amami to Okinawa, either in the notes or enclosure. Highlighting the differences in expectations the two sides held, Tsurumi stated that the Japanese side wished to have that reference omitted "so as to reassure the Japanese people and not disappoint the Okinawans who also desired reversion to Japan." Berger explained that "this was exactly the point that the U.S. wished to clarify—that the Amami transfer was not a first step and that other islands would be under full U.S. administration for an indefinite period." The participants agreed to further discussions in the Subcommittee on Military Rights meeting, to be held the next day.

Subsequently, the subcommittee met at the embassy in the morning of December 1 for its second meeting. The Japanese side, led by Tsurumi, submitted new proposals on military rights for the U.S. side to review and suggested that they should appear in the agreed official minutes "which should probably be unpublished." The U.S. side said that the draft "would probably be satisfactory" and that the Subcommittee should refer the issue to the General Meeting on December 2.

The Japanese side next delivered a revised draft to replace the U.S. enclosures, stating that the Japanese side had to "insist" on using the Joint Committee when obtaining facilities. However, it would be "prepared to give its fullest cooperation to the U.S. side on all matters affecting Amami," including "resort to eminent domain." The subcommittee agreed that this draft met "most of the points" raised by the U.S. side and that it would refer the matter to the General Meeting.

The Japanese side next submitted a three-part document meant to replace all of the other draft Agreed Minutes prepared by the U.S. side and asked that the contents be "adopted" by the Joint Committee as its official minutes. After some discussion of the contents, the subcommittee decided to recommend to the General Meeting that it "appeared" to be the "best obtainable solution under the circumstances."

To take up all of these matters, the Third General Meeting was held in the morning of the next day, December 3, at the Foreign Ministry.[57] However, due to the "flood of new written proposals . . . [and] close scheduling of the meetings," the U.S. side, Berger admitted, had little chance to give careful consideration to the Japanese proposals. Berger requested that the next General Meeting not be held until December 7 and reminded the Japanese side that the embassy had little authority to change the original U.S. proposals.

In light of all the activity, Allison, on December 4, went ahead and reported to Washington that the "Japanese [were] moving fast in [the] Amami negotiations."[58] Allison explained that the Japanese government was "anxious [for] exchange of notes [to] occur next week if possible" because ten days were needed to make necessary arrangements locally, and thus the "hope is [that] actual transfer can occur [on] December 20 at latest in advance of long New Year holiday." He noted that negotiations have been "intense" but "amicable," being "largely devoted to [finding] solution[s to] difficulties which substance [of] U.S. draft presents for Japan. [The] underlying principle of resistance encountered," Allison pointed out, is that the Japanese government "cannot go beyond [the] terms of [the] administrative agreement, Japanese constitution, or applicable laws." These differences were now "crystallized," the Ambassador reported, and "compromise wording on most points at issue is being finalized subject to Washington approval." He also pointed out that the essence of U.S. desires is being "obtained with only minor concessions," and he would send the text by telegram as soon as the agreed wording on individual items was settled by his negotiators. Allison requested "urgent action" on these telegrams in order to accommodate the Japanese side's good faith in the negotiations.

While these discussions were going on, Allison had been meeting with Gen. Hull to discuss the wording of a draft statement on Okinawa and Ogasawara to be made by the secretary of state at the time of the transfer of Amami. Both men, particularly Hull who had just come back from a visit to Okinawa, were concerned about "irrendentist activity" there and that the draft statement was "not adequate or affirmative enough to make our position clear."[59] In a November 28 telegram, Allison urged that a "positive statement," making clear the U.S. "intention [to] maintain indefinitely present rights" in Okinawa, be made and suggested that such a statement should be made in Washington by the secretary of state "in order to give the statement [the] full weight of [the] U.S. government."

On December 5, the ambassador sent a draft text to the Department for the Secretary's consideration.[60] A week later, Allison urged further consideration, arguing that it seemed to him that "frequent reiteration that United States may relinquish control [of] remaining islands is academic since there is no present intention of doing so and merely gives continuing impetus to irredentist elements."[61]

As Allison was discussing with Washington the larger geopolitical concerns, his staff continued negotiations with the Japanese side on the transfer arrangements, with financial and legal issues remaining somewhat complicated. Eventually, however, on December 18, the embassy sent the final negotiated text to Washington and recommended approval of it.[62]

Both the State and Defense Departments were dissatisfied with the recommendations, however, responding by telegram that they were "concerned" that the proposal would "effectuate [the] transfer" on December 25 based on an agreement "which Japanese [are] not finally committed [to] until after subsequent Diet approval."[63] The "implication is," the response continued, that the U.S. government had "surrendered [its] rights [under Article 3 of the Peace Treaty] without any legally binding guarantee [of] Japanese acceptance [of] conditions [for the] transfer." Dulles urged Allison to "explore with [the] Japanese side to fullest possible extent [the] use [of] language" other than what was contained in the embassy's recommendations. While the State Department's legal adviser had agreed that the language might "be acceptable in light [of the] urgency [of the] situation since [U.S.] rights [are] not finally relinquished until agreement effected," which would permit transfer by December 25, Dulles noted that the Defense Department argued that the U.S. government "should not agree [to the] transfer prior [to] final and authoritative Japanese government acceptance" of the agreement, "including Diet ratification if required."

Allison responded later that day after receiving Dulles' message and informed the State Department that the embassy was discussing the issue with the Japanese side.[64] The matter became all the more pressing because of a leak from the Foreign Ministry that the transfer of the islands would take place on December 25, with the press calling for confirmation and residents in Amami celebrating based on the Foreign Ministry's information. Allison urged the State Department to "give us [its] final views" on the proposed agreement "so we can meet [the] dateline if at all possible."

In the meantime, the embassy got word that the Japanese government agreed to revise a paragraph to clearly bind the government to the agreement effective December 25.[65] Shimoda Takezo, chief of the Treaty Bureau of the Foreign Ministry, according to the telegram, explained that Diet action was an "internal Japanese affair" and that the Japanese government was "prepared [to] accept full political responsibility for committing Japan to [a] binding agreement." The embassy pointed out to the State Department that it believed the "unqualified character" of the revisions "meets [any] difficulty give rising [to your] concerns."[66]

Time was running out for reversion within the year, as the Diet was only in session for another few days (until December 24). Allison wrote to the secretary on the evening of December 21 to tell him that the Japanese Cabinet was meeting at that very moment to decide whether to submit the agreement to the Diet for approval prior to the signing of it by Japan.[67] As Allison explained, several ministers felt that because the Diet was in session (although not meeting), "constitutional precedent" necessitated the agreement to be submitted before signing. The Foreign ministry, Allison reported, was confident that if such were the case, a "Diet quorum" would be possible with "quick approval with support from all parties" except possibly the Communist Party and Left Socialists. To be on the safe side, Allison requested instructions before December 23 in order to meet Foreign Ministry desires for a U.S. decision by that day "at [the] latest" to permit Diet deliberations on the 24th.

Shortly after Allison sent off the telegram, the embassy received word from a Foreign Ministry official that the cabinet had, in fact, decided to convene a full Diet session on the 24th.[68] An embassy representative told the official, Allison explained, that the embassy "could give no assurance" that it would be authorized to conclude an agreement soon, "although every effort was being made to do so." Although Allison did not need to restate it again here, it is clear he hoped to meet the Japanese desires on the time schedule.

The State Department wrote to Allison later that day expressing "regret" that it was "impossible" to get final clearance that day, but that it "hope[d] to do so tomorrow."[69] Due to the time differences, "tomorrow" essentially meant late on the 23rd or early the 24th. Time was truly running short.

Dulles' approval came by telegram at 9:20 A.M. on the 24th, after a final flurry of exchanges.[70] It was conditioned on rewording of transfer documents to incorporate changes the State Department requested in the same telegram. Revised, the agreement was submitted by the Japanese government to the Diet on the 24th, being approved shortly after 5:00 P.M.

After a hectic day, at 6:30 P.M. at the Foreign Ministry, Allison and Okazaki, representing the United States and Japan respectively, signed the agreement returning the Amami Islands to Japan, bringing to an end some four and a half months of anxiety over the preparations for the return of the islands.[71]

At the time of the signing, Okazaki read the following prepared statement expressing his country's appreciation for the transfer of the islands:

The reunion of the Amami archipelago with the mainland of Japan has been long and eagerly awaited for not only by the 200,000 islanders but by the entire people of our country. To this fervent national aspiration of the Japanese people the American government has happily responded. It was on the 8th of

Figure 5.2. U.S. Ambassador John M. Allison and Japanese Foreign Minister Okazaki Katso at the Signing Ceremony, Foreign Ministry, December 24, 1953

August last that Mr. John Foster Dulles, while on his visit to Tokyo, announced his government's intention to relinquish its rights over those islands in favor of Japan, which finds a concrete expression in the instrument now ready for signature today. I am convinced that the action taken by the United States Government in this matter, manifesting America's good will and understanding toward Japan, will contribute vastly to the furtherance of the close bond of friendship existing between our two countries.

To this, Ambassador Allison expressed U.S. satisfaction with the transfer:

By this agreement, the United States of America relinquishes in favor of Japan the rights which the United States has exercised under the provisions of Article 3 of the Treaty of Peace signed at San Francisco on September 8, 1951. In a statement made at Tokyo on August 8, 1953, Secretary of State Dulles announced the intention of the United States to relinquish these rights to Japan. The intervening weeks have witnessed careful preparations by both Governments for this event. Our mutual desires have ever been to effect this transfer in such a manner as to cause the least possible disruption to the everyday lives of the inhabitants of the Amami Islands. I believe we can see the attainment of these desires in the agreement before us and in the arrangements which have been made to carry it into effect. On behalf of the United

States of America I extend to the Japanese citizens of the Amami Islands every good wish for the peace and prosperity of their islands in this, their reunion with the homeland of Japan.

That evening, Yoshida wrote to Dulles personally to let him know that the bill approving the agreement on the "Reunion of [the] Amami Islands" had just passed both Houses of the Diet by unanimous vote, along with resolutions of "Thanksgiving" in the House of Representatives and "Felicitations" in the Upper House.[72] "All Japanese are happy and grateful," Yoshida told Dulles. "Thanks to you for this big Xmas present."

While it was indeed an occasion for happiness, not only for the islanders but for the representatives of the U.S. and Japanese governments as a testimony to U.S. ideals and the strength of the bilateral relationship, the celebration was not long lasting, however, as discussed in the last chapter.

The Reversion Ceremony in Naze

Arrangements for the transfer of the islands had been proceeding at the local level for some time and, on December 25, U.S., Japanese, and local officials gathered at the American Cultural Center Hall to mark the occasion. James V. Martin Jr., U.S. consul general, Fukuoka, representing Ambassador Allison and later involved in the negotiations on the revision of the security treaty, Public Affairs Officer Clifton B. Forster, and Col. S. B. Dishman, Deputy Civil Adm., USCAR, representing Gen. Hull, and a contingent of military and civilian officials from Okinawa attended from the U.S. side with Maeda Kensaku, first secretary of the Foreign Ministry, representing the central government, and Kagoshima Gov. Shigenari, representing the prefectural government.[73]

The small, simple Reversion Ceremony began amid a heavy rain on Christmas morning. Perhaps due to the rain, the band that was scheduled to play the national anthems of both countries at the start of the ceremony failed to show up, and, after a five-minute delay, the ceremony began without music at 10:05 A.M.

Maeda began by making a brief speech, thanking the United States for the return of the islands and welcoming the people of the Amami Islands back to Japan, followed by a message from Ambassador Allison, read by Martin, himself born in Japan, congratulating the islanders on "this happy occasion," on "again becom[ing] an integral part of that great prefecture [of] Kagoshima and of the homeland of Japan."[74]

Martin's greetings were followed by those of Gen. Hull, read by Dishman.[75] Because it was the most eloquent and summarized the overall situation, inconsistencies and all, Hull's message is included here in full:

Figure 5.3.   Gov. Shigenari Kaku, Consul Gen. James V. Martin Jr., Col. S. B. Dishman, and Others at the Reversion Ceremony, Naze, December 25, 1953

On this occasion of your restoration to the Japanese nation, I send you cordial greetings. It is creditable to all concerned that a transfer of political authority has come to pass without the pressures of agitation and violence, without controversy, and without rancor. Not everywhere and not often does this happen.

The United States is not greedy for either land or power. In its obvious willingness to relinquish control of these islands, the United States has once again evidenced its sincerity and friendliness to other peoples. It does not seek to dictate their destinies. It does seek conditions of peace wherein men can prosper and be free from fear. Those areas over which we must retain control in order to bring about such peaceful conditions will be administered with due consideration to the spiritual and material welfare of the people involved.

My brief tenure as governor of your islands is at an end. In terminating it, I wish you well. Before you lies a new challenge to carry on the work of overcoming the economic difficulties which so long have beset you. I hope that what you have experienced under American administration will help you to make the most of this vital challenge.

To many of you who have contributed so much to the smoothness and effectiveness of our relations, I voice the appreciation and gratitude of myself and the American people. You deserve them in equal measure from all of your countrymen.

Though no longer your governor, I remain no less concerned with your security in my capacity as commander in chief of the United States Forces in Japan. Until there is adequate defensive strength under the flag of peaceful

Japan, these forces ensure you against aggression and the paralyzing fear of aggression. It gives me pleasure to know that in this way I shall continue to have a part in furthering your well-being.

After Hull's greetings and sobering message about the realities on which the administration of the islands had been predicated, Gov. Shigenari spoke, welcoming the islanders back to the prefecture.

Following the ceremony, which ended at 10:35 A.M., Shigenari, local, prefectural, and central government officials attended the first of several larger public rallies at 11:00 A.M. A parade, in which some 5,000 reportedly participated holding small paper and cloth *Hinomaru* flags, was held that day amid the rain and ended up by going down to the port to watch small airplanes, sent by newspaper companies on the mainland, do flyovers of the city and drop leaflets and special editions of the papers.

The site of these officials visiting Amami, the *Hinomaru* flags flying from every home, and the arrival of Japanese newspaper companies all brought home to the islanders the fact that eight years of U.S. administration had come to an end, and they were, in words of Izumi, "now returning home."

Notes

1. A truce was signed between United Nations' forces and North Korea on July 27, 1953, that brought an end to the fighting. A Demilitarized Zone (DMZ) was created 2.5 miles wide, although North Korea continued to violate it over the years.

2. "Memorandum of Conversation by the Director of the Office of Northeast Asian Affairs Kenneth T. Young, Jr. (August 13, 1953)," *FRUS, 1952–1954, Vol. 14, Part 2,* p. 1481.

3. Comments like the first one, which were meant to downplay the importance of Amami and emphasize why Okinawa could not be returned, were reported occasionally in the press and became the subject of criticism: "if the islands were not strategically important, then why were they occupied or detached from Japan in the first place?"

4. Dulles was only partly correct in saying that the necessary discussions regarding territorial delineation had not been worked out prior to the announcement. According to an August 5 memorandum, a detailed territorial definition of the Amami Islands had been prepared. See "Memorandum by Alice L. Dunning to McClurkin on the Definition of Amami Group (August 5, 1953)," Roll 5, Microfilm C-0044, Records of the Director of the Office of Northeast Asian Affairs, 1945–1953, RG 59.

5. See "Telegram No. 384 from Secretary of State to U.S. embassy, Tokyo (August 13, 1953)," Folder 322.3 Amami Islands, Jan.–Oct. 1953, Box 24, RG 84, Tokyo, and "Telegram No. 423 from Allison to Secretary of State (August 14, 1953)," in same collection. According to Allison, the Foreign Ministry desired to inform the public "to relieve uncertainty among Amami residents" as soon as possible. The embassy believed

the "release [of this information is] desirable" and requested Dulles on August 14 to send instructions. The Division of Far Eastern Affairs responded later that day on Dulles' behalf, stating "No objection [to] release." (See "Telegram No. 402 from State Department to U.S. embassy, Tokyo (August 14, 1953)," Central Decimal File, 1950–1954 (794c.0221/8-1353), RG 59.) At the same time, Vice Minister Okumura Katsuzo met with Counselor of Mission J. Graham Parsons, explaining that Japan naturally considered the islands that had been part of Kagoshima Prefecture at the end of the war to be returned and asked for an early decision. On August 15, likely based on Araki's report of his conversation with Dulles (as well as the above telephone call to Okumura from Parsons on August 14), the Cultural Affairs Division of the Foreign Ministry announced that the territorial delineation of the islands to be returned would in principle include the former territory of Kagoshima Prefecture. Parsons response did not come until August 17. See "Letter from J. Graham Parsons to Vice-Minister for Foreign Affairs Okumara (August 17, 1953)," Nansei Shoto Kizoku Mondai, Amami Gunto, Nichibeikan Henkan Kyotei Henkan Kyotei Kankei, Dai Rokkan, p. 109.

6. "Amami Gunto Henkan Keii," p. 22.

7. For more on the Liaison Council, see the file "Jimu Hikitsugu Renraku Kyogikai," Nansei Shoto Kizoku Mondai, Amami Gunto, Nichibeikan Henkan Kyotei Henkan Kyotei Kankei, Dai Gokan, pp. 1–60, esp. p. 33.

8. "Amami Gunto Henkan Keii," p. 101.

9. "Jimu Hikitsugu Renraku Kyogikai," p. 57.

10. *Ibid.*, pp. 58–62.

11. *Ibid.*, pp. 69–72. Also see "Amami Gunto Henkan Keii," p. 22; and "Amami Gunto no Fukki to Sono Go (The Return of the Amami Islands and After)," *Nanpo Renraku Jiho*, Vol. 1, No. 2 (November 1954), p. 14.

12. Murayama, *Amami Fukkishi*, p. 491.

13. *Ibid.*

14. "Jimu Hikitsugu Renraku Kyogikai," pp. 80–82.

15. *Ibid.*

16. "Telegram No. 403 from Allison to Secretary of State (August 13, 1953)," Folder 322.3 Amami Islands, Jan.–Oct. 1953, Box 24, RG 84, Tokyo.

17. "Telegram No. 402 from Allison to Secretary of State (August 13, 1953)," Folder 322.3 Amami Islands, Jan.–Oct. 1953, Box 24, RG 84, Tokyo.

18. An example of this positive feedback was seen in a visit to the embassy by members of the Tokyo Amami Rengo, including Okuyama, Kanai, Nishida, and their political supporters, such as Ito, in which they stated that "they were unable to find words to express their joy and gratitude." See "Memorandum of Conversation on Visit to the embassy by Amami Oshima Reversion Association (August 12, 1953)," Folder 322.3 Amami Islands, Jan.–Oct. 1953, Box 24, RG 84, Tokyo.

19. "Memorandum from J. J. Conroy to Samuel Berger on Okinawan Conferences on Amami Oshima Reversion (August 26, 1953)," Folder 322.3 Amami Islands, Jan.–Oct. 1953, Box 24, RG 84, Tokyo. In addition to Conroy, the conference was attended by Gillies, Woodyatt, Maj. Gen. David A. D. Ogden (commanding general,

Ryukyu Command, and deputy governor, Ryukyu Islands), Brig. Gen. Charles V. Brom-
ley (civil administrator), Col. David R. Patterson (assistant to commanding general,
RYCOM, and deputy governor), Stuart T. Baron (director, Economic and Finance Department, USCAR), and Thomas H. Murfin (consul general, Okinawa).

20. This five-page report can be found attached to Conroy's memorandum above.

21. "Memorandum from J. J. Conroy to Samuel Berger on Okinawan Conferences."

22. See appendix 3 for the Security Treaty and appendix 4 for the Administrative
Agreement.

23. "Amami Gunto Henkan Keii," p. 28.

24. "Dispatch No. 506, Arrangements for Transfer of Amami Oshima Islands (September 16, 1953)," Central Decimal File, 1950–1954 (794c.0221/9-1653), RG 59.

25. "Amami Gunto Henkan Keii," p. 28.

26. *Ibid.* Also see "Memorandum from Berger to Ambassador (September 14,
1953)," Folder 322.3 Amami Islands, Jan.–Oct. 1953, Box 24, RG 84, Tokyo.

27. "Telegram No. 721 from Department of State to U.S. embassy, Tokyo (September 23, 1953)," Central Decimal File, 1950–1954 (794c.0221/9-1653), RG 59.

28. "Dispatch No. 590, Arrangements for Transfer of Amami Oshima Islands
(October 2, 1953)," Central Decimal File, 1950–1954 (794c.0221/10-253), RG 59.
For reasons unclear, this conference is called the "third meeting," although the Sep-
tember 11 conference was also labeled the "third meeting."

29. "Dispatch No. 610, Arrangements for Transfer of Amami Oshima Islands
(October 2, 1953)," Central Decimal File, 1950–1954 (794c.0221/10-853), RG 59.

30. "Telegram No. 959 from Allison to Secretary of State (October 14, 1953),"
Central Decimal File, 1950–1954 (794c.0221/10-1453), RG 59.

31. "Telegram No. 957 from Allison to Secretary of State (October 14, 1953),"
Central Decimal File, 1950–1954 (794c.0221/10-1453), RG 59.

32. "Disptach No. 680, Memorandum of Conversation with Foreign Ministry Official on Amami Transfer Arrangements (October 20, 1953)," Central Decimal File,
1950–1954 (794c.0221/10-2053), RG 59; and "Amami Gunto Henkan Keii," p. 27. Tsurumi, who joined the Foreign Ministry in 1940, had a brilliant career but unfortunately
died relatively young while serving as ambassador in Geneva in November 1976.

33. "The Ambassador in Japan (Allison) to the Department of State (October 20,
1953)," *FRUS, 1952–1954, vol. 14, part 2*, pp. 1533–1534.

34. "Telegram No. 07010 from Dulles to Allison (October 21, 1953)," Central
Decimal File, 1950–1954 (794c.0221/10-2153), RG 59.

35. "Letter from Assistant Secretary of Defense Frank M. Nash to Assistant
Secretary of State for Far Eastern Affairs Robertson on Arrangements for Return
of Amami Island Group (October 26, 1953)," Central Decimal File, 1950–1954
(794c.0221/10-2653), RG 59.

36. The JSC conducted a number of studies on the issue of the disposition of the
Amami Islands and, in particular, the military requirements for islands. One study, on
which the above letter was based, included a set of seventeen demands. See "Study
by JSPC, Military Requirements on the Amami Island Group (September 10, 1953),"

Records of the Joint Chiefs of Staff, Part II, 1946–1953, The Far East (Bethesda, Md.: University Publications of America, 1996), Reel 6, Frame 0944.

37. "Memorandum by the Assistant Secretary of State for Far Eastern Affairs Robertson to Undersecretary Smith on Status of Arrangements (October 21, 1953)," July–December 1953 (2) folder, Box 6, Bureau of Far Eastern Affairs, Miscellaneous Subject Files, 1953, RG 59.

38. "Telegram No. 1101 from Allison to Dulles (October 28, 1953)," Central Decimal File, 1950–1954 (794c.0221/10-2853), RG 59.

39. "Telegram No. 1038 from Secretary of State to embassy, Tokyo (October 30, 1953)," Central Decimal File, 1950–1954 (794c.0221/103053), RG 59.

40. "Letter from Assistant Secretary of State Robertson to Assistant Secretary of Defense Nash (November 13, 1953)," Central Decimal File, 1950–1954 (794c.0221/11-1353), RG 59.

41. "Telegram No. 1191 from embassy, Tokyo to Secretary of State (November 9, 1953)," Folder 322.3 Amami Islands, Nov.–Dec. 1953, Box 24, RG 84, Tokyo. Tsuchiya also proposed a formula that Okazaki was considering in which the bulk of the main issues (U.S. military rights, disposition of property owned or used by GRI and USCAR, establishment of conversion rate) would be resolved by December 1 to permit reversion, with smaller issues to be handled afterward, such as disposition of converted "B" yen currency, return of Japanese state property, obligations between Amami and Okinawa, status and treatment of Amami islanders remaining in Okinawa. Conroy, who met with Tsuchiya, expressed his inability to give a definite answer. In any case, officials from the Foreign Ministry had already begun telling representatives from Amami, including Izumi, who was visiting Tokyo, that reversion would likely take place on December 1. See Nankai Nichinichi Shimbun, ed., *Gojunenshi*, p. 166.

42. "Dispatch No. 805, Memorandum of Conversation—Amami Oshima Transfer Arrangements (November 17, 1953)," Central Decimal File, 1950–1954 (794c.0221/11-1753), RG 59.

43. "Memorandum from McClurkin to Drumright on Your Conversation This Afternoon with Minister Takeuchi (November 12, 1953)," Central Decimal File, 1950–1954 (794c.0221/11-1253), RG 59; and "Memorandum of Conversation on Arrangements for the Transfer to Japan of Control over the Amami Islands (November 12, 1953)," Central Decimal File, 1950–1954 (794c.0221/11-1253), RG 59.

44. "Telegram No. 1273 from Allison to Secretary of State (November 18, 1953)," Central Decimal File, 1950–1954 (794c.0221/11-1853) RG 59.

45. Murayama, *Amami Fukkishi*, pp. 495–499; and Nankai Nichinichi Shimbun, ed., *Gujunenshi*, p. 166.

46. "Letter from Assistant Secretary Nash to Robertson (November 20, 1953)," Central Decimal File, 1950–1954 (794c.0221/11-2053), RG 59.

47. "Telegram No. 1211 from Secretary of State to embassy, Tokyo (November 20, 1953)," Central Decimal File, 1950–1954 (794c.0221/11-1353), RG 59.

48. "Amami Gunto Henkan Keii," pp. 28–30. For the materials presented to the Foreign Ministry, see pp. 113–123.

49. "Memorandum from Robertson to Secretary of State on Amami Transfer Arrangements (November 18, 1953)," Central Decimal File, 1950–1954 (794c.0221/11-1853), RG 59.

50. Initially, Allison had expected to begin talks the day after he submitted the documents, but it seems the Foreign Ministry needed, understandably, some time to digest the contents. As a result, talks began on November 27 instead of November 25. See "Telegram No. 1305 from embassy, Tokyo to Secretary of State (November 23, 1953)," Central Decimal File, 1950–1954 (794c.0221/11-2353), RG 59. Also see "Telegram No. 1344 from embassy, Tokyo to Secretary of State (November 28, 1953)," Central Decimal File, 1950–1954 (794c.0221/11-2853), RG 59; and "Dispatch No. 867 Arrangements for the Transfer of the Amami Islands (December 1, 1953)," Central Decimal File, 1950–1954 (794c.0221/12-153), RG 59.

51. "Dispatch No. 867 Arrangements for the Transfer of the Amami Islands."

52. *Ibid.* Also see "Telegram No. 1354 from embassy, Tokyo to Secretary of State (November 30, 1953)," Central Decimal File, 1950–1954 (794c.0221/11-3053), RG 59.

53. For more on Yasukawa, see his memoirs, Yasukawa Takeshi, *Wasureenu Omoide to Korekara no Nichibei Gaiko* (*Unforgettable Memories and Japan–U.S. Diplomacy in the Future*), (Tokyo: Sekai no Ugokisha, 1991).

54. "Telegram No. 1354."

55. "Dispatch No. 867 Arrangements for the Transfer of the Amami Islands."

56. "Dispatch No. 873 Arrangements for the Transfer of the Amami Islands (December 3, 1953)," Central Decimal File, 1950–1954 (794c.0221/12-353), RG 59.

57. "Dispatch No. 925, Arrangements for the Transfer of the Amami Islands (December 17, 1953)," Central Decimal File, 1950–1954 (794c.0221/12-1753), RG 59.

58. "Telegram No. 1395 from embassy, Tokyo to Secretary of State (December 4, 1953)," Central Decimal File, 1950–1954 (794c.0221/12-453), RG 59.

59. "Telegram No. 1341 from embassy, Tokyo to Secretary of State (November 28, 1953)," Central Decimal File, 1950–1954 (794c.0221/11-2853), RG 59. Interestingly, Allison and Hull noted that such a statement would "go far [to] quiet" Republic of China's concerns voiced more and more loudly that the United States "might make further concessions to Japan in face of Japanese pressure." See "Telegram No. 302 from embassy, Taipei to Secretary of State (November 25, 1953)," Central Decimal File, 1950–1954 (794c.0221/11-2553), RG 59.

60. "Telegram No. 1399 from embassy, Tokyo to Secretary of State (December 5, 1953)," Central Decimal File, 1950–1954 (794c.0221/12-553), RG 59.

61. "Telegram No. 1434 from embassy, Tokyo to Secretary of State (December 10, 1953)," Central Decimal File, 1950–1954 (794c.0221/12-1053), RG 59.

62. "Telegram No. 1506 from embassy, Tokyo to the Secretary of State (December 18, 1953)," Central Decimal File, 1950–1954 (794c.0221/12-1853), RG 59.

63. "Telegram No. 1460 from Secretary of State to embassy, Tokyo (December 18, 1953)," Folder 322.3 Amami Islands, Nov.–Dec. 1953, Box 24, RG 84, Tokyo.

64. "Telegram No. 1524 from embassy, Tokyo to Secretary of State (December 19, 1953)," Central Decimal File, 1950–1954 (794c.0221/12-1953), RG 59.

65. "Telegram No. 1525 from embassy, Tokyo to Secretary of State (December 19, 1953)," Folder 322.3 Amami Islands, Nov.–Dec. 1953, Box 24, RG 84, Tokyo.

66. Shimoda later served as Japan's ambassador to the United States from 1967 to 1970. For more on his career, see Shimoda Takezo, *Sengo Nihon Gaiko No Shogen: Nihon wa Koshite Saisei* (*Testimony of Postwar Japanese Diplomacy: This is How Japan Was Reborn*), (Tokyo: Gyosei Mondai Kenkyujo, 1984).

67. "Telegram No. 1540 from embassy, Tokyo to Secretary of State (December 21, 1953)," Central Decimal File, 1950–1954 (794c.0221/12-2153), RG 59.

68. "Telegram No. 1555 from embassy, Tokyo to Secretary of State (December 22, 1953)," Folder 322.3 Amami Islands, Nov.–Dec. 1953, Box 24, RG 84, Tokyo.

69. "Telegram No. 1500 from Secretary of State to embassy, Tokyo (December 22, 1953)," Folder 322.3 Amami Islands, Nov.–Dec. 1953, Box 24, RG 84, Tokyo.

70. "Telegram No. 1509 from Secretary of State to embassy, Tokyo (December 23, 1953)," Folder 322.3 Amami Islands, Nov.–Dec. 1953, Box 24, RG 84, Tokyo.

71. "Amami Gunto Henkan Keii," p. 39.

72. "Telegram from Yoshida Shigeru to John Foster Dulles (December 24, 1953)," Central Decimal File, 1950–1954 (794c.0221/12-2453), RG 59.

73. "Dispatch No. 47, Observations on Amami Oshima's Return to Japan (January 8, 1954)," Central Decimal File, 1950–1954 (794c.0221/1-854), RG 59; author's interviews with James V. Martin Jr., January 30, 1999, Washington, D.C., and Clifton B. Forster, December 7, 1999, Tiburon, California. Also see Murayama, pp. 520–529; and Nankai Nichinichi Shimbun, ed., *Gojunenshi*, pp. 166–171.

74. "Dispatch No. 1007, Statements by Japanese and United States Representatives on the Occasion of the Transfer of the Amami Islands (January 5, 1954)," Central Decimal File, 1950–1954 (794c.0221/1-554), RG 59.

75. "Dispatch No. 1007."

~

Conclusion

"If the Japanese had developed otherwise, I would have taken a stronger position for the restoration of Japanese administration in the other Ryukyuan islands. However, as it is, I do not want to encourage this. Nothing that has happened will prevent the United States from changing its mind later, if this seems desirable."

—John Foster Dulles, U.S. Secretary of State,
Letter to former colleague Dean Rusk, December 29, 1953

As alluded to in the introduction and discussed throughout this book, the return of the Amami Islands was a natural, albeit belated, outcome of U.S. ideals and specific policy toward Japan. Because the islands were viewed as strategically important due to their location in between Okinawa and mainland Japan, the road to the realization of those ideals and the implementation of that policy was a rocky one and was influenced, sometimes, by factors outside of U.S. control in the Cold War.

In this sense, the return of the Amami Islands was properly an occasion of great celebration, first and foremost by the people of the Amami Islands, living there and in mainland Japan, and secondly, by the government and people of Japan. Yoshida's expression of thanks to Dulles, mentioned in the last chapter, those of Gov. Shigenari, sent directly to President Eisenhower and Secretary Dulles on Christmas day, and that of Okuyama Hachiro of *Amami Rengo*, clearly reflect this feeling.[1]

The road ahead for the people of the islands would not be easy—trying to reintegrate socially, politically, administratively, and economically after years of separation from mainland Japan—and no one expected it to be so. Nevertheless, it was the clear desire of the people of the islands to return to *sokoku*, or "the fatherland," and that wish was granted by the United States in a peaceful manner—an unusual event in international affairs. For this, not only gratitude but admiration was felt by all observers and participants at the time.

At the same time, however, a major issue was left unresolved, which detracted from celebrations over the return of the Amami Islands. The issue, of course, was the U.S. decision to maintain the status quo with regard to Okinawa and Ogasawara.

The announcement of that decision was made simultaneously in Washington, D.C., and Tokyo (at 10:00 A.M. on December 24 and 12:01 A.M. on December 25, respectively) at the time of reversion, although its contents had been known to some degree beforehand.[2] Namely, Dulles explained the decision of the U.S. government to maintain its rights over the other islands as per Article 3 of the Peace Treaty in the following way.

1. By arrangements concluded today in Tokyo, the government of the United States has relinquished in favor of Japan its rights under Article III of the Japanese Peace Treaty over the Amami Oshima group of the Ryukyu Islands.
2. Questions have been raised regarding the intentions of the United States with respect to the remaining islands specified in Article III of the Peace Treaty.
3. The United States government believes that it is essential to the success of the cooperative effort of the free nations of Asia and of the world in the direction of peace and security, that the United States continue to exercise its present powers and rights in the remaining Ryukyu Islands and in the other islands specified in Article III of the Peace Treaty so long as conditions of threat and tension exist in the Far East.
4. The United States earnestly hopes that progress can be made in reducing tensions, and we will spare no effort toward that end. But, until conditions of genuine stability and confidence are created, the need of the free nations to preserve an armed vigilance will remain imperative. It would be an abdication of responsibility to the common effort of these free nations, including Japan, for the United States to adopt any other course than here set out, since the remaining Ryukyuan and other islands specified in Article III of the Peace Treaty constitute an essential link in the strategic defense of the whole Pacific area. Accordingly, the

United States intends to remain as custodian of these islands for the forseeable future. However, in exercising its treaty rights, the United States will not only do all in its power to improve the welfare and well-being of the inhabitants of the Ryukyus, but it will continue to safeguard economic and cultural intercourse throughout the Archipelago.

Allison, who, as we saw earlier, had encouraged Dulles to make such a statement, showed Okazaki a copy of the advance text of the statement on December 24 that had been worked out between the embassy and the State Department in the run-up to the signing ceremony.[3] Symbolic of the desire of Japan to see Okinawa returned, Okazaki disappointedly looked at Allison and "said grimly" that he "guess[ed] it could not be helped." Later, during conversation following the signing ceremony, Okazaki referred to a statement attributed to President Manuel L. Quezon of the Philippines regarding the desire for independence, that "it was better to live in poverty and be independent than be prosperous and be under foreign rule." Simply put, it was a warning that the people of Japan and Okinawa would not be satisfied until reversion of Okinawa and Ogasawara was realized. Allison, who was sympathetic, probably was expecting such an opinion to be held, but to hear it stated so no doubt surprised him. "On [the] whole," however, Allison informed Dulles, "Okazaki was . . . philosophical on [the] matter and recognized realities of [the] situation."

Okazaki's comments did bother Dulles tremendously, for he personally wrote to Allison that "the Japanese are constantly asking more and more from [the] U.S. without feeling any obligation themselves to do what is necessary to promote security in Asia."[4] Dulles noted he recalled Yoshida's statement at the San Francisco Peace Conference that "he hoped administration would be restored to Japan 'in the not too distant future with the reestablishment of world security—especially the security of Asia.' If that reestablishment of security now seems much more distant than Yoshida apparently then hoped, that is in no small part due to the fact that Japan itself has not made the contribution to restoring security which we had hoped."

Dulles made a similar comment, he informed Allison, to Chargé d'Affaires Izeki Yujiro when the latter came in to express his appreciation to Dulles for the return of the islands. Dulles told him that he thought "it was time that the Japanese leaders realized they cannot expect forever to be on the receiving end without any corresponding effort on their part."[5] In describing this scene to Allison, Dulles added that he "still ha[s] confidence that the Japanese people possess qualities necessary to enable them to play a major role, but so far they certainly have succeeded in keeping these qualities under wraps."

Dulles it seems was contemplating another letter that same day, lamenting Japan's lack of active cooperation in the field of defense and the effect it had on America's Okinawa policy, namely the necessity to retain administrative rights over Okinawa. On December 29, he wrote to Dean Rusk, then-president of the Rockefeller Foundation, responding to Rusk's letter on Okinawan matters of December 18. "You doubtless have seen," Dulles began, "the statement I have issued with reference to the return of the Amami Islands and the retention of our position in the other islands. I accept this," Dulles continued,

> largely because I am terribly disappointed at the way things have been going in Japan. There has not been any rebirth of moral strength, as in the case of Germany. The Communists are infiltrating deeply into labor unions, the Government is weak and vacillating, and those who can afford to do so are squandering their windfall from the Korean War and the Government dares not impose any austerity.
>
> If the Japanese had developed otherwise, I would have taken a stronger position for the restoration of Japanese administration in the other Ryukyuan islands. However, as it is, I do not want to encourage this. Nothing that has happened will prevent the United States from changing its mind later, if this seems desirable.[6]

Eventually, the "other Ryukyuan islands," including Okinawa, and the Ogasawara Islands were returned in 1972 and 1968 respectively, but it was not during Dulles' time in office or even during his life (he retired in April 1959 and died that May from cancer).

According to Allison, Dulles' December 24 statement, while remaining a "clear definition" of the U.S. position, was "unfortunately" not given "top coverage" in the press and in "many" instances was "headlined misleadingly . . . to suggest that the reversion of the other islands is also contemplated."[7] Allison referred to stories titled "Return of All Ryukyus Seen" and "Japan is Seen Slated to Get Ryukyus Back," which included comments by "certain" American officials that the return of the Amami Islands had set a "precedent."[8] Specifically, an article by United Press correspondent Stewart Hensley, based in Washington, D.C., which stated that U.S. officials had indicated that the government was considering the return of other islands, "took much of the force from" the secretary's statement, Allison lamented, because "its emphasis is on the future return of the Ryukyus rather than indefinite American administration."[9]

Ironically, although the return of the Amami Islands had in fact set a precedent, and a very important one at that, Allison and the State Department, not to mention the U.S. military, hoped that the Dulles statement, followed by similar statements by other officials both public and private, would ease pressure for reversion. In this regard, it seems they had underestimated the strong desire that existed to see the other islands returned.

A month later, however, the embassy slowly became aware that it would "undoubtedly . . . in the future . . . be subjected to a renewal of the flow of letters and petitions on the return of the other islands."[10] Moreover, newspaper editorials, which had first expressed its gratitude over the return, gradually began to question why Okinawa and Ogasawara were not returned, and in some cases became strongly critical of U.S. policy. One, which appeared as "An Open Letter to the Ambassador" and was published in the *Yomiuri Shimbun* and carried in the English-language *Tokyo Evening News*, took the following tone:

> I have the honor of addressing you in print, and state the following in regard to the agreement between the United States and Japan concerning the return of the Amami Oshima Islands.
>
> I don't mean to say that the Amami Oshima Islands simply have been returned where they rightfully belong, and we frankly and gladly accept this Christmas present as an American expression of goodwill. No matter how poor and barren those islands may be, they are Japanese territory inhabited by our Japanese brethren.
>
> But we cannot forget that Japan remains deprived of some territories which have belonged to Japan since olden times and were not acquired through "war and aggression." They are the Ryukyu and Bonin Islands, Habomai, Shikotan. . . . Because our land is so narrow, we are prone to get excited about any island, no matter how small—even about a little reef which may be wiped out by a submarine volcanic eruption.
>
> That is why we can't stop thinking about the territories taken away from us in a manner that fails to convince us.
>
> It seems that the United States wants to hold on to the control and administration of the Ryukyus and Bonins in order to maintain its strategic setup in the entire Pacific area.
>
> But why would it be strategically inopportune to return those islands to Japan? Isn't Japan offering even its homeland to the United States for military bases?
>
> I don't think it would inconvenience the Americans in their defense setup for the Pacific area if the islands were returned to Japan and arrangements made under the United States–Japan Security Pact and Administrative Agreement. If America could return them without strings attached, and then discuss the use of the islands, this would deeply impress the Japanese people with the goodwill of America, and help to strengthen further the unity of the two nations.
>
> I deem it a great honor to inform Your Excellency that the above viewpoint is shared by the majority of the Japanese people.[11]

Interestingly, the writer touched on a point that the State Department had long argued in favor of—namely, the return of Okinawa upon the securing of base rights.

In Okinawa, too, public opinion, while happy for their cousins in Amami to the north and encouraged by the precedent that the return of the islands had established, was bothered by the fact that Okinawa was not included. Indeed, combined with the fact that just at that time the military was forcibly seizing lands in Okinawa for base expansion, the situation would become even more explosive over the coming months and years.

As seen in discussions between Dulles and Ambassador Araki, Allison and Okazaki, and at the working level during the negotiations, the U.S. and Japanese sides essentially had two different agendas in the talks on the reversion of Amami (although the goal of strengthening the bilateral relationship through the reversion was the same). The American side wished that the return of Amami would put a stop (however temporary) to calls for the return of Okinawa, which was, in the U.S. opinion, not feasible while international tensions prevailed, the Japanese defense posture remained weak, and Japan continued to be politically reluctant to play a larger regional role. The Japanese side, on the other hand, viewed the return of the Amami Islands as the first step in securing the return of its other lost territories, Okinawa and Ogasawara. The agreement to return the Amami Islands, in other words, formed a precedent by which it could be done. The fact that Okinawa and Ogasawara were not returned at this time only ended up encouraging people in mainland Japan and Okinawa more, not less—an irony of history perhaps.

Nevertheless, while the undefined status of Okinawa became one of the main issues, if not the biggest problem, in U.S.–Japan relations over the years, the importance of the return of the Amami Islands—politically, symbolically, diplomatically—cannot and should not be overlooked. Namely, the Amami Islands were returned peacefully, within the framework of Article 3, and thus did, in fact, create such a precedent—the so-called *Amami Hoshiki*, or "Amami Formula"—by which Okinawa and Ogasawara could also be later returned, and which, in fact, were returned.[12]

In the case of Amami, the leadership of Eisenhower, who involved himself in the decision to return the Amami Islands at the NSC meeting in June 1953 and had developed his own personal views on the issue based on his own experiences as a military strategist, supreme commander (in Europe) in charge of the occupation, and Army chief-of-staff in Washington, was vital. He judged the costs of the occupation of the Amami Islands too high for little strategic value, especially when weighed against the importance of the relationship with Japan.

Dulles, on the other hand, while knowing that the decision to return the Amimi Islands was the right thing to do, wanted more from Japan and was extremely disappointed in Japan's failure to contribute more positively to the security of the Western Alliance through rearmament and an increase in its defense budget. The issue of Japan's reluctance to rearm on a scale Dulles desired would make him somewhat bitter, although, as he noted in his letter to Rusk after the transfer of the islands, he still hoped to be able to permit the return of Okinawa at some point in the future.

His colleagues in the State Department, particularly Ambassador Allison, were more moderate and perhaps cautious on Japanese rearmament, hoping to see the Amami Islands returned without any overt *quid pro quo* in defense matters. Nevertheless, inherently such a trade-off, spoken or unspoken, was necessary, then and later. In other words, U.S. forces would not unilaterally withdraw or scale down their presence and see a vacuum created. There had to be some sort of increased Japanese role to make up in some way (although it could never be absolute) for the changes in force structure. This issue would become more apparent at the time of the return of Ogasawara in 1968 and Okinawa in 1972, and still, in my opinion, affects the situation today in the early twenty-first century with the continued large presence of U.S. forces in Okinawa. To bring about a reasonable reduction of U.S. forces (if that is what the governments of both countries desire), then a corresponding increase in Japan's role in the region—political, diplomatic, economic, and, yes, military—will be even more necessary. This may be just one of the many things that the Amami reversion process has taught us.

However, most important, and most gratifying to me—an American scholar of U.S.–Japan relations in Japan—is the fact that with the U.S. decision to return the Amami Islands, the U.S. government was both living up to American ideals and pursuing the maintenance (if not improvement) of friendly relations with its vital partner in the Pacific. The "Christmas present" of the return of the Amami Islands was one enjoyed not only by the people of Amami and the rest of Japan, but by the peoples of both countries.

Notes

1. "Telegram from Governor Shigenari of Kagoshima Prefecture Japan to the President (December 25, 1953)," Central Decimal File, 1950–1954 (794c.022/12-2553), RG 59. Shigenari's telegram read: "Deeply Moved By Welcoming the Day of the Return of Amami Oshima to Japan STOP Representing Two Million People of Kagoshima Prefecture Express Sincere Gratitude to Dear President and All People of USA STOP." Okuyama's message, also addressed to Eisenhower, read: "I Have Honor

to Express, on Behalf of All Amami People, Our Heartfelt Gratitude to Your Good Office for Return of Amami Islands from United States to Japan." See "Telegram from Chairman Hachiro Okuyama to the President (December 25, 1953)," Central Decimal File, 1950–1954 (794c.022/12-2553), RG 59.

2. "U.S. Returns Islands to Japanese Control: Statement by Secretary of State John Foster Dulles," *Department of State Bulletin*, Vol. 30, No. 758 (January 4, 1954), p. 17.

3. "Telegram No. 1586 from Allison to Secretary of State (December 26, 1953)," Central Decimal File, 1950–1954 (794c.022/12-2653), RG 59.

4. "Confidential Telegram from Dulles to Allison (December 28, 1953)," *FRUS, 1952–1954, Vol. 14, Part 2*, p. 1572. Dulles told Allison that the telegram had "no Departmental clearance" and was sent to "give you my thinking, which you can discreetly [be] let known to extent, if any, you think appropriate. Happy New Year."

5. *Ibid.*, p. 1573.

6. "Personal Letter from Dulles to Dean Rusk (December 29, 1953)," John Foster Dulles Chronological File, December 1953 (1) folder, Box 6, John Foster Dulles Chronological Series, John Foster Dulles Papers, 1951–1959, Dwight D. Eisenhower Presidential Library, Abilene, KS.

7. "Dispatch No. 1082, Japanese Press Reaction to Transfer of Amami Islands (January 21, 1954)," Folder 322.3 Amami, Box 24, RG 84, Tokyo.

8. "Telegram No. 1586."

9. *Ibid.* "Return of Entire Chain of Ryukyus is Predicted," *The Mainichi*, December 26, 1953.

10. "Dispatch No. 1082."

11. *Ibid.* Also see "Henshu techo (musings)," Yomiuri Shimbun, December 26, 1953.

12. It is unclear where the phrase "Amami Hoshiki" originated from, but it was used commonly in the 1960s. Kanai refers to it in his book, attributing it to Deputy Chief Executive Kohagura Seiko during interpellations in the Ryukyu Legislature on May 25, 1965, being the first. However, Kanai also notes that Chief Executive Ota Seisaku (1959–1964) also said he used that expression. See Kanai, *Fukki Undo Kaikoroku*, p. 12.

~

Agreement Between Japan and the United States Concerning the Amami Islands

Signed December 24, 1953

WHEREAS the United States of America desires, with respect to the Amami Islands, to relinquish in favor of Japan all rights and interests under Article 3 of the Treaty of Peace with Japan signed at the city of San Francisco on September 8, 1951, as announced by the Secretary of State on August 8, 1953; and

WHEREAS Japan is willing to assume full responsibility and authority for the exercise of all powers of administration, legislation arid jurisdiction over the territory and inhabitants of the Amami Islands;

THEREFORE, the Government of Japan and the Government of the United States of America have determined to conclude this Agreement, and have accordingly appointed their respective representatives for this purpose, who have agreed as follows:

Article I

1. With respect to the Amami Islands, the United States of America relinquishes in favor of Japan all rights and interests under Article 3 of the Treaty of Peace with Japan signed at the city of San Francisco on September 8, 1951, effective from December 25, 1953. Japan, as of such date, assumes full responsibility and authority for the exercise of all and any powers of administration, legislation and jurisdiction over the territory and inhabitants of the Amami Islands.

2. For the purpose of this Agreement, the term "Amami Islands" shall mean the group of islands, including their territorial waters, as defined in the attached Annex.

Article II

1. The two installations and sites presently utilized by the United States of America in the Amami Islands will be used by the United States armed forces in accordance with the procedures set forth in the Administrative Agreement, as amended, under Article III of the Security Treaty between Japan and the United States of America, signed at Tokyo on February 28, 1952. However, in the event that, due to unavoidable delays, it is impossible to comply with the above procedures by December 25, 1953, Japan grants to the United States of America the continued use of those particular installations and sites, pending the completion of the said procedures.

2. The Government of Japan will take over the operation of the weather station at Naze, Amami Oshima, and shall furnish to the Government of the United States of America weather observations as may be agreed upon through consultations by the Joint Committee as provided for in Article XXVI of the Administrative Agreement. In the event that due to unavoidable delays, it is impossible for the Government of Japan to take over the operation on December 25, 1953, it is agreed that the present operation will be continued until such time as the Government of Japan is prepared to assume this responsibility.

Article III

1. On December 25, 1953, the Government of Japan shall begin to withdraw from circulation in the Amami Islands all "B" yen and issue, in its stead, Japanese yen at the rate of 3 Japanese yen for 1 "B" yen. This exchange of currency shall be accomplished as speedily as possible. The "B" yen so withdrawn from circulation shall be returned to the United States Civil Administrator at Naha, Okinawa, without obligation by the Government of the United States of America to reimburse the Government of Japan in any manner for it or for the Japanese yen issued in the islands.

2. Existing budgetary and fiscal arrangements for collection of funds and payment of obligations will be maintained through December 24, 1953, after which time the Government of Japan shall assume full fiscal responsibility in the Amami Islands.

3. The Government of Japan shall assume all financial obligations of the postal system in the Amami Islands. Accounts between the postal system in the Amami Islands and the postal system in the remaining islands of the Nansei Shoto shall be settled as agreed upon at a later date between the Government of Japan and the Government of the United States of America taking into calculation other assets of the postal system in the Amami Islands and the prewar assets and obligations of the Japanese Government postal system in the remaining islands of the Nansei Shoto.

4. Property of the Government of the Ryukyu Islands, including papers, archives and evidentiary materials, existing in the Amami Islands on December 25, 1953, shall be transferred to the Government of Japan on that date without compensation.

5. Property of the Government of Japan, including local governments, existing in the Amami Islands on December 25, 1953 which have been under the custody of the Government of the United States of America prior to that date, shall be returned to the Government of Japan on that date without compensation.

6. As of December 25, 1953, there will exist certain current accounts payable owed by various agencies and institutions in the Amami Islands to governmental and other agencies in the remaining islands of the Nansei Shoto arising from shipment of goods to the Amami Islands, and certain long-term obligations owed by individuals and institutions in the Amami Islands to the Ryukyu Reconstruction Finance Fund. The balances of these accounts and identities of debtors and creditors shall be confirmed by the two Governments as soon as possible. The Government of the United States of America shall transfer and assign, without compensation, to the Government of Japan all rights and interests in the accounts so confirmed.

7. There will be as of December 25, 1953 obligations owed by or to individuals, including juridical persons, in the Amami Islands to or from individuals, including juridical persons, in the remaining islands of the Nansei Shoto. The two Governments agree to establish procedures that will expedite the settlement of these obligations.

Article IV

1. Japan waives all claims of Japan and its nationals against the United States of America arid its nationals and against the local authorities of the Ryukyu Islands (Nansei Shoto) and its predecessors arising out of

the war or out of actions taken because of the existence of a state of war, and waives all claims arising from the presence, operations or actions of forces or authorities of the United States of America which shall have occurred in or have any effect upon the Amami Islands prior to December 25, 1953. The foregoing waiver does not, however, include any Japanese claims specifically recognized in the laws of the United States of America or the local laws of the Ryukyu Islands (Nansei Shoto) enacted since September 2, 1945.

2. Japan recognizes the validity of all acts and omissions done during the period of occupation and during the period of military government or of the United States Civil Administration of the Amami Islands under or in consequence of directives of the occupying authorities, the military government or the United States Civil Administration or authorized by existing law during that time, and will take no action subjecting United States nationals or residents of the islands of the Nansei Shoto to civil or criminal liability arising out of such acts or omissions.

Article V

1. Japan recognizes the validity of, and will continue in full force and effect:

(a) judgments in civil cases rendered by any court in the Amami Islands prior to December 25, 1953, in respect of which there was no recourse or right to review under preexisting law, and;

(b) final judgments in civil cases rendered by the Ryukyuan Court of Appeals in Okinawa, prior to December 25, 1953, in respect to those cases which originated in any court in the Amami Islands, provided that in both instances such recognition or continuation would not be contrary to public policy.

2. Without in any way adversely affecting the substantive rights and positions of the litigants concerned Japan will assume jurisdiction over and continue to judgment and execution any civil cases pending as of December 25, 1953 in any court in the Amami Islands or any civil cases originating in any such court which are pending in the Ryukyuan Court of Appeals as of the above date.

Article VI

Japan may, in accordance with its laws and procedures, exercise criminal jurisdiction over those persons in the Amami Islands who are serving sentences imposed by any Ryukyuan court prior to December 25, 1953, or over any person in the Amami Islands whose case is pending before such court or the Ryukyuan Court of Appeals in Okinawa as of the above date, provided that where such person is in custody as of the same date, he shall continue to remain in the custody of the Japanese authorities pending appropriate disposition. The Japanese authorities will, in the exercise of criminal jurisdiction over such person, give due faith and credit to the evidentiary data and material used by the Ryukyuan court or by the Ryukyuan Court of Appeals in Okinawa in their exercise of criminal jurisdiction over the person concerned.

Article VII

Treaties, conventions and other international agreements to which Japan is a party, including the Treaty of Peace with Japan signed at the city of San Francisco on September 8, 1951, the Security Treaty between Japan and the United States of America signed on the same date and the Administrative Agreement thereunder as amended, the Notes exchanged on the same date between the Prime Minister of Japan and the Secretary of State of the United States of America, and the Treaty of Friendship, Commerce and Navigation between Japan and the United States of America signed at Tokyo on April 2, 1953, shall be applicable to the Amami Islands as from the date of coming into force of this Agreement.

Article VIII

Any matter relating to the execution of this agreement shall be agreed upon through consultation between the two Governments or the competent authorities thereof.

Article IX

This Agreement shall come into force on December 25, 1953.

IN WITNESS THEREOF, the undersigned, being duly authorized by their respective Governments, have signed this Agreement.

DONE at Tokyo, this twenty-fourth day of December 1953, in duplicate in the Japanese and English languages, both equally authentic.

FOR JAPAN:
(Signed) Katsuo Okazaki

FOR THE UNITED STATES OF AMERICA:
(Signed) John M. Allison

Annex

The Amami Islands are defined as all of those islands, islets, atolls, and rocks situated in an area bonded by 29° north latitude on the north, 27° north latitude on the south, 128° 18 minutes east longitude on the west and 130° 13 minutes east longitude on the east.

~

Exchange of Notes on the Signing of the Agreement Between the U.S. and Japan Concerning the Amami Islands

American Embassy,
Tokyo, December 24, 1953

Excellency:

I have the honor to refer to the Agreement between the United States of America and Japan concerning the Amami Islands, signed today and to state as follows:

The Amami Islands and their territorial waters, because of their proximity to both the mainland of Japan and to the military installations of the United States of America in the remaining islands of the Nansei Shoto, bear a unique relationship to the defense and security of the Far East. It is understood that the Government of Japan, cognizant of this unique relationship, will take into consideration those requirements which the United States of America considers necessary to preserve, strengthen and facilitate the defense of the remaining islands of the Nansei Shoto.

Accept, Excellency, the renewed assurance of my most distinguished consideration.

His Excellency
Katsuo Okazaki,
Minister for Foreign Affairs,
Tokyo

(signed) John M. Allison

(Translation)
Tokyo, December 24, 1953

Monsieur l'Ambassadeur,

I have the honour to acknowledge the receipt of Your Excellency's Note of today's date in which Your Excellency has informed me as follows:

"I have the honor to refer to the Agreement between the United States of America and Japan concerning the Amami Islands, signed today and to state as follows:

The Amami Islands and their territorial waters, because of their proximity to both the mainland of Japan and to the military installations of the United States of America in the remaining islands of the Nansei Shoto, bear a unique relationship to the defense and security of the Far East. It is understood that the Government of Japan, cognizant of this unique relationship, will take into consideration those requirements which the United States of America considers necessary to preserve, strengthen and facilitate the defense of the remaining islands of the Nansei Shoto."

I have further the honour to take note of Your Excellency's statement, and to inform Your Excellency that the understanding set forth in the above-quoted paragraph is also the understanding of the Government of Japan.

I avail myself of this opportunity to renew to Your Excellency, Monsieur l'Ambassadeur, the assurance of my highest consideration.

His Excellency
Mr. John M. Allison
Ambassador Extraordinary
and Plenipotentiary of the
United States of America
to Japan

(signed) Katsuo Okazaki
Minister for Foreign Affairs

APPENDIX THREE

~

Unpublished Minutes of the U.S.–Japan Joint Committee Meeting, December 24, 1953

(Phrases in italics represent final changes made to original draft text prepared by U.S. representatives in November.)

1. *The United States representative made the following statement:*
   "Article II, paragraph 1, of the Administrative Agreement is understood to constitute recognition that the unique relationship of the Amami Islands to the defense and security of both Japan and the United States *of America* may require that additional facilities and areas in the Amami Islands (including sites for navigational aids, devices, and aircraft control and warning sites needed to insure complete radio and radar coverage) be granted to the United States *of America on an urgent basis.*"

   The Japanese representative replied: "With due appreciation of the importance of the Amami Islands for the defense and security of the two countries, the Japanese Government will give as prompt and favorable consideration as possible if and when such requests are specifically and case by case made through the Sub-committee for Facilities and Areas."

2. *The United States representative stated:*
   "It is understood that in connection with carrying out the Security Treaty the United States Forces be extended freedom of air space to all areas over the Amami Islands and their territorial waters *and the utilization of the territorial waters of the Amami Islands."*

The Japanese representative replied: "The Japanese Government confirms this understanding and will allow it to be extended in conformity with the current practices in these respects under the Administrative Agreement."

3. *The United States representative made the following statement:*
"It is desired that authorized personnel of the United States of America may promptly conduct preliminary site surveys in the Amami Islands in connection with the selection of land areas for additional facilities as may be requested in the future."

The Japanese representative replied: "The Japanese Government is ready to enter into consultation through the Sub-committee for Facilities and Areas as to the establishment of such machinery as may be required to meet the desire of the United States."

4. *The representatives of both sides have agreed:*
"In accordance with the relevant provisions of the Administrative Agreement, the Japanese authorities, upon detection or upon request of the United States Forces, will take immediate and adequate measures in the areas of the Amami Islands for removing or destroying any hostile or nuisance device such as, but not limited to, electronic-jamming facilities which might interfere with effective security or protection of the United States military forces and installations. The United States of America may, upon request by the competent authorities of the Government of Japan, furnish them with such assistance as may be necessary to accomplish the above."

~

Security Treaty Between Japan and the United States of America

Signed September 8, 1951

Japan has this day signed a Treaty of Peace with the Allied Powers. On the coming into force of that Treaty, Japan will not have the effective means to exercise its inherent right of self-defense because it has been disarmed.

There is danger to Japan in this situation because irresponsible militarism has not yet been driven from the world. Therefore Japan desires a Security Treaty with the United States of America to come into force simultaneously with the Treaty of Peace between Japan and the United States of America.

The Treaty of Peace recognizes that Japan as a sovereign nation has the right to enter into collective security arrangements, and further, the Charter of the United Nations recognizes that all nations possess an inherent right of individual and collective self-defense.

In exercise of these rights, Japan desires, as a provisional arrangement for its defense, that the United States of America should maintain armed forces of its own in and about Japan so as to deter armed attack upon Japan.

The United States of America, in the interest of peace and security, is presently willing to maintain certain of its armed forces in and about Japan, in the expectation, however, that Japan will itself increasingly assume responsibility for its own defense against direct and indirect aggression, always avoiding any armament which could be an offensive threat or serve other than to promote peace and security in accordance with the purposes and principles of the United Nations Charter.

Accordingly, the two countries have agreed as follows:

Article I

Japan grants, and the United States of America accepts, the right, upon the coming into force of the Treaty of Peace and of this Treaty, to dispose United States land, air and sea forces in and about Japan. Such forces may be utilized to contribute to the maintenance of international peace and security in the Far East and to the security of Japan against armed attack from without, including assistance given at the express request of the Japanese Government to put down large-scale internal riots and disturbances in Japan, caused through instigation or intervention by an outside power or powers.

Article II

During the exercise of the right referred to in Article I, Japan will not grant, without the prior consent of the United States of America, any bases or any rights, powers or authority whatsoever, in or relating to bases or the right of garrison or of maneuver, or transit of ground, air or naval forces to any third power.

Article III

The conditions which shall govern the disposition of armed forces of the United States of America in and about Japan shall be determined by administrative agreements between the two Governments.

Article IV

This Treaty shall expire whenever in the opinion of the Governments of Japan and the United States of America there shall have come into force such United Nations arrangements or such alternative individual or collective security dispositions as will satisfactorily provide for the maintenance by the United Nations or otherwise of international peace and security in the Japan Area.

Article V

This Treaty shall be ratified by Japan and the United States of America and will come into force when instruments of ratification thereof have been exchanged by them at Washington.

IN WITNESS WHEREOF the undersigned Plenipotentiaries have signed this Treaty.

DONE in duplicate at the city of San Francisco, in the Japanese and English languages, this eighth day of September, 1951.

FOR JAPAN:
Shigeru Yoshida

FOR THE UNITED STATES OF AMERICA:
Dean Acheson
John Foster Dulles
Alexander Wiley
Styles Bridges

~

Administrative Agreement, February 28, 1952

Under Article III of the Security Treaty between the United States of America and Japan

Preamble

Whereas the United States of America and Japan on September 8, 1951, signed a Security Treaty which contains provisions for the disposition of United States land, air and sea forces in and about Japan;

And whereas Article III of that Treaty states that the conditions which shall govern the disposition of the armed forces of the United States in and about Japan shall be determined by administrative agreements between the two Governments;

And whereas the United States of America and Japan are desirous of concluding practical administrative arrangements which will give effect to their respective obligations under the Security Treaty and will strengthen the close bonds of mutual interest and regard between their two peoples;

Therefore, the Governments of the United States of America and of Japan have entered into this Agreement in terms as set forth below:

Article I

In this Agreement the expression

    (a) "members of the United States armed forces" means the personnel on active duty belonging to the land, sea or air armed services of the United States of America when in the territory of Japan.

    (b) "civilian component" means the civilian persons of United States nationality who are in the employ of, serving with, or accompanying the United States armed forces in Japan, but excludes persons who are ordinarily resident in Japan or who are mentioned in paragraph 1 of Article XIV. For the purposes of this Agreement only, dual nationals, United States and Japanese, who are brought to Japan by the United States shall be considered as United States nationals.

    (c) "dependents" means

Spouse, and children under 21;

Parents, and children over 21, if dependent for over half their support upon a member of the United States armed forces or civilian component.

Article II

1. Japan agrees to grant to the United States the use of the facilities and areas necessary to carry out the purposes stated in Article I of the Security Treaty. Agreements as to specific facilities and areas, not already reached by the two Governments by the effective date of this Agreement, shall be concluded by the two Governments through the Joint Committee provided for in Article XXVI of this Agreement. "Facilities and areas" include existing furnishings, equipment and fixtures necessary to the operation of such facilities and areas.

2. At the request of either party, the United States and Japan shall review such arrangements and may agree that such facilities and areas shall be returned to Japan or that additional facilities and areas may be provided.

3. The facilities and areas used by the United States armed forces shall be returned to Japan whenever they are no longer needed for purposes of this Agreement, and the United States agrees to keep the needs for facilities and areas under continual observation with a view toward such return.

4. (a) When facilities and areas such as target ranges and maneuver grounds are temporarily not being used by the United States armed forces, interim use may be made by Japanese authorities and na-

tionals provided that it is agreed that such use would not be harmful to the purposes for which the facilities and areas are normally used by the United States armed forces.

(b) With respect to such facilities and areas as target ranges and maneuver grounds which are to be used by United States armed forces for limited periods of time, the Joint Committee shall specify in the agreements covering such facilities and areas the extent to which the provisions of this Agreement shall apply.

Article III

1. The United States shall have the rights, power and authority within the facilities and areas which are necessary or appropriate for their establishment, use, operation, defense or control. The United States shall also have such rights, power and authority over land, territorial waters and airspace adjacent to, or in the vicinities of such facilities and areas, as are necessary to provide access to such facilities and areas for their support, defense and control. In the exercise outside the facilities and areas of the rights, power and authority granted in this Article, there should be, as the occasion requires, consultation between the two Governments through the Joint Committee.

2. The United States agrees that the above-mentioned rights, power and authority will not be exercised in such a manner as to interfere unnecessarily with navigation, aviation, communication, or land travel to or from or within the territories of Japan. All questions relating to frequencies, power and like matters used by apparatus employed by the United States designed to emit electric radiation shall be settled by mutual arrangement. As a temporary measure the United States armed forces shall be entitled to use, without radiation interference from Japanese sources, electronic devices of such power, design, type of emission, and frequencies as are reserved for such forces at the time this Agreement becomes effective.

3. Operations in the facilities and areas in use by the United States armed forces shall be carried on with due regard for the public safety.

Article IV

1. The United States is not obliged, when it returns facilities and areas to Japan on the expiration of this Agreement or at an earlier date, to restore the facilities and areas to the condition in which they were at the

time they became available to the United States armed forces, or to compensate Japan in lieu of such restoration.

2. Japan is not obliged to make any compensation to the United States for any improvements made in the facilities and areas or for the buildings or structures left thereon on the expiration of this Agreement or the earlier return of the facilities and areas.

3. The foregoing provisions shall not apply to any construction which the United States may undertake under special arrangements with Japan.

Article V

1. United States and foreign vessels and aircraft operated by, for, or under the control of the United States for official purposes shall be accorded access to any port or airport of Japan free from toll or landing charges. When cargo or passengers not accorded the exemptions of this Agreement are carried on such vessels and aircraft, notification shall be given to the appropriate Japanese authorities, and such cargo or passengers shall be entered according to the laws and regulations of Japan.

2. The vessels and aircraft mentioned in paragraph 1, United States Government-owned vehicles including armor, and members of the United States armed forces, the civilian component, and their dependents shall be accorded access to and movement between facilities and areas in use by the United States armed forces and between such facilities and areas and the ports of Japan.

3. When the vessels mentioned in paragraph 1 enter Japanese ports, appropriate notification shall, under normal conditions, be made to the proper Japanese authorities. Such vessels shall have freedom from compulsory pilotage, but if a pilot is taken pilotage shall be paid for at appropriate rates.

Article VI

1. All civil and military air traffic control and communications systems shall be developed in close coordination and shall be integrated to the extent necessary for fulfillment of collective security interests. Procedures, and any subsequent changes thereto, necessary to effect this coordination and integration will be established by mutual arrangement.

2. Lights and other aids to navigation of vessels and aircraft placed or established in the facilities and areas in use by United States armed forces and in territorial waters adjacent thereto or in the vicinity

thereof shall conform to the system in use in Japan. The United States and Japanese authorities which have established such navigation aids shall notify each other of their positions and characteristics and shall give advance notification before making any changes in them or establishing additional navigation aids.

Article VII

The United States armed forces shall have the right to use all public utilities and services belonging to, or controlled or regulated by the Government of Japan, and to enjoy priorities in such use, under conditions no less favorable than those that may be applicable from time to time to the ministries and agencies of the Government of Japan

Article VIII

The Japanese Government undertakes to furnish the United States armed forces with the following meteorological services under present procedures, subject to such modifications as may from time to time be agreed between the two Governments or as may result from Japan's becoming a member of the International Civil Aviation Organization or the World Meteorological Organization:

(a) Meteorological observations from land and ocean areas including observations from weather ships assigned to positions known as "X" and "T".

(b) Climatological information including periodic summaries and the historical data of the Central Meteorological Observatory.

(c) Telecommunications service to disseminate meteorological information required for the safe and regular operation of aircraft.

(d) Seismographic data including forecasts of the estimated size of tidal waves resulting from earthquakes and areas that might be affected thereby.

Article IX

1. The United States shall have the right to bring into Japan for purposes of this Agreement persons who are members of the United States armed forces, the civilian component, and their dependents.

2. Members of the United States armed forces shall be exempt from Japanese passport and visa laws and regulations. Members of the

United States armed forces, the civilian component, and their dependents shall be exempt from Japanese laws and regulations on the registration and control of aliens, but shall not be considered as acquiring any right of permanent residence or domicile in the territories of Japan.

3. Upon entry into or departure from Japan members of the United States armed forces shall be in possession of the following documents:
   (a) personal identity card showing name, date of birth, rank and number, service, and photograph; and
   (b) individual or collective travel order certifying to the status of the individual or group as a member or members of the United States armed forces and to the travel ordered.

   For purposes of their identification while in Japan, members of the United States armed forces shall be in possession of the foregoing personal identity card.

4. Members of the civilian component, their dependents, and the dependents of members of the United States armed forces shall be in possession of appropriate documentation issued by the United States authorities so that their status may be verified by Japanese authorities upon their entry into or departure from Japan, or while in Japan.

5. If the status of any person brought into Japan under paragraph 1 of this Article is altered so that he would no longer be entitled to such admission, the United States authorities shall notify the Japanese authorities and shall, if such person be required by the Japanese authorities to leave Japan, assure that transportation from Japan will be provided within a reasonable time at no cost to the Japanese Government.

Article X

1. Japan shall accept as valid, without a driving test or fee, the driving permit or license or military driving permit issued by the United States to a member of the United States armed forces, the civilian component, and their dependents.

2. Official vehicles of the United States armed forces and the civilian component shall carry distinctive numbered plates or individual markings which will readily identify them.

3. Privately owned vehicles of members of the United States armed forces, the civilian component, and their dependents shall carry Japanese number plates to be acquired under the same conditions as those applicable to Japanese nationals.

Article XI

1. Save as provided in this Agreement, members of the United States armed forces, the civilian component, and their dependents shall be subject to the laws and regulations administered by the customs authorities of Japan.

2. All materials, supplies and equipment imported by the United States armed forces, the authorized procurement agencies of the United States armed forces, or by the organizations provided for in Article XV, for the official use of the United States armed forces or for the use of the members of the United States armed forces, the civilian component, and their dependents, and materials, supplies and equipment which are to be used exclusively by the United States armed forces or are ultimately to be incorporated into articles or facilities used by such forces, shall be permitted entry into Japan; such entry shall be free from customs duties and other such charges. Appropriate certification shall be made that such materials, supplies and equipment are being imported by the United States armed forces, the authorized procurement agencies of the United States armed forces, or by the organizations provided for in Article XV, or, in the case of materials, supplies and equipment to be used exclusively by the United States armed forces or ultimately to be incorporated into articles or facilities used by such forces, that delivery thereof is to be taken by the United States armed forces for the purposes specified above.

3. Property consigned to and for the personal use of members of the United States armed forces, the civilian component, and their dependents, shall be subject to customs duties and other such charges, except that no duties or charges shall be paid with respect to:

   (a) Furniture and household goods for their private use imported by the members of the United States armed forces or civilian component when they first arrive to serve in Japan or by their dependents when they first arrive for reunion with members of such forces or civilian component, and personal effects for private use brought by the said persons upon entrance.

   (b) Vehicles and parts imported by members of the United States armed forces or civilian component for the private use of themselves or their dependents.

   (c) Reasonable quantities of clothing and household goods of a type which would ordinarily be purchased in the United States for everyday use for the private use of members of the United States armed forces, civilian component, and their dependents, which are mailed into Japan through United States military post offices.

4. The exemptions granted in paragraphs 2 and 3 shall apply only to cases of importation of goods and shall not be interpreted as refunding customs duties and domestic excises collected by the customs authorities at the time of entry in cases of purchases of goods on which such duties and excises have already been collected.

5. Customs examination shall not be made in the following cases:
   (a) Units and members of the United States armed forces under orders entering or leaving Japan;
   (b) Official documents under official seal;
   (c) Mail in United States military postal channels and military cargo shipped on a United States Government bill of lading.

6. Except as such disposal may be authorized by the Japanese and United States authorities in accordance with mutually agreed conditions, goods imported into Japan free of duty shall not be disposed of in Japan to persons not entitled to import such goods free of duty.

7. Goods imported into Japan free from customs duties and other such charges pursuant to paragraphs 2 and 3, may be re-exported free from customs duties and other such charges.

8. The United States armed forces, in cooperation with Japanese authorities, shall take such steps as are necessary to prevent abuse of privileges granted to the United States armed forces, members of such forces, the civilian component, and their dependents in accordance with this Article.

9. (a) In order to prevent offenses against laws and regulations administered by the customs authorities of the Japanese Government, the Japanese authorities and the United States armed forces shall assist each other in the conduct of inquiries and the collection of evidence.
   (b) The United States armed forces shall render all assistance within their power to ensure that articles liable to seizure by, or on behalf of, the customs authorities of the Japanese Government are handed to those authorities.
   (c) The United States armed forces shall render all assistance within their power to ensure the payment of duties, taxes, and penalties payable by members of such forces or of the civilian component, or their dependents.

(d) Vehicles and articles belonging to the United States armed forces seized by the customs authorities of the Japanese Government in connection with an offense against its customs or fiscal laws or regulations shall be handed over to the appropriate authorities of the force concerned.

Article XII

1. The United States shall have the right to contract for any supplies or construction work to be furnished or undertaken in Japan for purposes of, or authorized by, this Agreement, without restriction as to choice of supplier or person who does the construction work.
2. Materials, supplies, equipment and services which are required from local sources for the maintenance of the United States armed forces and the procurement of which may have an adverse effect on the economy of Japan shall be procured in coordination with, and, when desirable, through or with the assistance of, the competent authorities of Japan.
3. Materials, supplies, equipment and services procured for official purposes in Japan by the United States armed forces, or by authorized procurement agencies of the United States armed forces upon appropriate certification shall be exempt from the following Japanese taxes:
   (a) Commodity tax
   (b) Travelling tax
   (c) Gasoline tax
   (d) Electricity and gas tax
4. Materials, supplies, equipment and services procured for ultimate use by the United States armed forces shall be exempt from commodity and gasoline taxes upon appropriate certification by the United States armed forces. With respect to any present or future Japanese taxes not specifically referred to in this Article which might be found to constitute a significant and readily identifiable part of the gross purchase price of materials, supplies, equipment and services procured by the United States armed forces, or for ultimate use by such forces, the two Governments will agree upon a procedure for granting such exemption or relief there from as is consistent with the purposes of this Article.
5. Local labor requirements of the United States armed forces or civilian component shall be satisfied with the assistance of the Japanese authorities.

6. The obligations for the withholding and payment of income tax and of social security contributions, and, except as may otherwise be mutually agreed, the conditions of employment and work, such as those relating to wages and supplementary payments, the conditions for the protection of workers, and the rights of workers concerning labor relations shall be those laid down by the legislation of Japan.

7. Members of the civilian component shall not be subject to Japanese laws or regulations with respect to terms and conditions of employment.

8. Neither members of the United States armed forces, civilian component, nor their dependents, shall by reason of this Article enjoy any exemption from taxes or similar charges, relating to personal purchases of goods and services in Japan chargeable under Japanese legislation.

9. Except as such disposal may be authorized by the Japanese and United States authorities in accordance with mutually agreed conditions, goods purchased in Japan exempt from the taxes referred to in paragraph 3, shall not be disposed of in Japan to persons not entitled to purchase such goods exempt from such tax.

Article XIII

1. The United States armed forces shall not be subject to taxes or similar charges on property held, used or transferred by such forces in Japan.

2. Members of the United States armed forces, the civilian component, and their dependents shall not be liable to pay any Japanese taxes to the Japanese Government or to any other taxing agency in Japan on income received as a result of their service with or employment by the United States armed forces, or by the organizations provided for in Article XV. The provisions of this Article do not exempt such persons from payment of Japanese taxes on income derived from Japanese sources, nor do they exempt United States citizens who for United States income tax purposes claim Japanese residence from payment of Japanese taxes on income. Periods during which such persons are in Japan solely by reason of being members of the United States armed forces, the civilian component, or their dependents shall not be considered as periods of residence or domicile in Japan for the purpose of Japanese taxation.

3. Members of the United States armed forces, the civilian component, and their dependents shall be exempt from taxation in Japan on the holding, use, transfer inter se, or transfer by death of movable property,

tangible or intangible, the presence of which in Japan is due solely to the temporary presence of these persons in Japan, provided that such exemption shall not apply to property held for the purpose of investment or the conduct of business in Japan or to any intangible property registered in Japan. There is no obligation under this Article to grant exemption from taxes payable in respect of the use of roads by private vehicles.

Article XIV

1. Persons, including corporations organized under the laws of the United States, and their employees who are ordinarily resident in the United States and whose presence in Japan is solely for the purpose of executing contracts with the United States for the benefit of the United States armed forces shall, except as provided in this Article, be subject to the laws and regulations of Japan.
2. Upon certification by appropriate United States authorities as to their identity, such persons and their employees shall be accorded the following benefits of this Agreement:
   (a) Rights of accession and movement, as provided for in Article V, paragraph 2;
   (b) Entry into Japan in accordance with the provisions of Article IX;
   (c) The exemption from customs duties, and other such charges provided for in Article XI, paragraph 3, for members of the United States armed forces, the civilian component, and their dependents;
   (d) If authorized by the United States Government, the right to use the services of the organizations provided for in Article XV;
   (e) Those provided for in Article XIX, paragraph 2, for members of the armed forces of the United States, the civilian component, and their dependents;
   (f) If authorized by the United States Government, the right to use military payment certificates, as provided for in Article XX;
   (g) The use of postal facilities provided for in Article XXI;
   (h) Exemption from the laws and regulations of Japan with respect to terms and conditions of employment.
3. Such persons and their employees shall be so described in their passports and their arrival, departure and their residence while in Japan shall from time to time be notified by the United States armed forces to the Japanese authorities.

4. Upon certification by an authorized officer of the United States armed forces depreciable assets except houses, held, used, or transferred, by such persons and their employees exclusively for the execution of contracts referred to in paragraph 1 shall not be subject to taxes or similar charges of Japan.

5. Upon certification by an authorized officer of the United States armed forces, such persons and their employees shall be exempt from taxation in Japan on the holding, use, transfer by death, or transfer to persons or agencies entitled to tax exemption under this Agreement, of movable property tangible or intangible, the presence of which in Japan is due solely to the temporary presence of these persons in Japan, provided that such exemption shall not apply to property held for the purpose of investment or the conduct of other business in Japan or to any intangible property registered in Japan. There is no obligation under this Article to grant exemption from taxes payable in respect of the use of roads by private vehicles.

6. The persons and their employees referred to in paragraph 1 shall not be liable to pay income or corporation taxes to the Japanese Government or to any other taxing agency in Japan on any income derived under a contract made in the United States with the United States Government in connection with the construction, maintenance or operation of any of the facilities or areas covered by this Agreement. The provisions of this paragraph do not exempt such persons from payment of income or corporation taxes on income derived from Japanese sources, nor do they exempt such persons and their employees who, for United States income tax purposes, claim Japanese residence, from payment of Japanese taxes on income. Periods during which such persons are in Japan solely in connection with the execution of a contract with the United States Government shall not be considered periods of residence or domicile in Japan for the purposes of such taxation.

7. Japanese authorities shall have the primary right to exercise jurisdiction over the persons and their employees referred to in paragraph 1 of this Article in relation to offenses committed in Japan and punishable by the law of Japan. In those cases in which the Japanese authorities decide not to exercise such jurisdiction they shall notify the military authorities of the United States as soon as possible. Upon such notification the military authorities of the United States shall have the right to exercise such jurisdiction over the persons referred to as is conferred on them by the law of the United States.

Article XV

1. (a) Navy exchanges, post exchanges, messes, social clubs, theaters, newspapers and other non-appropriated fund organizations authorized and regulated by the United States military authorities may be established in the facilities and areas in use by the United States armed forces for the use of members of such forces, the civilian component, and their dependents. Except as otherwise provided in this Agreement, such organizations shall not be subject to Japanese regulations, License, fees, taxes or similar controls.

   (b) When a newspaper authorized and regulated by the United States military authorities is sold to the general public, it shall be subject to Japanese regulations, License, fees, taxes or similar controls so far as such circulation is concerned.

2. No Japanese tax shall be imposed on sales of merchandise and services by such organizations, except as provided in paragraph 1 (b), but purchases within Japan of merchandise and supplies by such organizations shall be subject to Japanese taxes.

3. Except as such disposal may be authorized by the United States and Japanese authorities in accordance with mutually agreed conditions, goods which are sold by such organizations shall not be disposed of in Japan to persons not authorized to make purchases from such organizations.

4. The obligations for the withholding and payment of income tax and of social security contributions, and, except as may otherwise be mutually agreed, the conditions of employment and work, such as those relating to wages and supplementary payments, the conditions for the protection of workers, and the rights of workers concerning labor relations shall be those laid down by the legislation of Japan.

5. The organizations referred to in this Article shall provide such information to the Japanese authorities as is required by Japanese tax legislation.

Article XVI

It is the duty of members of the United States armed forces, the civilian component, and their dependents to respect the law of Japan and to abstain from any activity inconsistent with the spirit of this Agreement, and, in particular, from any political activity in Japan.

Article XVII

1. Upon the coming into force with respect to the United States of the "Agreement between the Parties to the North Atlantic Treaty regarding the Status of their Forces," signed at London on June 19, 1951, the United Sates will immediately conclude with Japan, at the option of Japan, an agreement on criminal jurisdiction similar to the corresponding provisions of that Agreement.

2. Pending the coming into force with respect to the United States of the North Atlantic Treaty Agreement referred to in paragraph 1, the United States service courts and authorities shall have the right to exercise within Japan exclusive jurisdiction over all offenses which may be committed in Japan by members of the United States armed forces, the civilian component, and their dependents, excluding their dependents who have only Japanese nationality. Such jurisdiction may in any case be waived by the United States.

3. While the jurisdiction provided in paragraph 2 is effective, the following provisions shall apply:

   (a) Japanese authorities may arrest members of the United States armed forces, the civilian component, or their dependents outside facilities and areas in use by United States armed forces for the commission or attempted commission of an offense, but in the event of such an arrest, the individual or individuals shall be immediately turned over to the United States armed forces. Any person fleeing from the jurisdiction of the United States armed forces and found in any place outside the facilities and areas may on request be arrested by the Japanese authorities and turned over to the United States authorities.

   (b) The United States authorities shall have the exclusive right to arrest within facilities and areas in use by United States armed forces. Any person subject to the jurisdiction of Japan and found in any such facility or area will, on request, be turned over to the Japanese authorities.

   (c) The United States authorities may, under due process of law, arrest, in the vicinity of such a facility or area, any person in the commission or attempted commission of an offense against the security of that facility or area. Any such person not subject to the jurisdiction of the United States armed forces shall be immediately turned over to Japanese authorities.

   (d) Subject to the provisions of paragraph 3 (c), the activities outside the facilities and areas of military police of the United States armed forces shall be limited to the extent necessary for maintaining order and discipline of and arresting members of the United States armed forces, the civilian component, and their dependents.

(e) The authorities of the United States and Japan shall cooperate in making available witnesses and evidence for criminal investigations and other criminal proceedings in their respective tribunals and shall assist each other in the making of investigations. In the event of a criminal contempt, perjury, or an obstruction of justice before a tribunal which does not have criminal jurisdiction over the individual committing the offense, he shall be tried by a tribunal which has jurisdiction over him as if he had committed the offense before it.

(f) The United States armed forces shall have the exclusive right of removing from Japan members of the United States armed forces, the civilian component, and their dependents. The United States will give sympathetic consideration to a request by the Government of Japan for the removal of any such person for good cause.

(g) Japanese authorities shall have no right of search or seizure, with respect to any persons or property, within facilities and areas in use by the United States armed forces, or with respect to property of the United States armed forces wherever situated. At the request of the Japanese authorities the United States authorities undertake, within the limits of their authority, to make such search and seizure and inform the Japanese authorities as to the results thereof. In the event of a judgment concerning such property, except property owned or utilized by the United States Government, the United States will turn over such property to the Japanese authorities for disposition in accordance with the judgment. Japanese authorities shall have no right of search or seizure outside facilities and areas in use by the United States armed forces with respect to the persons or property of members of the United States armed forces, the civilian component, or their dependents, except as to such persons as may be arrested in accordance with paragraph 3 (a) of this Article, and except as to cases where such search is required for the purpose of arresting offenders under the jurisdiction of Japan.

(h) A death sentence shall not be carried out in Japan by the United States armed forces if the legislation of Japan does not provide for such punishment in a similar case.

4. The United States undertakes that the United States service courts and authorities shall be willing and able to try and, on conviction, to

punish all offenses against the laws of Japan which members of the United States armed forces, civilian component, and their dependents may be alleged on sufficient evidence to have committed in Japan, and to investigate and deal appropriately with any alleged offense committed by members of the United States armed forces, the civilian component, and their dependents, which may be brought to their notice by Japanese authorities or which they may find to have taken place. The United States further undertakes to notify the Japanese authorities of the disposition made by United States service courts of all cases arising under this paragraph. The United States shall give sympathetic consideration to a request from Japanese authorities for a waiver of its jurisdiction in cases arising under this paragraph where the Japanese Government considers such waiver to be of particular importance. Upon such waiver, Japan may exercise its own jurisdiction.

5. In the event the option referred to in paragraph 1 is not exercised by Japan, the jurisdiction provided for in paragraph 2 and the following paragraphs shall continue in effect. In the event the said North Atlantic Treaty Agreement has not come into effect within one year from the effective date of this Agreement, the United States will, at the request of the Japanese Government, reconsider the subject of jurisdiction over offenses committed in Japan by members of the United States armed forces, the civilian component, and their dependents.

Article XVIII

1. Each party waives all its claims against the other party for injury or death suffered in Japan by a member of its armed forces, or a civilian governmental employee, while such member or employee was engaged in the performance of his official duties in cases where such injury or death was caused by a member of the armed forces, or a civilian employee of the other party acting in the performance of his official duties.

2. Each party waives all its claims against the other party for damage to any property in Japan owned by it, if such damage was caused by a member of the armed forces or a civilian governmental employee of the other party in the performance of his official duties.

3. Claims, other than contractual, arising out of acts or omissions of members of, or employees of the United States armed forces in the performance of official duty or out of any other act, omission or occurrence for which the United States armed forces is legally responsible, arising incident to non-combat activities and causing injury, death, or

property damage in Japan to third parties shall be dealt with by Japan in accordance with the following provisions:

(a) Claims shall be filed within one year from the date on which they arise and shall be considered and settled or adjudicated in accordance with the laws and regulations of Japan with respect to claims arising from the activities of its own employees.

(b) Japan may settle any such claims, and payment of the amount agreed upon or determined by adjudication shall be made by Japan in yen.

(c) Such payment, whether made pursuant to a settlement or to adjudication of the case by a competent tribunal of Japan, or the final adjudication by such a tribunal denying payment, shall be binding and conclusive.

(d) The cost incurred in satisfying claims pursuant to the preceding subparagraphs shall be shared on terms to be agreed by the two Governments.

(e) In accordance with procedures to be established, a statement of all claims approved or disapproved by Japan pursuant to this paragraph, together with the findings in each case, and a statement of the sums paid by Japan, shall be sent to the United States periodically, with a request for reimbursement of the share to be paid by the United States. Such reimbursement shall be made within the shortest possible time in yen.

4. Each party shall have the primary right, in the execution of the foregoing paragraphs, to determine whether its personnel were engaged in the performance of official duty. Such determination shall be made as soon as possible after the arising of the claim concerned. When the other party disagrees with the results of such determination, that party may bring the matter before the Joint Committee for consultation under the provisions of Article XXVI of this Agreement.

5. Claims against members of or employees of the United States armed forces arising out of tortious acts or omissions in Japan not done in the performance of official duty shall be dealt with in the following manner:

(a) The Japanese authorities shall consider the claim and assess compensation to the claimant in a fair and just manner, taking into account all the circumstances of the case, including the conduct of the injured person, and shall prepare a report on the matter.

(b) The report shall be delivered to the United States authorities, who shall then decide without delay whether they will offer an ex gratia payment, and if so, of what amount.

(c) If an offer of ex gratia payment is made, and accepted by the claimant in full satisfaction of his claim, the United States authorities shall make the payment themselves and inform the Japanese authorities of their decision and of the sum paid.

(d) Nothing in this paragraph shall affect the jurisdiction of the Japanese courts to entertain an action against a member or employee of the United States armed forces, unless and until there has been payment in full satisfaction of the claim.

6. (a) Members of and civilian employees of the United States armed forces, excluding those employees who have only Japanese nationality, shall not be subject to suit in Japan with respect to claims specified in paragraph 3, but shall be subject to the civil jurisdiction of Japanese courts with respect to all other types of cases.

(b) In case any private movable property, excluding that in use by the United States armed forces, which is subject to compulsory execution under Japanese law, is within the facilities and areas in use by the United States armed forces, the United States authorities shall, upon the request of Japanese courts, possess and turn over such property to the Japanese authorities.

(c) The United States authorities shall cooperate with the Japanese authorities in making available witnesses and evidence for civil proceedings in Japanese tribunals.

7. Disputes arising out of contracts concerning the procurement of materials, supplies, equipment, services, and labor by or for the United States armed forces, which are not resolved by the parties to the contract concerned, may be submitted to the Joint Committee for conciliation, provided that the provision of this paragraph shall not prejudice any right which the parties to the contract may have to file a civil suit.

Article XIX

1. Members of the United States armed forces, the civilian component, and their dependents, shall be subject to the foreign exchange controls of the Japanese Government.

2. The preceding paragraph shall not be construed to preclude the transmission into or outside of Japan of United States dollars or dollar instruments representing the official funds of the United States or realized as a result of service or employment in connection with this Agreement by members of the United States armed forces and the

civilian component, or realized by such persons and their dependents from sources outside of Japan.

3. The United States authorities shall take suitable measures to preclude the abuse of the privileges stipulated in the preceding paragraph or circumvention of the Japanese foreign exchange controls.

Article XX

1. (a) United States military payment certificates denominated in dollars may be used by persons authorized by the United States for internal transactions within the facilities and areas in use by the United States armed forces. The United States Government will take appropriate action to insure that authorized personnel are prohibited from engaging in transactions involving military payment certificates except as authorized by United States regulations. The Japanese Government will take necessary action to prohibit unauthorized persons from engaging in transactions involving military payment certificates and with the aid of United States authorities will undertake to apprehend and punish any person or persons under its jurisdiction involved in the counterfeiting or uttering of counterfeit military payment certificates.

   (b) It is agreed that the United States authorities will apprehend and punish members of the United States armed forces, the civilian component, or their dependents, who tender military payment certificates to unauthorized persons and that no obligation will be due to such unauthorized persons or to the Japanese Government or its agencies from the United States or any of its agencies as a result of any unauthorized use of military payment certificates within Japan.

2. In order to exercise control of military payment certificates the United States shall have the right to designate certain American financial institutions to maintain and operate, under United States supervision, facilities for the use of persons authorized by the United States to use military payment certificates. Institutions authorized to maintain military banking facilities will establish and maintain such facilities physically separated from their Japanese commercial banking business, with personnel whose sole duty is to maintain and operate such facilities. Such facilities shall be permitted to maintain United States currency bank accounts and to perform all financial transactions in connection therewith including receipt and remission of funds to the extent provided by Article XIX, paragraph 2, of this Agreement.

Article XXI

The United States shall have the right to establish and operate, within the facilities and areas in use by the United States armed forces, United States military post offices for the use of members of the United States armed forces, the civilian component, and their dependents, for the transmission of mail between United States military post offices in Japan and between such military post offices and other United States post offices.

Article XXII

The United States shall have the right to enroll and train all eligible United States citizens, residing in Japan, in the reserve organizations of the armed forces of the United States, except that the prior consent of the Japanese Government shall be obtained in the case of persons employed by the Japanese Government.

Article XXIII

The United States and Japan will cooperate in taking such steps as may from time to time be necessary to ensure the security of the United States armed forces, the members thereof, the civilian component, their dependents, and their property. The Japanese Government agrees to seek such legislation and to take such other action as may be necessary to ensure the adequate security and protection within its territory of installations, equipment, property, records and official information of the United States, and for the punishment of offenders under the applicable laws of Japan.

Article XXIV

In the event of hostilities, or imminently threatened hostilities, in the Japan area, the Governments of the United States and Japan shall immediately consult together with a view to taking necessary joint measures for the defense of that area and to carrying out the purposes of Article 1 of the Security Treaty.

Article XXV

1. It is agreed that the United States will bear for the duration of this Agreement without cost to Japan all expenditures incident to the

maintenance of the United States armed forces in Japan except those to be borne by Japan as provided in paragraph 2.

2. It is agreed that Japan will:

(a) Furnish for the duration of this Agreement without cost to the United States and make compensation where appropriate to the owners and suppliers thereof all facilities, areas and rights of way, including facilities and areas jointly used such as those at airfields and ports, as provided in Articles II and III.

(b) Make available without cost to the United States, until the effective date of any new arrangement reached as a result of periodic reexamination, an amount of Japanese currency equivalent to $155 million per annum for the purpose of procurement by the United States of transportation and other requisite services and supplies in Japan. The rate of exchange at which yen payments will be credited shall be the official par value, or that rate considered most favorable by the United States which on the day of payment is available to any party, authorized by the Japanese Government or used in any transaction with any party by the Japanese Government or its agencies or by Japanese banks authorized to deal in foreign exchange, and which, if both countries have agreed par values with the International Monetary Fund, is not prohibited by the Articles of Agreement of the Fund.

3. It is agreed that arrangements will be effected between the Governments of the United States and Japan for accounting applicable to financial transactions arising out of this Agreement.

Article XXVI

1. A Joint Committee shall be established as the means for consultation between the United States and Japan on all matters requiring mutual consultation regarding the implementation of this Agreement. In particular, the Joint Committee shall serve as the means for consultation in determining the facilities and areas in Japan which are required for the use of the United States in carrying out the purposes stated in Article I of the Security Treaty.

2. The Joint Committee shall be composed of a representative of the United States and of Japan, each of whom shall have one or more deputies and a staff. The Joint Committee shall determine its own procedures, and arrange for such auxiliary organs and administrative services as may be required. The Joint Committee shall be so organized

that it may meet immediately at any time at the request of the representative of either the United States or Japan.

3. If the Joint Committee is unable to resolve any matter, it shall refer that matter to the respective Governments for further consideration through appropriate channels.

Article XXVII

1. This Agreement shall come into force on the date on which the Security Treaty between the United States and Japan enters into force.

2. Each party to this Agreement undertakes to seek from its legislature necessary budgetary and legislative action with respect to provisions of this Agreement which require such action for their execution.

Article XXVIII

Either party may at any time request the revision of any Article of this Agreement, in which case the two Governments shall enter into negotiation through appropriate channels.

Article XXIX

This Agreement, and agreed revisions thereof, shall remain in force while the Security Treaty remains in force unless earlier terminated by agreement between the parties.

In witness whereof the representatives of the two Governments, duly authorized for the purpose, have signed this Agreement.

Done at Tokyo, in duplicate, in the English and Japanese languages, both texts authentic, this twenty-eighth day of February, 1952.

FOR THE GOVERNMENT OF THE UNITED STATES OF AMERICA:

Dean Rusk
Earl Johnson

FOR THE GOVERNMENT OF JAPAN:

K. Okazaki

~

Exchanged Notes Regarding Administrative Agreement, February 28, 1952

Under Article III of the Security Treaty between the United States of America and Japan

Excellency:

I have the honor to refer to our discussion on the terms of the Administrative Agreement signed today, in which Your Excellency stated as the opinion of the Japanese Government that, as the occupation of Japan by the Allied Powers comes to an end on the coming into force of the Treaty of Peace with Japan, the use of facilities and areas by United States forces on the basis of occupation requisition also comes to an end on the same date; thereafter, the use of facilities and areas by United States forces must be based upon agreement between the two Governments, subject to the rights which each might have under the Treaty of Peace with Japan, the Security Treaty, and the Administrative Agreement. I hereby confirm that such is also the opinion of the United States Government.

In Article II, paragraph 1, of the Administrative Agreement it is stipulated that, "Agreements as to specific facilities and areas, not already reached by the two Governments by the effective date of this Agreement, shall be concluded by the two Governments through the Joint Committee provided for in Article XXVI of this Agreement." The United States Government is confident that our two Governments are agreed that consultation shall be on an urgent basis in order to complete such arrangements at the earliest possible date.

With this in mind, the United States Government is prepared to join with the Japanese Government in constituting a Preliminary Working Group, consisting of a representative and the necessary staff from each Government, to begin such consultations immediately, with the understanding that the arrangements made by the Preliminary Working Group shall be put into effect as agreed and that the task of the Preliminary Working Group would be taken over by the Joint Committee upon the effective date of the Administrative Agreement.

However, unavoidable delays may arise in the determination and preparation of facilities and areas necessary to carry out the purposes stated in Article I of the Security Treaty. It would be much appreciated, therefore, if Japan would grant the continued use of those particular facilities and areas, with respect to which agreements and arrangements have not been completed by the expiration of ninety days after the effective date of the Treaty of Peace with Japan, pending the completion of such agreements and arrangements. Accept, Excellency, the assurances of my highest consideration.

Dean Rusk

His Excellency Katsuo Okazaki, Minister of State, Tokyo.
The Gaimusho
Tokyo
February 28, 1952.

Excellency:

I have the honor to acknowledge the receipt of Your Excellency's Note of today's date in which Your Excellency has informed me as follows:
(The American note deleted)
The Japanese Government fully shares the desire of the United States Government to initiate consultations on an urgent basis in order to complete arrangements for the use of facilities and areas at the earliest possible date. The Japanese Government agrees, therefore, to the immediate constitution of the Preliminary Working Group referred to in Your Excellency's Note, with the understanding that the arrangements made by the Preliminary Working Group shall be put into effect as agreed and that the task of the Preliminary Working Group would be taken over by the Joint Committee upon the effective date of the Administrative Agreement.

With full appreciation of the contents of Your Excellency's Note, I have the honor, on behalf of the Japanese Government, to confirm that the Japanese Government will grant to the United States the continued use of those particular facilities and areas, with respect to which agreements and arrangements have not been completed by the expiration of ninety days after the effective date of the Treaty of Peace with Japan, pending the completion of such agreements and arrangements.

Accept, Excellency, the assurances of my highest consideration.

sd/Katsuo Okazaki

~

Bibliography

Articles and Books

Aketagawa, Toru. *Nichibei Gyosei Kyotei no Seijishi: Nichibei Chii Kyotei Kenkyu Josetsu* (*The Political History of the U.S.–Japan Administrative Agreement: Introductory Study of the U.S.–Japan Status of Forces Agreement*). Tokyo: Hosei Daigaku Shuppankai, 1999.

Allison, John M. *Ambassador from the Prairie or Allison Wonderland*. Boston: Houghton Mifflin, 1973.

Amakawa, Akira. "Nihon Hondo no Senryo to Okinawa no Senryo," *Yokohama Kokusai Keizai Hogaku*, Vol. 1, No. 1 (March 1993), pp. 37–65.

Amami Senkyo 100 Shunen Kinenshi Henshubu. *Katorikku Amami 100 Nen* (*100 Years of Catholicism in Amami*). Naze: Amami Senkyo 100 Shunen Jikko Iinkai, 1992.

Amami Kyodo Kenkyukai, ed. *Gunseika no Amami: Nihon Fukki Sanju Shunen Kinenshi* (*Amami Under Military Government: Report on the Occasion of the 30th Anniversary of the Return to Japan*). Naze: Amami Kyodo Kenkyukai, 1983.

Amos, Paul S. "Okinawa and the Liuchius," *Department of State Bulletin*, Vol. 12, No. 304 (April 22, 1945), pp. 743–748.

Arasaki, Moriteru. *Okinawa Gendaishi e no Shogen* (*Testimony to Modern Okinawa History*), Vol. 2. Naha: Okinawa Taimususha, 1982.

Aston, W. G. *Nihongi: Chronicles of Japan from the earliest times to A.D. 697* (as translated from the original Chinese and Japanese). London: Kegan Paul, Trench, Trubner, 1924.

Ballantine, Joseph W. "The Future of the Ryukyus," *Foreign Affairs*, Vol. 31, No.4 (July 1953), pp. 663–674.

Barrett, George. "Report on Okinawa: A Rampart We Built," *New York Times Magazine*, September 21, 1952, pp. 9–11, 63, 65.

Bennet, Com. Henry Stanley. "The Impact of Invasion and Occupation on the Civilians of Okinawa," *U.S. Naval Institute Proceedings*, Vol. 72 (February 1946), pp. 262–275.

Bess, Demaree. "Okinawa—American Island," *Saturday Evening Post*, Vol. 226, No. 1 (July 11, 1953), pp. 26–27, 86–88.

Berger, Graenum. *A Not So Silent Envoy: A Biography of Ambassador Samuel David Berger*. Private Publisher.

Bogan, Eugene F. "Government of the Trust Territory of the Pacific Islands," *The Annals of the American Academy of Political and Social Science*, Vol. 267 (January 1950), pp. 164–174.

Borton, Hug. *Spanning Japan's Modern Century: The Memoirs of Hugh Borton*. Lanham, Md.: Lexington, 2002.

Braibanti, Ralph J. D. "The Outlook for the Ryukyus," *Far Eastern Survey*, Vol. 22, No. 7 (June 1953), pp. 73–78.

Braibanti, Ralph J. D. "The Role of Administration in the Occupation of Japan," *The Annals of the American Academy of Political and Social Science*, Vol. 267 (January 1950), pp. 154–163.

Bradley, Omar N. *A General's Life: An Autobiography*. New York: Simon and Schuster, 1983.

Bowie, Robert R., and Richard H. Immerman. *Waging Peace: How Eisenhower Shaped an Enduring Cold War Strategy*. New York: Oxford University Press, 1998.

Blumenson, Martin. *Mark Clark: The Last of the Great World War II Commanders*. New York: Congdon and Weed, 1984.

Caldwell, John T. "Okinawa 1945–1946" in Committee Members for the Watkins Paper Publication, ed. *Papers of James T. Watkins IV: Historical Records of Postwar Okinawa: The Begining of U.S. Occupancy* [sic]. Ginowan: Ryokurindo Shoten, 1993.

Cary, Otis. *A History of Christianity in Japan: Roman Catholic, Greek Orthodox, and Protestant Missions*. Tokyo: Charles E. Tuttle, 1976.

Chang, Hsia-hai. "The Treaty With Japan: A Chinese View," *Foreign Affairs*, Vol. 26, No. 3 (April 1948), pp. 505–514.

Clark, Mark W. *From the Danube to the Yalu*. New York: Harper and Brothers , 1954.

Committee Members for the Watkins Paper Publication, ed. *Papers of James T. Watkins IV: Historical Records of Postwar Okinawa: The Begining of U.S. Occupancy* [sic]. Ginowan: Ryokurindo Shoten, 1993.

Connor, Sydney. "The Navy's Entry into Military Government," *The Annals of the American Academy of Political and Social Science*, Vol. 267 (January 1950), pp. 8–18.

Cutler, Robert. *No Time for Rest*. Boston: Little, Brown and Co., 1965.

Cutler, Robert. "The Development of the National Security Council," *Foreign Affairs*, Vol. 34, No. 4 (April 1956), pp. 441–458.

Davidonis, A. C. "Some Problems of Military Government," *The American Political Science Review*, Vol. 38, No. 3 (June 1944), pp. 460–474.

Department of State. *Foreign Relations of the United States, 1942, China*. Washington, D.C.: Government Printing Office, 1956.

Department of State. *Foreign Relations of the United States, 1943, The Conferences at Cairo and Tehran*. Washington, D.C.: Government Printing Office, 1961.

Department of State. *Foreign Relations of the United States, 1945, Vol. 1, General; The United Nations*. Washington, D.C.: Government Printing Office, 1967.

Department of State. *Foreign Relations of the United States, 1945, Vol. 6, The British Commonwealth, The Far East*. Washington, D.C.: Government Printing Office, 1969.

Department of State. *Foreign Relations of the United States, 1946, Vol. 1, General; The United Nations*. Washington, D.C.: Government Printing Office, 1972.

Department of State. *Foreign Relations of the United States, 1946, Vol. 8, The Far East*. Washington, D.C.: Government Printing Office, 1971.

Department of State. *Foreign Relations of the United States, 1947, Vol. 1, General; The United Nations*. Washington, D.C.: Government Printing Office, 1973.

Department of State. *Foreign Relations of the United States, 1947, Vol. 6, The Far East*. Washington, D.C.: Government Printing Office, 1972.

Department of State. *Foreign Relations of the United States, 1948, Vol. 1, General; The United Nations (in two parts) Part 2*. Washington, D.C.: Government Printing Office, 1976.

Department of State. *Foreign Relations of the United States, 1948, Vol. 6, The Far East and Australasia*. Washington, D.C.: Government Printing Office, 1974.

Department of State. *Foreign Relations of the United States, 1949, Vol. 7, The Far East and Australasia (in two parts) Part 2*. Washington, D.C.: Government Printing Office, 1976.

Department of State. *Foreign Relations of the United States, 1950, Vol. 6, East Asia and the Pacific*. Washington, D.C.: Government Printing Office, 1976.

Department of State. *Foreign Relations of the United States, 1951, Vol. 6, Asia and the Pacific (in two parts) Part 1*. Washington, D.C.: Government Printing Office, 1977.

Department of State. *Foreign Relations of the United States, 1952–1954, Vol. 14, China and Japan (in two parts) Part 2*. Washington, D.C.: Government Printing Office, 1985.

Dickinson, Fred R. "Nichibei Anpo Taisei no Henyo: MSA Kyotei ni Okeru Saigunbi ni Kansuru Ryokai" (United States–Japan Security System in Transition: The 1954 Mutual Defense Assistance Agreement and Japanese Rearmament), *Hogaku Ronso (Kyoto Law Review)*, Vol. 121, No. 4 (July 1987)–Vol. 122, No. 3 (December 1987), pp. 60–82, 103–131.

Dower, John W. *Empire and Aftermath: Yoshida Shigeru and the Japanese Experience, 1878–1954.* Cambridge, Mass.: Council on East Asian Studies, 1988.

Dulles, Foster Rhea, and Gerald E. Ridinger. "The Anti-Colonial Policies of Franklin D. Roosevelt," *Political Science Quarterly*, Vol. 70, No. 1 (March 1955), pp. 1–18.

Dulles, John Foster. "Policy for Security and Peace," *Foreign Affairs*, Vol. 32, No. 4 (April 1954), pp. 353–364.

Dulles, John Foster. "Security in the Pacific," *Foreign Affairs*, Vol. 30, No. 2 (January 1952), pp. 175–187.

Dulles, John Foster. *War or Peace.* New York: Macmillan, 1950.

Dunn, Frederick S. *Peace-Making and the Settlement with Japan.* Princeton: Princeton University Press, 1963.

Eisenhower, Dwight D. *The White House Years, 1953–1956: Mandate for Change.* Garden City, N.Y.: Doubleday, 1963.

Eldridge, Robert D. "'Fukki Undo' no Kessokuryoku ni Manabu" (Learning from the Unity [Seen] in the 'Reversion Movement'), in Nankai Nichinichi Shimbun, ed. *Sorezore no Amami Ron 50: Amami 21 Seiki e no Joso (50 Essays on Amami: Prelude to Amami in the 21st Century).* Kagoshima: Nanpo Shinsha, 2001, pp. 110–114.

Eldridge, Robert D. "Ogasawara to Nichibei Kankei, 1945–1968" (Ogasawara and U.S.–Japan Relations, 1945–1968), in Daniel Long, ed., *Ogasawara Gaku Koto Hajime (An Introduction to Ogasawara Studies).* Kagoshima: Nanpo Shinsha, 2002, pp. 245–272.

Eldridge, Robert D. "San Furanshisuko Kowa to Okinawa no Shori: 'Senzai Shuken' o Meguru Yoshid–Daresu no 'Kosho' (The San Francisco Peace Treaty and the Disposition of Okinawa: The Yoshida–Dulles 'Negotiations' over 'Residual Sovereignty')." *Yomiuri Rondan Shinjinsho Saiyushusho (Yomiuri Newspaper 1999 First Place Award Article), Yomiuri Rondan Shinjin Ronbunshu,* 1999, pp. 6–33.

Eldridge, Robert D. "Showa Tenno to Okinawa: 'Tenno Messeeji' no Saikosatsu" (The Showa Emperor and Okinawa: The 'Tenno Message' Reexamined), *Chuo Koron,* Vol. 114, No. 3 (March 1999), pp. 152–171.

Eldridge, Robert D. "The Amami Reversion Movement: Its Origins, Activities, Impact, and Meaning," *Asian Cultural Studies,* No. 27 (March 2001), pp. 77–98.

Eldridge, Robert D. "The Japanese Government, the San Francisco Peace Treaty, and the Disposition of Okinawa, 1945–1952," *The Transactions of the Asiatic Society of Japan,* Fourth Series, Vol. 14 (1999), pp. 123–141.

Eldridge, Robert D. *The Origins of the Bilateral Okinawa Problem: Okinawa in Postwar U.S.–Japan Relations, 1945–1952.* New York: Garland, 2001.

Eldridge, Robert D. "40 Nenmae Togo Keikaku ni Manabu" (Learning from the Consolidation Plans of 40 Years Ago), *Ryukyu Shimpo,* January 19–February 2, 2001 series.

Eldridge, Robert D., and Ayako Kusunoki. "To Base or Not to Base? Yoshida Shigeru, the 1950 Ikeda Mission, and Post-Treaty Japanese Security Conceptions," *Kobe University Law Review,* No. 33 (1999), pp. 97–126.

Emerson, Rupert. "American Policy Toward Pacific Dependencies," *Pacific Affairs*, Vol. 20 (September 1947), pp. 259–275.

Emerson, Rupert. *From Empire to Nation: The Rise to Self-Assertion of Asian and African Peoples*. Boston: Beacon Press, 1960.

Fisch, Arnold G., Jr. *Military Government in the Ryukyu Islands, 1945–1950*. Washington, D.C.: Center of Military History, 1988.

Foltos, Lester J. "The New Pacific Barrier: America's Search for Security in the Pacific, 1945–1947," *Diplomatic History*, No. 13 (Summer 1989), pp. 317–342.

Ford, Clellan S. "Occupation Experiences on Okinawa," *The Annals of the American Academy of Political and Social Science*, Vol. 267 (January 1950), pp. 175–182.

Foreign Office, Japanese Government, ed. *Minor Islands Adjacent to Japan Proper: Part II Ryukyu and Other Nansei Islands*. Tokyo: Foreign Office, Japanese Government, March 1947.

Fujiwara, Nanpu. *Shin Amamishi (New Amami History)*. Naze: Amami Shunjusha, 1980.

Fukunaga, Fumio, ed. *GHQ Minseikyoku Shiryo, Vol. 2 Senryo Kaikaku: Senkyoho-Seijishikin Kiseiho (Government Section, GHQ Materials, Vol. 2 Occupation Reforms: Election Law and Political Funds Law.)* Tokyo: Maruzen, 1997.

Gabe, Masaaki. *Nichibei Kankei no Naka no Okinawa (Okinawa in Postwar Japan–U.S. Relations)*. Tokyo: Sanichi Shobo, 1996.

Gabe, Masao. "Senryo Shoki no Okinawa ni Okeru Seigun Kankei" (Civil–Military Relations in Okinawa Under U.S. Occupation), *Nenpo Seijigaku* (1989), pp. 47–73.

Gaddis, John Lewis. *The United States and the Origins of the Cold War, 1941–1947*. New York: Columbia University Press, 1972.

Gallicchio, Marc S. *The Cold War Begins in Asia: American East Asian Policy and the Fall of the Japanese Empire*. New York: Columbia University Press, 1988.

Gilchrist, Huntington. "The Japanese Islands: Annexation or Trusteeship?" *Foreign Affairs*, Vol. 22, No. 4 (July 1944), pp. 635–642.

Government Section, Supreme Commander for the Allied Powers, ed., *Political Reorientation of Japan, September 1945 to September 1948, Volume 2*. Washington, D.C.: Government Printing Office, 1949; reprint edition, Westport, Conn.: Greenwood Press, 1970.

Greenstein, Fred I., and Richard H. Immerman. "Effective National Security Advising: Recovering the Eisenhower Legacy," *Political Science Quarterly*, Vol. 115, No. 3 (Fall 2000), pp. 335–345.

Greenstein, Fred I. *The Hidden-Hand Presidency: Eisenhower as Leader*. Baltimore, Md.: Johns Hopkins University Press, 1994.

Hagiwara, Toru. *Kowa to Nihon (The Peace Settlement and Japan)*. Tokyo: Yomiuri Shimbunsha, 1950.

Halperin, Morton H. *Bureaucratic Politics and Foreign Policy*. Washington, D.C.: The Brookings Institution, 1974.

Hara, Kimie. *Japanese–Soviet/Russian Relations Since 1945: A Difficult Peace*. London, U.K.: Routledge, 1998.

Hareven, Tamara K. *Eleanor Roosevelt: An American Conscience*. New York: Da Capo Press, 1975.

Haring, Douglas G. "Amami Gunto: Forgotten Islands," *Far Eastern Quarterly*, Vol. 21, No. 16 (November 19, 1952), pp. 170–172.

Haring, Douglas G. *Scientific Investigations in the Ryukyu Islands (SIRI): Progress Report on Anthropological Study? The Island of Amami Oshima in the Northern Ryukyus*. Washington, D.C.: Pacific Science Board, National Research Council, November 1951.

Haring, Douglas G. *Scientific Investigations in the Ryukyu Islands (SIRI): The Island of Amami Oshima in the Northern Ryukyus*. Washington, D.C.: Pacific Science Board, National Research Council, October 1952.

Hata, Ikuhiko. *Hirohito Tenno Itsutsu no Ketsudan* (*The Five Decisions of Emperor Hirohito*). Tokyo: Kodansha, 1984 (later revised several years after Hirohito's death as *Showa Tenno Itsutsu no Ketsudan* (*The Five Decisions of the Showa Emperor*). Tokyo: Bungei Shunjusha, 1994).

Hata, Ikuhiko. *Shiroku Saigunbi* (*A Record of Japan's Rearmament*). Tokyo: Bungei Shunju, 1976.

Hayward, Edwin J. "Coordination of Military and Civilian Affairs Planning," *The Annals of the American Academy of Political and Social Science*, Vol. 267 (January 1950), pp. 19–27.

Higa, Mikio. *Politics and Parties in Postwar Okinawa*. Vancouver: University of British Columbia, 1963.

Hiyane, Teruo. *Kindai Okinawa no Seishinshi* (*Modern Okinawa's Psychological History*). Tokyo: Shakai Hyoronsha, 1996.

Hosoya, Chihiro. "Japan's Response to U.S. Policy on the Japanese Peace Treaty: The Dulles–Yoshida Talks of January–February 1951," *Hitotsubashi Journal of Law and Politics* (December 1981), pp. 15–27.

Hosoya, Chihiro. *San Furanshisuko Kowa e no Michi* (*The Road to the San Francisco Peace Treaty*). Tokyo: Chuo Koronsha, 1984.

Hyneman, Charles S. "The Army's Civil Affairs Training Program," *The American Political Science Review*, Vol. 38, No. 2 (April 1944), pp. 342–353.

Igarashi, Takeshi. "American–Japanese Peace-Making and the Cold War, 1947–1951," *Amerika Kenkyu*, Vol. 13 (March 1979), pp. 166–187.

Igarashi, Takeshi. "Peace-Making and Party Politics: The Formation of the Domestic Foreign-Policy System in Postwar Japan," *Journal of Japanese Studies*, Vol. 11, No. 2 (Summer 1985), pp. 323–356.

Igarashi, Takeshi. *Tainichi Kowa to Reisen* (*The Treaty of Peace with Japan and the Cold War*). Tokyo: Tokyo Daigaku Shuppankai, 1986.

Ikeda, Hayato. *Kinko Zaisei fu Senryoka Sannen no Omoide* (*Balanced Finance and Memories of Three Years Under Occupation*). Tokyo: Chuo Koron Shinsha, 1999.

Ikeda, Shintaro. "Jon Arison to Nihon Saigunbi, 1952–1953" (John Allison and Japanese Rearmament, 1952–1953), *Gaiko Jiho* (*Diplomatique Revue*), No. 1343 (November–December 1997), pp. 109–125.

Inoki, Masamichi. *Hyoden Yoshida Shigeru* (*Yoshida Shigeru: A Biography*). Tokyo: Yomiuri Shimbunsha, 1981.

Iokibe, Makoto. *Beikoku no Nihon Senryo Seisaku* (*U.S. Occupation Policy for Japan*). Tokyo: Chuo Koronsha, 1985.

Iokibe, Makoto. *Nichibei Senso to Sengo Nihon* (*The Japan–U.S. War and Postwar Japan*). Osaka: Osaka Shoseki, 1989.

Iokibe, Makoto. *Sengo Nihon Gaikoshi* (*A History of Postwar Japanese Diplomacy*). Tokyo: Yuhikaku, 1999.

Iokibe, Makoto. *Senryoki: Shushotachi no Shin Nippon* (*The Occupation Period: The Prime Ministers and the New Japan*). Tokyo: Yomiuri Shimbunsha, 1997.

Iokibe, Makoto, ed. *The Occupation of Japan: U.S. Planning Documents, 1942–1945.* Bethesda, Md.: Congressional Information Service, Inc., 1987.

Iokibe, Makoto, ed. *The Occupation of Japan, Part 2: U.S. and Allied Policy, 1945–1952.* Bethesda, Md.: Congressional Information Service, Inc., 1989.

Iokibe, Makoto, ed. *The Occupation of Japan, Part 3: Reform, Recovery and Peace, 1945–1952.* Bethesda, Md.: Congressional Information Service, Inc., 1991.

Izumi Horo Shotoku Kinenzo Kenritsu Kinen Iinkai, ed. *Imazo Sokoku e: Izumi Horo Shotoku Kinenzo Kenritsu Kinenshi* (*And Now, to the Fatherland: A Journal Recording the Creation of the Izumi Horo Memorial Statue*). Isen: Izumi Horo Shotoku Kinenzo Kenritsu Kinen Iinkai, 1998.

Johnson, Robert H. "The National Security Council: The Relevance of its Past to Its Future." *Orbis*, Vol. 13, No. 3 (Fall 1969), pp. 714–717.

Johnstone, William C. "Trusteeship for Whom?" *Far Eastern Survey*, Vol. 14, No. 12 (June 20, 1945), pp. 156–159.

Kagoshima Kenritsu Tankidaigaku Chiiki Kenkyusho, ed. *Amami Gunto no Keizai Shakai no Henyo* (*Changes in the Economic Society of the Amami Islands*). Kaghoshima: Kagoshima Kenritsu Tankidaigaku Chiiki Kenkyusho, 1999.

Kaitei Nazeshishi Hensan Iinkai, ed. *Kaitei Nazeshishi* (*Revised History of Naze City*), Vol. 1. Naze: Nazeshiyakusho, 1996.

Kajiura, Atsushi. "Amami Shoto no Henkan o Meguru Beikoku no Tainichi/Taisokan" (The Views of the U.S. Toward Japan and the Soviet Union in the Reversion of the Amami Islands), *Kokusai Seiji* (*International Relations*), No. 105 (January 1994), pp. 112–126.

Kalischer, Peter. "Our Gibraltar in the Pacific," *Collier's* (October 11, 1952), pp. 22–26.

Kamiya, Yuji. *Amami, Motto Shiritai* (*Learning More about Amami*). Kagoshima: Nanpo Shinsha, 2001.

Kanai, Masao, ed. *Amami Oshima Fukki Undo Kaikoroku* (*Recollections on the Amami Oshima Reversion Movement*). Tokyo: Yamamotosha, 1966.

Kanai, Masao. "Amami Oshima No Sokoku Fukki Naru" (The Successful Return of Amami Oshima to the Fatherland), in Terebi Tokyo, ed. *Shogen: Watashino Showashi* (*Testimony: My Showa History*), Vol. 6. Tokyo: Gakugei Shorin, 1969.

Karasik, Daniel D. "Okinawa: A Problem in Administration and Reconstruction," *Far Eastern Quarterly*, Vol. 7, No. 3 (May 1948), pp. 254–267.

Kayo, Yasuharu. *Okinawa Minseifu: Hitotsu no Jidai no Kiseki* (*Okinawa Civil Administration: The Foundation of an Era*). Tokyo: Kume Shobo, 1986.

Keesing, Felix M. "The Former Japanese Mandated Islands," *Far Eastern Survey*, Vol. 14, No. 19 (September 26, 1945), pp. 269–271.

Kennan, George F. *Memoirs, Volume I: 1925–1950*. Boston: Little, Brown, 1967.

Kennan, George F. *Memoirs, Volume II: 1950–1963*. Boston: Little, Brown, 1972.

Kerr, George H. *Okinawa: The History of an Island People*. Rutland, Vt.: Charles E. Tuttle, 1958.

Kojima, Noboru. *Kowa Joyaku* (*The Peace Treaty*). Tokyo: Shinchosha, 1992.

Kokusaiho Jirei Kenkyukai, ed. *Nihon no Kokusaiho Jirei Kenkyu, 3: Ryodo* (*Digest of Japanese Practice of International Law, Vol. 3: Territory*). Tokyo: Keio Tsushin, 1990.

Kono, Yasuko. *Okinawa Henkan o Meguru Seiji to Gaiko Nichibei Kankeishi no Bunmyaku* (*Politics and Diplomacy Over the Reversion of Okinawa in the Context of the History of Japan–U.S. Relations*). Tokyo: Tokyo Daigaku Shuppankai, 1994.

Korb, Lawrence J. *The Joint Chiefs of Staff: The First Twenty-Five Years*. Bloomington: Indiana University Press, 1976.

Kusunoki, Ayako. "Senryoka Nihon no Anzen Hosho Koso: Gaimusho ni Okeru 'Yoshida Dokutorin' no Keisei Katei" (Japanese Security Conceptions During the Occupation: The Foreign Ministry and the Formation of the 'Yoshida Doctrine'), *Rokkodai Ronshu*, Vol. 45, No. 3 (March 1999), pp. 1–55.

Lash, Joseph P. *Eleanor: The Years Alone*. New York: W. W. Norton, 1972.

Lattimore, Eleanor. "Pacific Ocean or American Lake?" *Far Eastern Survey*, Vol. 14, No. 22 (November 7, 1945), pp. 313–315.

Lawrence, William (Neal) Henry. "Emergency Visit to Amami Oshima, 1946." (Unpublished essay, 2002).

Lawrence, Neal Henry. "Okinawa: Battle and Regeneration," *The Transactions of the Asiatic Society of Japan*, Fourth Series, Vol. 12 (1997), pp. 1–17.

Maki, John M. "US Strategic Area or UN Trusteeship," *Far Eastern Survey*, Vol. 16, No. 15 (August 13, 1947), pp. 175–178.

Mason, John Brown. "Lessons of Wartime Military Government Training," *The Annals of the American Academy of Political and Social Science*, Vol. 267 (January 1950), pp. 183–192.

Masumi, Junnosuke. *Postwar Politics in Japan, 1945–1955*. Berkeley, Calif.: Institute of East Asian Studies, 1985.

Matsuda, Kiyoshi. *Amami Oshima Nihon Fukki Undoshiryo* (*Historical Materials On the Return of Amami Oshima to Japan*). Naze: Nankai Nichinichi Shambun Sha, 1968.

Matsudo, Kiyoshi. *Amami Shakai Undoshi* (*A History of Amami Social Movement*). Tokyo: JCA Shuppan, 1979.

Matsushita, Shiro. *Kindai Amami no Shihai to Shakai* (*The Control of Modern Amami and its Society*). Tokyo: Daiichi Shobo, 1983.

Megumi, Juji. *Senkyo 35 Nenshi* (*35 Years of Elections*). Naze: Nankai Nichinichi Shimbun Sha, 1981.

Migita, Shoshin. *Amami no Gunzo: Tokyo Amami Kai 100 Nen o Toru* (*The Amami Clan: Capturing 100 Years of the Tokyo Amami Kai*). Tokyo: Kobunsha, 2000.

Migita, Shoshin. *Tokyo ni Okeru Amami no Fukki Undo* (*The Reversion Movement in Tokyo*). Tokyo: Shinko Sendensha, 1966.

Minamura, Takeichi. *Sengo Nihon no Keisei to Hatten: Senryo to Kaikakuno Hikaku Kenkyu* (*The Formation and Development of Postwar Japan: Comparative Studies of Occupation and Reform*). Tokyo: Nihon Keizai Hyoronsha, 1995.

Miyashita, Masaaki. *Seido no Hinomaru* (*The Cathedral's Hinomaru Flag*). Kagoshima: Nanpo Shinsha, 1999.

Miyazato, Seigen. *Amerika no Okinawa Seisaku* (*America's Okinawa Policy*). Naha: Nirai sha, 1986.

Miyazato, Seigen. *Amerika no Okinawa Tochi* (*America's Administration of Okinawa*). Tokyo: Iwanami Shoten, 1966.

Miyazato, Seigen. *Amerika no Taigai Seisaku Kettei Katei* (*America's Foreign Policy-Making Process*). Tokyo: Sanichi Shobo, 1981.

Miyazawa, Kiichi. *Tokyo–Washinton Mitsudan* (*Secret Talks Between Tokyo and Washington*). Tokyo: Jitsugyo no Nihonsha, 1956.

Murakawa, Ichiro. *Daresu to Yoshida Shigeru* (*Dulles and Yoshida Shigeru*). Tokyo: Kokusho Kankokai, 1991.

Murayama, Iekuni. *Amami Fukkishi* (*The History of the Amami Reversion*). Naze: Nankai Nichinichi Shimbunsha, 1971.

Murphy, Robert D. *Diplomat Among Warriors*. Garden City, N.Y.: Doubleday, 1964.

Nakachi, Kiyoshi. *Ryukyu–U.S.–Japan Relations 1945–1972: The Reversion Movement Political, Economic, and Strategical* [sic] *Issues*. Quezon City, Philippines: Hiyas Press, 1989.

Nakamura, Yasutaro. *Sokoku e No Michi: Kobei 8 Nen Amami no Fukki Undoshi* (*The Road to the Fatherland: Opposing the U.S. for 8 Years, A History of the Amami Reversion Movement*). Kyoto: Tosho Shuppan, 1984.

Nakano, Yoshio, ed. *Sengo Shiryo: Okinawa* (*Postwar Materials: Okinawa*). Tokyo: Nihon Hyoronsha, 1969.

Nakayoshi, Ryoko. *Nihon Fukki Undoki* (*A Record of the Reversion Movement*). Naha: Okinawa Taimususha, 1964.

Nankai Nichinichi Shimbun Gojunenshi Hensan Iinkai, ed. *Nankai Nichinichi Shimbun Gojunenshi* (*50 Years of the Nankai Nichinichi Newspaper*). Naze: Nankai Nichinichi Shimbun sha, 1997.

Nelson, Anne Kasten. *The State Department Policy Planning Staff Papers, 1947*. New York: Garland Publishing, 1983.

Nelson, Anna Kasten, ed. *The State Department Policy Planning Staff Papers, Vol. 2: 1948.* New York: Garland Publishing, 1983.

Nelson, Anna Kasten, ed. *The State Department Policy Planning Staff Papers, Vol. 3: 1949.* New York: Garland Publishing, 1983.

Newman, Marshall T., and Ransom L. Eng. "The Ryukyu People: A Cultural Appraisal," *Smithsonian Report for 1947*, pp. 379–406.

Nihon Kyosanto Amami Chiku Iinkai, ed. *Amami no Noroshi: Amami Kyosantoshi, 1947–1953 (The Beacon of Amami: A History of the Amami Communist Party, 1947–1953).* Naze: Nihon Kyosanto Amami Chiku Iinkai, 1984.

Nishimura, Kumao. *Nihon Gaikoshi, 27: San Furanshisuko Heiwa Joyaku (Japanese Diplomatic History, Vol. 27: The San Francisco Peace Treaty).* Tokyo: Kajima Heiwa Kenkyusho, 1971.

Nishimura, Kumao. "Okinawa Kizoku no Kimaru Made—Motomeru ni Isoideatta Nihon no Seron" (Until the Reversion of Okinawa is Decided—Public Opinion Demanded [the Return of the Islands] Too Quickly), *Asahi Jaanaru*, Vol. 1, No. 15 (June 21, 1959), pp. 18–21.

Nishimura, Kumao. "San Franshisuko no Omoide" (Memories of San Francisco), *Chuo Koron*, Vol. 72, No. 6 (May 1957), pp. 74–80.

Nishimura, Tomiaki. *Amami Gunto no Kingendaishi (A Modern History of the Amami Islands).* Tokyo: Kaifusha, 1993.

Nixon, Richard. *The Memoirs of Richard Nixon.* New York: Grosset and Dunlap, 1978.

Nobori, Shomu. *Dai Amami Shi (The History of Greater Amami)*, rev. ed. Tokyo: Hara Shobo, 1975.

O'Flaherty, Edward. *Okinawa: Twenty-seven Years of American Stewardship (First Draft).* Unpublished manuscript, 1975.

Oikawa, Nagaho. *Kusetsu 8 Nen ni Omou (Reflecting on 8 Difficult Years).* Private Publisher, 1954.

Okazaki, Katsuo. "Gyosei Kyotei no Rakuyaura: Anpo Joyaku no Tsureko o Bengo Suru" (Behind the Optimists of the Administrative Agreement: Defending the Child that Accompanied the Security Treaty), *Bungei Shunju*, Vol. 40, No. 9 (September 1956), pp. 70–78.

"Okinawa and the Luchu Archipelago," *The World Today*, Vol. 3 (July 1947), pp. 363–370.

"Okinawa: Base to Dominate Asia," *U.S. News & World Report*, Vol. 30 (June 22, 1951), pp. 25–26.

"Okinawa: Forgotten Island," *Time*, Vol. 54, No. 22 (November 28, 1949), pp. 24–27.

"Okinawa: Junkyard of the Pacific," *Life*, Vol. 27 (December 19, 1949), pp. 19–23.

Okinawaken, ed. *Okinawa: Sengo 50 Nen no Ayumi (Okinawa: 50 Years of the Postwar).* Naha: Okinawaken, 1995.

Okinawa Ogasawara Henkan Domei Amami Shibu. *Nihonjin ha Nihon ni Kaese: Amami no Sokoku Fukki Undo no Kiroku (Return Japanese to Japan: A Record of the*

Amami Reversion Movement to the Fatherland). Naze: Okinawa Ogasawara Henkan Domei Amami Shibu, 1966.

"On the Alert at Okinawa," *New York Times Magazine* (September 16, 1951), pp. 10–11.

Packard, George R., III. *Protest in Tokyo: The Security Treaty Crisis of 1960.* Westport, Conn.: Greenwood Press, 1966.

"People of Amami–Oshima Cry for Return to Japan," *The Mainichi*, November 18, 1952.

Post World War II Foreign Policy Planning: State Department Records of Harley Notter, 1939–1945. Bethesda, Md.: Congressional Information Service, 1985.

Radford, Arthur W. (edited by Stephen Jurika Jr.). *From Pearl Harbor to Vietnam: The Memoirs of Admiral Arthur W. Radford.* Stanford, Calif.: Hoover Institution Press, 1980.

Records of the Joint Chiefs of Staff, Part II, 1946–1953, The Far East. Bethesda, Md.: University Publications of America, 1996.

"Reds in 'Cold War' in Japanese Isles: U.S. Catholic Mission Vies with Leftist Unit in Good Works for Ryukyu Needy," *New York Times*, January 19, 1958.

Reischauer, Edwin O. *The United States and Japan.* Cambridge, Mass.: Harvard University Press, 1950.

Reischauer, Edwin O. *My Life Between Japan and America.* Tokyo: John Weatherhill, Inc., 1986.

"Return of Entire Chain of Ryukyus is Predicted," *The Mainichi*, December 26, 1953.

Richard, Dorothy E. *The United States Naval Administration of the Trust Territories of the Pacific Islands.* Washington, D.C.: Office of Chief of Naval Operations, Department of the Navy, 1957.

Roosevelt, Eleanor. *The Autobiography of Eleanor Roosevelt.* New York: Harper and Brothers Publishers, 1958.

Ryukyu Ginko Chosabu, ed. *Sengo Okinawa Keizaishi (Postwar Okinawa Economic History).* Naze: Ryukyu Ginko, 1984.

Sakaguchi, Tokutaro. *Amami Oshima Shi (A History of Amami Oshima),* Rev. Ed. Tokyo: Maruyama Gakugei Tosho, 1984.

Sakamoto, Kazuya. "Aizenhaua no Gaiko Senryaku to Nihon, 1953–1954" (Eisenhower, the New Look and Japan Policy), *Hogaku Ronso (Kyoto Law Review),* Vol. 122, No. 3 (December 1987), pp. 59–77; Vol. 123, No. 3 (December 1988), pp. 71–94.

Sakamoto, Kazuya. *Nichibei Domei no Kizuna: Anpo Joyaku to Sogosei no Mosaku (The Bonds of the Japan–U.S. Alliance: The Security Treaty and the Search for Mutuality).* Tokyo: Yuhikaku, 2000.

Sakida, Saneyoshi. *Beigunsei no Teppeki o Koete: Watashi no Shogen to Kiroku de Tsuzuru Amami no Fukki Undoshi (Overcoming the Iron Curtain of the U.S. Military Occupation: A History of the Reversion Movement based on My Testimony and Records).* Naze: Amami Rurikakesu no Kai, 1997.

Saneshima, Ryuzo. *Ano Hi, Ano Toki* (*That Day, That Time*). Naze: Nankai Nichinichi Shimbunsha, 1996.

Saneshima, Ryuzo. "U.S. Military Rule in Amami," in Okinawa Prefectural Government, ed. *Okinawa: 50 Years of the Postwar Era*. Naha: Okinawaken, 1995.

Sarantakes, Nicholas E. *Keystone: The American Occupation of Okinawa and U.S.–Japanese Relations*. College Station: Texas A&M University Press, 2000.

Satake, Kyoko. *Gunseika Amami no Mikko-Mitsu Boeki* (*Smuggling and Secret Travels in Amami During the Occupation*). Kagoshima: Nanpo Shinsha, 2003.

Satohara, Akira. *Amerika Gunseika no Amami Oshima ni Okeru "Bunka Katsuo Nenpyo"* (*"Chronology of Cultural Activities" in Amami Oshima during the American Military Occupation*). Private publisher, copy in possession of author.

Satohara, Akira. *Ryukyuko Amami no Sengo Seishinshi: Amerika Gunseika no Shiso–Bunka no Kiseki* (*The Postwar Psychological History of Amami–Ryukyu: Thought and Culture during the American Military Occupation*). Tokyo: Satsuki Shobo, 1994.

Schaller, Michael. *Altered States: The United States and Japan Since the Occupation*. New York: Oxford University Press, 1997.

Schaller, Michael. *The American Occupation of Japan: The Origins of the Cold War in Asia*. New York: Oxford University Press, 1985.

Schoenbaum, Thomas J. *Waging Peace and War: Dean Rusk in the Truman, Kennedy, and Johnson Years*. New York: Simon and Schuster, 1988.

Schonberger, Howard B. *Aftermath of War: Americans and the Remaking of Japan, 1945–1952*. Kent, Ohio: The Kent State University Press, 1989.

Scientific Investigations in the Ryukyu Islands (SIRI), Pacific Science Board, National Research Council. "The Reversion Movement on Amami Oshima: Final Report." Unpublished report for CI&E Department, USCAR, March 1952.

Sebald, William J. *With MacArthur in Japan: A Personal History of the Occupation*. New York: W. W. Norton, 1965.

Seidensticker, Edward G. "Japanese Views on Peace," *Far Eastern Survey*, Vol. 20, No. 12 (June 13, 1951), pp. 119–124.

Shibayama, Futoshi. "Japan, An Ally of What Kind in the U.S.–Japanese Military Relations? The Negotiations Surrounding the Administrative Agreement to Implement the U.S.–Japan Security Treaty, 1951–1952," *Journal of Information and Policy Studies*, Vol. 1 (March 1999), pp. 1–24.

Shidehara, Akira. *Nanto Enkaku Shiron* (*Studies on the History of the Southern Islands*). Tokyo: Toyamabo, 1900.

Shimao, Toshio. "Neglected Islands," *Japan Quarterly*, Vol. 14, No. 1 (January 1969), pp. 72–75.

Shimoda, Takezo. *Sengo Nihon Gaiko No Shogen: Nihon wa Koshite Saisei Shita* (*Testimony of Postwar Japanese Diplomacy: This is How Japan Was Reborn*). Tokyo: Gyosei Mondai Kenkyujo, 1984.

Shindo, Eiichi. "Bunkatsu Sareta Ryodo—Okinawa, Chishima, Soshite Anpo" (Separated Territories—Okinawa, Chishima, and the Security Treaty), *Sekai*, No. 401 (April 1979), pp. 31–51, later translated as "Divided Territories and the Origin of the Cold War," *Tsukuba Hosei*, No. 13 (1990), pp. 244–273.

Shindo, Eiichi. "'Tenno Messeeji' no Sairon: Sengo Gaiko Shiryo no Yomikata" ('The Tenno Message' Revisited—Ways to Read Postwar Diplomatic Materials), *Sekai*, No. 407 (October 1979), pp. 104–113.

Slover, Robert H. "Military Government—Where Do We Stand Today?" *The Annals of the American Academy of Political and Social Science*, Vol. 267 (January 1950), pp. 193–200.

Smith, Howard. "Economy of the Ryukyu Islands," *Far Eastern Survey*, Vol. 20, No. 10 (May 1951).

Sone, Eki. *Watashi no Memoaaru: Kasumigaseki Kara Nagatacho e* (My Memoirs: From Kasumigaseki to Nagatacho). Tokyo: Nikkan Kogyo Shinbunsha, 1974.

Suzuki, Tadakatsu. *Nihon Gaikoshi, 26: Shusen Kara Kowa Made* (Japanese Diplomatic History: From the End of the War Until the Peace Treaty). Tokyo: Kajima Kenkyujo Shuppankai, 1973.

Taira, Koji. "Troubled National Identity: The Ryukyuans/Okinawans," in Michael Weiner, ed., *Japan's Minorities: The Illusion of Homogeneity*. London, U.K.: Routledge, 1997, pp. 140–177.

Takada, Toshisada. *Unmei no Shimajima Amami to Okinawa* (Destiny's Islands: Amami and Okinawa). Kagoshima: Amamisha, 1956.

Takayasu, Shigemasa. *Okinawa–Amami Henkan Undoshi* (A History of the Reversion Movement on Okinawa and Amami). Yokohama: Okinawa Amamishi Chosa Iinkai, 1975.

Takemae, Eiji. *Senryo Sengoshi: Tainichi Kanri Seisakuno Zenyo* (Occupation Postwar History: An Overview of the Occupation Policies Toward Japan). Tokyo: Sofusha, 1980.

Tanaka, Akihiko. *Anzen Hosho: Sengo 50 Nen no Mosaku* (Security: 50 Years of Searching in the Postwar). Tokyo: Yomiuri Shinbunsha, 1997.

Tanigawa, Kenichi, ed. *Okinawa, Amami, to Japan* (Okinawa, Amami, and Japan). Tokyo: Doseisha, 1986.

Teruya, Eiichi. *Okinawa Gyosei Kiko Hensenshi: Meiji 12 Nen kara Showa 59 Nen* (The History of the Changes in Okinawa's Administrative Organization: From 1879 to 1984). Private Publisher, 1984.

Tokyo Amami Kai 80 Shunen Henshu Iinkai, ed. *Tokyo Amamikai 80 Nen no Ayumi* (80 Years of the Tokyo Amami Kai). Tokyo: Tokyo Amami Kai, 1984.

Tokyo Amami Kai 100 Shunen Henshu Iinkai, ed. *Tokyo Amamikai 100 Nen no Ayumi* (100 Years of the Tokyo Amami Kai). Tokyo: Tokyo Amami Kai, 1999.

Toyoshita, Narahiko. *Anpo Joyaku no Ronri: Sono Seisei to Tenkai* (The Logic of the Security Treaty: Its Birth and Development). Tokyo: Kashiwa Shobo, 1999.

"The Okinawa Junk Heap," *Life*, Vol. 27 (December 19, 1949), pp. 29–23.

"The United States, Japan, and the Ryukyu Islands," *The World Today*, Vol. 8 (August 1952), pp. 352–360.

U.S. Amami Civil Administration Team, ed. *Amami Oshima*. Naze: U.S. Amami Civil Administration, 1952.

"U.S. Returns Islands to Japanese Control: Statement by Secretary of State John Foster Dulles," *Department of State Bulletin*, Vol. 30, No. 758 (January 4, 1954), p. 17.

Ushiomi, Toshitaka. "Amami Oshima Oboegaki" (Memorandum on Amami Oshima), *Horitsu Jiho*, Vol. 26, No. 3 (March 1954), pp. 71–76.

Veith, Ilza. "The Strategic Bonins," *Far Eastern Survey*, Vol. 14, No. 21 (October 24, 1945), pp. 307–309.

Vinacke, Harold M. "United States Far Eastern Policy," *Pacific Affairs*, Vol. 13, No. 4 (December 1946), pp. 346–353.

Wakabayashi, Chiyo. "Occupation and 'Self-Government' 1945–1946," *Social Science Japan*, No. 14 (November 1998), pp. 17–18.

Warner, Gordon. *The Okinawa Reversion Story: War, Peace, Occupation, Reversion, 1945–1972*. Naha: The Executive Link, 1995.

Watanabe, Akio. *The Okinawa Problem: A Chapter in Japan–U.S. Relations*. Melbourne: Melbourne University Press, 1970.

Watanabe, Akio, and Seigen Miyazato, eds. *San Franshisuko Kowa* (*The San Francisco Peace Settlement*). Tokyo: Tokyo Daigaku Shuppankai, 1986.

Watson, Robert J. *History of the Joint Chiefs of Staff: The Joint Chiefs of Staff and National Policy, 1953–1954*. Washington, D.C.: Office of Joint History Office of the Chairman of the Joint Chiefs of Staff, 1998.

Weinstein, Martin E. *Japan's Postwar Defense Policy, 1947–1968*. New York: Columbia University Press, 1971.

Welfield, John. *An Empire in Eclipse: Japan in the Postwar American Alliance System*. London: The Athlone Press, 1988.

Yamashita, Fumitake. *Amami no Rekishi Samazama* (*Various Aspects of Amami's History*). Sumiyoson: Amami Bunka Zaidan, 1994.

Yamashita, Yasuo, "Amami Gunto no Fukki" (The Return of Amami Gunto), in Nanpo Doho Engokai, ed. *Nanpo Shoto no Hoteki Chii* (*The Legal Status of the Southern Islands*). Tokyo: Nanpo Doho Engokai, 1958.

Yasukawa, Takeshi. *Wasureenu Omoide to Korekara no Nichibei Gaiko* (*Unforgettable Memories and Japan–U.S. Diplomacy in the Future*). Tokyo: Sekai no Ugokisha, 1991.

Yasuoka, Okiharu. "Daitenkanki ni Fukaketsu na 'Rinengata Kokka Keiei no Seiji'" (Politics for Managing a Value-Based Country that are Necessary in a Time of Great Change)," *Jiyu Minshu*, No. 591 (June 2002), pp. 74–90.

Yoshida, Keiki, ed. *Amami no Nihon Fukki Undo Shiryo* (*Materials on the Return of Amami to Japan*). Private Publisher.

Yoshida, Kensei. *Democracy Betrayed: Okinawa Under U.S. Occupation.* Bellingham: Western Washington University, 2002.

Yoshida Shien Tsuito Bunshu Kanko Iinkai, ed. *Kaiso Yoshida Shien* (*Remembering Yoshida Shien*). Tokyo: Yoshida Shien Tuito Bunshu Kanko Iinkai Honbu, 1990.

Yoshida, Shigeru. *Kaiso Junen* (*Recollections of Ten Years*). Tokyo: Shinchosha, 1957.

Yoshida, Shigeru. *The Yoshida Memoirs: The Story of Japan in Crisis.* Tokyo: Sekkasha, 1962.

Yoshitsu, Michael M. *Japan and the San Francisco Peace Settlement.* New York: Columbia University Press, 1983.

Correspondence/Interviews

Araki Eikichi (family of), Fujisawa-shi, Kanagawa Prefecture, Japan, November 29, 1999.

Robert A. Fearey, Bethesda, Maryland, and Washington, D.C., 1997–2001.

Richard B. Finn, Bethesda, Maryland, 1997–1998.

Clifton B. Forster, Tiburon, California, December 7, 1999.

Dr. Iwao Ishino, by fax and e-mail, August 13, 2002, and August 21, 2002.

Christian Herter Jr., Washington, D.C., January 5, 2000.

George F. Kennan, Princeton, New Jersey, September 5, 1997.

Kusuda Toyoharu, Naze-shi, Kagoshima Prefecture, Japan, July 17, 1999.

Father Neal Henry Lawrence, by letter, e-mail, and fax, August 2002.

Dr. James V. Martin Jr., Washington, D.C., January 30, 1999.

Migita Shoshin, Fujisawa-shi, Kanagawa Prefecture, Japan, April 19, 2000.

Sakida Saneyoshi, Naze-shi, Kagoshima Prefecture, Japan, July 19, 1999.

Yamashita Takefumi, Naze-shi, Kagoshima Prefecture, Japan, July 18, 1999.

Oral Histories

John M. Allison, April 20, 1969 (John Foster Dulles Oral History Project, Seeley G. Mudd Manuscript Library, Princeton University, Princeton, New Jersey).

Hugh Borton (Oral History Research Office, Columbia University, New York).

W. Walton Butterworth, September 8, 1965 (John Foster Dulles Oral History Project, Seeley G. Mudd Manuscript Library, Princeton University, Princeton, New Jersey).

W. Walton Butterworth, July 6, 1971 (Truman Library Oral History Program, Harry S. Truman Presidential Library, Independence, Missouri).

Eugene H. Dooman (Oral History Research Office, Columbia University, New York).

U. Alexis Johnson, September 8, 1966 (John Foster Dulles Oral History Project, Seeley G. Mudd Manuscript Library, Princeton University, Princeton, New Jersey).

U. Alexis Johnson, June 19, 1975 (Truman Library Oral History Program, Harry S. Truman Presidential Library, Independence, Missouri).

Katsuo Okazaki, October 2, 1964 (John Foster Dulles Oral History Project, Seeley G. Mudd Manuscript Library, Princeton University, Princeton, New Jersey).

Jeff Graham Parsons, July 1, 1974 (Truman Library Oral History Program, Harry S. Truman Presidential Library, Independence, Missouri).

Douglas W. Overton, October 18, 1960 (Oral History Research Office, Columbia University, New York).

Walter S. Robertson, July 23–24, 1967 (John Foster Dulles Oral History Project, Seeley G. Mudd Manuscript Library, Princeton University, Princeton, New Jersey).

Walter S. Robertson, April 19, 1967 (Dwight D. Eisenhower Presidential Library, Abilene, Kansas).

William J. Sebald (John Foster Dulles Oral History Project, Seeley G. Mudd Manuscript Library, Princeton University, Princeton, New Jersey).

William J. Sebald, 3 Volumes, 1977 (Special Collections Division, Nimitz Library, U.S. Naval Academy, Annapolis, Maryland).

Yoshida Shigeru, September 30, 1964 (John Foster Dulles Oral History Project, Seeley G. Mudd Manuscript Library, Princeton University, Princeton, New Jersey).

Personal Papers/Collections

Araki Eikichi (personal, shared with author by family).

Joseph W. Ballantine (Hoover Institution Archives, Stanford University, Stanford, California).

Samuel D. Berger (Special Manuscripts Division, Lauinger Library, Georgetown University, Washington, D.C.).

Niles W. Bond (personal, shared with author).

John T. Caldwell (Hoover Institution Archives, Stanford University, Stanford, California).

Eugene H. Dooman (Hoover Institution Archives, Stanford University, Stanford, California).

John Foster Dulles (Seeley G. Mudd Manuscript Library, Princeton University, Princeton, New Jersey).

Robert A. Fearey (personal, shared with author).

Richard B. Finn (personal, shared with author).

Edward O. Freimuth (personal, shared with author prior to Freimuth's passing; to be made available for use at the Okinawa Prefectural Archives, Okinawa, Japan, in 2003).

George H. Kerr (Hoover Institution Archives, Stanford University, Stanford, California).

Nakano Yoshio (Okinawa Bunka Kenkyujo, Hosei University, Tokyo).

Richard M. Nixon (Richard Nixon Library, Yorba Linda, California).

Jeff Graham Parsons (Special Manuscripts Division, Lauinger Library Georgetown University, Washington, D.C.).

Edward O'Flaherty (U.S. National Archives II, College Park, Maryland).

Walter S. Robertson (Division of Manuscripts and Archives, Virginia Historical Society, Richmond, Virginia).

William J. Sebald (Special Collections Division, Nimitz Library, U.S. Naval Academy, Annapolis, Maryland).

Joseph W. Stilwell (Hoover Institution Archives, Stanford University, Stanford, California).

Tokonami Tokuji (Kindai Nihon Hosei Shiryo Senta, Faculty of Law, Tokyo University, Tokyo).

James T. Watkins (Hoover Institution Archives, Stanford University, California, and Okinawa Prefectural Archives, Okinawa, Japan).

Official Documents and Other Materials

U.S. Government Documents

Dwight D. Eisenhower Presidential Library, Abilene, Kansas
Papers of Dwight D. Eisenhower, Daily Appointments
Papers of Dwight D. Eisenhower, Diaries
Papers of John Foster Dulles
White House Office File, National Security Council Staff Papers, 1948–1961
White House Office Files, Office of the Special Assistant for National Security Affairs Records, 1952–1961
White House Office File, Office of the Staff Secretary, 1952–1961

Harry S. Truman Presidential Library, Independence, Missouri
Papers of Harry S. Truman, Central Files
Papers of Harry S. Truman, President's Official File
Papers of Harry S. Truman, President's Secretary File
Papers of Harry S. Truman, Records of the National Security Council

National Archives II, College Park, Maryland
Record Group 59, General Records of the Department of State
Record Group 84, Records of the Foreign Service Posts of the Department of State
Record Group 218, Records of the Joint Chiefs of Staff
Record Group 260, Records of the U.S. Civil Administration of the Ryukyu Islands
Record Group 319, Records of the Army Staff
Record Group 331, Records of GHQ/SCAP

Japanese Government Documents

Foreign Ministry Archives, Azabu, Tokyo
7th Opening, 1982 (Records on the Treaty of Peace With Japan)
11th Opening, 1991 (Records on the Reversion of Amami Oshima)

Amami Reversion Movement and Local Administration Materials

Amami Branch, Kagoshima Prefectural Library, Naze-shi, Kagoshima-ken
Amami Oshima Nihon Fukki Undo Shiryo (Materials on the Amami Reversion Movement to Japan)

Index

A

Acheson, Dean G., 18, 42

Adair, Hugh D., 9, 37

Allied Council of Japan, 28n61, 49, 53

Allies, xxviii, 19, 34, 40, 49, 53, 79, 80–81

Allison, John M., 22, 64, 77n160, 81, 97–98, 104–109, 110n1, 110n3, 110n5, 112n28, 112n30, 112n32, 118, 126–127, 130, 136–139, 146n50, 146n59, 151–155

Alsace-Lorraine, xv–xvi

Amami Gunto Jimu Hikitsugu Renraku Kyogikai (Liaison Council for the Transition of Administration of the Amami Islands), 117–118

Amami Gunto Kaigi (Amami Legislature), 49, 72n91

Amami Islands: bombing of (in WWII), xxvi; Catholicism in, xxiv; differences between Okinawa and, xxvi; early history of, xxii–xxiv; fortification of, xxiv–xxv; geographical description of, xx–xxii, xxviiin1; hurricane destruction on, 67n38; modern history of, xxiv–xxvi; population of, xx; postwar history of, brief description, xxvi–xxviii; relations with Japan, xxii–xxvii; relations with Kagoshima, xxii–xxvii; relations with Ryukyu Kingdom, xxii–xxiii

Amami Kyosanto (Amami Communist Party), 42, 47, 63, 66n26, 68n41, 69n65

"*Amami Kyosanto Jiken* (Amami Communist Party Incident)," 42

Amami Oshima Nihon Fukki Kakushin Doshikai (Progressive Brotherhood for the Return of Amami Oshima to Japan), 63

Amami Oshima Nihon Fukki Kyogikai (Council for the Reversion of Amami to Japan), 31, 47, 48, 49, 51, 55–59, 63–64

Amami Oshima Shakai Minshuto (Amami Oshima Social Democratic Party), 46–49, 71n85, 73n100

Amami Rengo (Amami Federation). *See Zenkoku Amami Rengo Sohonbu*

215

About the Author

Robert D. Eldridge is an Associate Professor of Japanese Political and Diplomatic History at the School of International Public Policy, Osaka University (OSIPP) in Osaka, Japan, and a Fellow at the Research Institute for Peace and Security (*Heiwa Anzen Hosho Kenkyusho*) in Tokyo. He specializes in U.S.–Japan relations and, in particular, the historical and contemporary aspects of Okinawa-related issues. He graduated cum laude with high departmental honors in International Relations from Lynchburg College in Virginia in 1990, following a semester abroad in Paris and another semester in Washington, D.C. After participating in the Japan Exchange and Teaching Program from 1990 to 1992, he earned his M.A. and Ph.D. from Kobe University in Japan in 1996 and 1999, respectively. He has been a Special Research Fellow for the Japan Society for the Promotion of Science (*Nihon Gakujutsu Shinkokai*), a Postdoctoral Fellow at the Suntory Foundation (*Suntory Bunka Zaidan*), where he began this study on the Amami Islands, and a Research Fellow at the Research Institute for Peace and Security before joining the faculty of Osaka University in 2001. He has published extensively and in 1999 was awarded the prestigious *Yomiuri Rondan Shinjinsho* (New Opinion Leader of the Year Award) from the *Yomiuri Shimbun*, the first time the honor has been given to a non-Japanese citizen. In 2001, he published his first book, *The Origins of the Bilateral Okinawa Problem: Okinawa in Postwar U.S.–Japan Relations, 1945–1952*, and is working on a follow-up study to be titled *The Road to Reversion: Okinawa in Postwar U.S.–Japan Relations, 1952–1972*.